C. G. Jung and Hans Urs von Balthasar

This book brings together the work of Carl Gustav Jung and Hans Urs von Balthasar, two of the most creative thinkers in psychology and theology in the twentieth century, to critically compare their ideas on the perennial question of God's involvement with evil.

In later life Jung embarked on a project relating to Christianity, with psychotherapeutic and theological intentions, forming his collection of essays, *Symbolik des Geistes*, in which God and evil was a major theme. Balthasar gave significant attention to Jung's psychology in his own theological trilogy, but opposed the approach to God and evil that Jung presented.

In this book Les Oglesby provides a thorough examination of convergences and divergences in Jung and Balthasar's thinking, their different approaches to the origins and reality of evil, and their alternative theological orientations. The book culminates in a study of each man's understanding of the central event of Christianity, Christ's death on the Cross and his descent to the dead, and discusses how Balthasar's 'vertical' and Jung's 'horizontal' approach to this major happening can be held together fruitfully with one another.

Illustrating how analytical psychology and Christian theology can mutually enrich one another when they are held in creative tension, this book invites reflection on the meaning of the central symbol of Christianity and God's involvement with evil as an aid to integrated psychological living and theological maturity. It will prove fascinating for students of psychology and religion as well as for Jungian analysts and practical theologians.

Les Oglesby was Director of Ministry in the Diocese of Ely, and has now retired. He gained his Lambeth PhD in Psychology and Theology in 2012.

Research in Analytical Psychology and Jungian Studies Series
Series Advisor: Andrew Samuels, *Professor of Analytical Psychology, Essex University, UK.*

The *Research in Analytical Psychology and Jungian Studies* series features scholarly works that are, broadly speaking, of an empirical nature. The series comprises research-focused volumes involving qualitative and quantitative research, historical/archival research, theoretical developments, heuristic research, grounded theory, narrative approaches, collaborative research, practitioner-led research, and self-study. The series also includes focused works by clinical practitioners, and provides new research-informed explorations of the work of C. G. Jung that will appeal to researchers, academics and scholars alike.

Books in this series:

Time and Timelessness
Temporality in the theory of Carl Jung
Angeliki Yiassemides

Apophatic Elements in the Theory and Practice of Psychoanalysis
Pseudo-Dionysius and C. G. Jung
David Henderson

C. G. Jung and Hans Urs von Balthasar
God and evil – A critical comparison
Les Oglesby

C. G. Jung and Hans Urs von Balthasar

God and evil – A critical comparison

Les Oglesby

Routledge
Taylor & Francis Group
LONDON AND NEW YORK

First published 2014
by Routledge
2 Park Square, Milton Park, Abingdon, Oxfordshire OX14 4RN

and by Routledge
711 Third Avenue, New York, NY 10017

First issued in paperback 2016

Routledge is an imprint of the Taylor & Francis Group, an informa business

British Library Cataloguing in Publication Data
A catalogue record for this book is available from the British Library

Library of Congress Cataloging in Publication Data
Oglesby, Les.
C. G. Jung and Hans Urs von Balthasar: God and evil—a critical comparison / Les Oglesby.
pages cm
Includes bibliographical references and index.
1. Jung, C. G. (Carl Gustav), 1875–1961. 2. Balthasar, Hans Urs von, 1905–1988. 3. Good and evil—Psychological aspects. 4. Good and evil—Religious aspects—Christianity. I. Title.
BJ1401O45 2014
214—dc23
2013018314

ISBN 13: 978-0-415-79178-6 (pbk)
ISBN 13: 978-0-415-87057-3 (hbk)

Typeset in Bembo
by Book Now Ltd, London

For Dorothy

Contents

Foreword

It is a pleasure to accept Les Oglesby's invitation to write a brief Foreword for his book, *C. G. Jung and Hans Urs von Balthasar: God and evil – A critical comparison*. It is always gratifying to learn that one's own work has stimulated others and planted a seed for further developments in a chosen field of enquiry, but in this case it is more than that, because Les Oglesby's work far exceeds one's modest hopes in this regard. His is a work of extraordinary intellectual rigour and broad scholarship. Much more than that, however, it takes up what is, in my mind, the most pressing issue for contemporary Christian theology and Jungian psychology alike: the problem of evil.

For theology, this has to do with how to move forward in theological reflection after the Holocaust; for Jungian psychology, it is how to deal with collective shadow and to treat traumas caused by man and nature. On the one side, God must be considered and in some fashion be held accountable; on the other side, the human psyche must be recognized not only as a source of wisdom and creativity but also as capable of generating evil on a scale impossible to accept. Both sides have a problem here, but can they help each other?

Les Oglesby meticulously lays the groundwork for how Christian theology, as represented by the Swiss Catholic theologian Hans Urs von Balthasar, might enter into a constructive dialogue with the depth psychology of Swiss psychoanalyst C. G. Jung regarding the problem of evil. In a sense, this work is a prolegomenon for further constructive work to come. It lays the foundations for a bridge, and in the process it clears away a great many inhibiting misconceptions and misinterpretations on both sides of the gap between theology and psychology, which in the past have hindered construction of the much-desired exchange. This also requires setting solidly in place the positions on either side of the divide, theological presuppositions on the one side and psychological ones on the other.

One of Les Oglesby's great virtues is that he shows precise understanding of both sides and is even-handed and without prejudice with regard to both. The position of Balthasar as what he terms a 'contextualizing theologian' is shown to be open to consideration of extra-theological reflections and modern scientific views while retaining theological integrity within the purview of Roman

Catholic tradition. The position of Jung as a 'reinterpretive psychologist' is similarly shown to be open to extra-psychological doctrines and teachings, including traditional Roman Catholic dogma, while retaining scientific integrity on its side. Once these positions have been carefully examined and exposed, the question is: What is possible by way of mutual enrichment through dialogue? Can theology gain from such a dialogue with Jungian psychology? Can Jungian psychology benefit from dialogue with traditional Christian theology?

Les Oglesby does not overestimate the possibilities of such an exchange. Many have tried, all of whom he mentions in this extensively researched work, and so far all have failed to offer a convincing and reliable structure for such dialogue to bear much fruit. The most famous example of failure is the attempted dialogue between Jung and the Dominican priest Victor White, which broke down precisely over the problem of evil and how to conceptualize it. Les Oglesby thinks the possibilities for dialogue might be greater between Jung and the Jesuit-trained priest Balthasar, and he ingeniously brings the discussion to the point concerning the symbols of the Cross and the *descensus*. Here, perhaps, Christian theology, which offers a vertical perspective of transcendence, and Jungian psychology, which offers a horizontal perspective of psychological reality – on the subjects of evil, God's involvement in evil, and the meaning of suffering the tension of opposites in the excruciating conflict between good and evil for individuation and spiritual development – can be brought together to offer complementary truths.

I would take the argument a step further and say that both need the other, and precisely at this point. Psychology has a hard time getting off the ground and easily gets bogged down in description and diagnosis, and theology has a hard time reaching the ground because of its commitments to metaphysical realities, but between them they might find a point of contact that can assist them both. While Jungian psychology can bring us to awareness of the darkest and deepest corners of human evil and suffering (recognition of the shadow and 'absolute evil') and speculate about the authorship of this aspect of existence, Christian theology may be able to offer the possibility for hope and redemption (through divine love and intimate participation in human suffering) and challenge psychology to take a leap of faith.

This, at least, is the glimpse of the promised land offered by Les Oglesby's brilliant contribution to a possible dialogue between Christian theology and Jungian psychology.

Murray Stein
Goldiwil, Switzerland, June 2013

Preface

My general interest in the link between theology and psychology, during my ministry in the Church of England, in parishes, in theological education and in ministerial training, has been stimulated and informed by more people than it would be possible to acknowledge. The decision to explore a Jungian contribution to a dialogue with theology was sparked by Murray Stein's work on *Jung's Treatment of Christianity* and encouraged initially through conversations with Eric Hutchison (1921–2009), Anglican priest and Jungian analyst.

I had the opportunity to be part of the first cohort using the new provision to work for a research doctorate within the Archbishop's Examination in Theology and I am grateful for the support of successive directors of the Academic Board, Michael Kitchen and Jeremy Morris, and particularly that of the AET registrar, Maureen Palmer. My supervisors, Ben Quash and Chris MacKenna, were very patient in letting me find my own way to discover the focus of my work, making many pertinent suggestions along the way. My doctoral thesis, on which this book is based, was examined in 2012 by David Law (University of Manchester) and Lucy Huskinson (University of Bangor), and I thank them both for their challenge and encouragement. It made a significant difference to be able to access the resources of the Cambridge University Library and to receive financial support from the Continuing Ministerial Education fund of the Diocese of Ely and the Ely Theological College Trust. It has been important for me also to have the interested support of colleagues and friends in the Diocese of Ely and in the Cambridge Jungian Circle (and the help of Jack Herbert in translating some German texts). I have received considerable help from the staff at Routledge, particularly Jane Madeley and Clare Ashworth.

This work is dedicated to my wife, Dorothy, who has been most lovingly generous in making room for the time and energy that the doctoral thesis and the book have called for, as well as sharing, over the last forty-five years, an ongoing interest in the interplay between psychology and theology.

Acknowledgements

In this book I have made particular reference to the following works:

Razing the Bastions: On the Church in this Age by Hans Urs von Balthasar, translated by B. McNeil, copyright © 1993 Ignatius Press, San Francisco. Used by permission of Ignatius Press, San Francisco. *Theo-Drama: Theological Dramatic Theory, vol. I: Prolegomena* by Hans Urs von Balthasar, translated by G. Harrison, copyright © 1988 Ignatius Press, San Francisco. Used by permission of Ignatius Press, San Francisco. *Theo-Drama: Theological Dramatic Theory, vol. III: Dramatis Personae: Persons in Christ* by Hans Urs von Balthasar, translated by G. Harrison, copyright © 1992 Ignatius Press, San Francisco. Used by permission of Ignatius Press, San Francisco. *Theo-Drama: Theological Dramatic Theory, vol. IV: The Action* by Hans Urs von Balthasar, translated by G. Harrison, copyright © 1994 Ignatius Press, San Francisco. Used by permission of Ignatius Press, San Francisco. *Theo-Drama: Theological Dramatic Theory, vol. V: The Last Act* by Hans Urs von Balthasar, translated by G. Harrison, copyright © 1998 Ignatius Press, San Francisco. Used by permission of Ignatius Press, San Francisco. *Theo-Logic: Theological Logical Theory, vol. II: Truth of God* by Hans Urs von Balthasar, translated by A. J. Walker, copyright © 2004 Ignatius Press, San Francisco. Used by permission of Ignatius Press, San Francisco. Copyright © Hans Urs von Balthasar 1990 *Mysterium Paschale: The Mystery of Easter*, translated by A. Nichols, T & T Clark, an imprint of Bloomsbury Publishing Plc. Used by permission of Bloomsbury Publishing plc, London. *Aion: Researches into the Phenomenology of the Self* (*Collected Works*, vol. 9, part II) by C. G. Jung, translated by R. F. C. Hull, 2nd edition © 1969 Princeton University Press. Used by permission of Princeton University Press. *Psychology and Religion: West and East* (*Collected Works*, vol. 11) by C. G. Jung, translated by R. F. C. Hull, 2nd edition, copyright © 1969 Princeton University Press, published in the UK by Routledge. Used by permission of Princeton University Press and Taylor & Francis Books (UK). *The Symbolic Life: Miscellaneous Writings* (*Collected Works*, vol. 18) by C. G. Jung, translated by R. F. C. Hull © 1977 the Heirs of C. G. Jung. Used by permission of Princeton University Press and Taylor & Francis Books (UK).

Abbreviations

Jung

Quotations are cited with reference to the following abbreviations:

CW *Collected Works*, edited by Sir Herbert Read, M. Fordham, G. Adler and William McGuire, translated by R. F. C. Hull, 20 volumes, London: Routledge and Kegan Paul, 1953–1983. Cited in the text with volume number. Essays from the *Collected Works* are cited in the text separately, some with date, others with the abbreviations below, and page reference. Their relevant volume number is indicated in the bibliography.

CWA *The Zofingia Lectures*, (*Collected Works*, Supplementary Volume A), translated by J. van Heurck, London: Routledge and Kegan Paul, 1983.

CWB *Psychology of the Unconscious* (*Collected Works*, Supplementary Volume B), translated by B. M. Hinkle, Princeton: Princeton University Press, 1991.

L1 *C. G. Jung Letters: I, 1906–1950*, edited by G. Adler with A. Jaffé, translated by R. F. C. Hull, Princeton: Princeton University Press, 1973.

L2 *C. G. Jung Letters: II, 1951–1961*, edited by G. Adler, translated by J. Hulen, Princeton: Princeton University Press, 1975.

MDR *Memories, Dreams, Reflections*, recorded and edited by A. Jaffé, translated by R. and C. Winston, London: Fontana Press, 1995.

PADT *A Psychological Approach to the Dogma of the Trinity* (1942/1948) in *CW*11: 107–200.

PCT *On the Psychology of the Concept of the Trinity*, translated by G.V. Hartman, *Quadrant: Journal of the C. G. Jung Foundation for Analytical Psychology*, 1998.

PRTL *Psychology and Religion* (1938/1940) in *CW*11:3–105.

PSF *The Phenomenology of the Spirit in Fairytales* (1945/1948) in *CW*9(i): 207–54.

RBLN *The Red Book: Liber Novus*, translated by M. Kyburz, J. Peck, and S. Shamdasani, S. Shamdasani (ed.), New York and London: W. W. Norton and Company, 2009.
SM *The Spirit Mercurius* (1943/1948) in *CW*13: 191–250.
SOT *Satan in the Old Testament*, by R. S. Kluger, translated by H. Nagel, Evanston: Northwestern University Press, 1967.

Balthasar

Quotations are cited with reference to the following abbreviations:

EP *Epilogue*, translated by E. T. Oakes, San Francisco: Ignatius Press, 2004b.
GL *The Glory of the Lord: A Theological Aesthetics*, seven volumes, edited by J. Fession (vol. 1), B. McNeil (vol. 5), and J. Riches (vols 1–7) translated by O. Davies (vols 4–5), E. Leiva-Merikakis (vols 1 and 6), A. Louth (vols 2–5), F. McDonagh (vol. 2), B. McNeil (vols 2, and 4–7), J. Saward (vols 3–5), M. Simon (vol. 3) and R. Williams (vols 3–5), San Francisco: Ignatius Press, 1982–91. Cited in the text by volume number.
MP *Mysterium Paschale: The Mystery of Easter*, translated by A. Nichols, San Francisco, Ignatius Press, 2005b.
RBCA *Razing the Bastions: On the Church in this Age*, translated by B. McNeil, San Francisco: Ignatius Press, 1993.
TD *Theo-Drama: Theological Dramatic Theory*, five volumes, translated by G. Harrison, San Francisco: Ignatius Press, 1988–98. Cited in the text by volume number.
TL *Theo-Logic: Theological Logical Theory*, three volumes, translated by A. J. Walker (vols 1–2) and G. Harrison (vol. 3), San Francisco: Ignatius Press, 2000–05. Cited in the text by volume number.

Biblical quotations

Where biblical material is set within quotations from other authors, those authors' text and referencing system are reproduced unaltered. In my own text, unless otherwise stated, quotations are from the *New Revised Standard Version* (Metzger and Murphy, 1991), using its abbreviation system (ibid.: xxvii–xxviii).

Chapter 1

Introduction

This book aims to make a contribution to the dialogue between Jungian psychology and Christian theology, by means of a critical comparison, drawing on the works of C. G. Jung and Hans Urs von Balthasar, on the question of God's involvement with evil. For both men this was a particular concern. It was a key theme of Jung's 1948 collection of essays, *Symbolik des Geistes*, published as the opening phase of Jung's project in relation to Christianity. Balthasar saw Jung as a representative of a contemporary response to this issue which was different from his own.

The first two parts of this book set the scene, constructing a framework and outlining bases for the critical comparison undertaken in the third and fourth parts. In chapter two, I give an introductory outline of each man's life and work, of Jung's project in relation to Christianity and of the theological project of Balthasar's multi-volume trilogy. In chapter three, I offer a typological framework within which Balthasar can be read as a contextualizing theologian and Jung as a reinterpretive psychologist. There are bases for a critical comparison in the similarities between Jung's map of the psyche and Balthasar's theological anthropology and also in their divergent theological orientations (in chapter four) and different approaches to the questions of analogy and polarity (in chapter five). These divergent approaches are illustrated at the end of chapter five by using the essay in Jung's *Symbolik des Geistes* collection on Satan in the Old Testament as a case study.

The critical comparison of Jung and Balthasar on the question of God's involvement with evil begins, in chapter six, with an exploration of their views on the origin and reality of evil, highlighting the struggles each has with this issue within their own framework of ideas. Chapter seven looks at Jung's essay on the Trinity in *Symbolik des Geistes* as the culmination of his psychotherapeutic and theological contribution to the Christian understanding of God's involvement with evil. This seems to end with little possibility for creative dialogue with Balthasar. However, in chapter eight, I make use of a critical comparison of each man's understanding of the Cross as the basis, in chapter nine, for the construction of a model for holding together in tension a 'vertical' with a 'horizontal' reflection on the question of God and evil.

In a final chapter, I summarize the outcomes of this critical comparison and make some suggestions for further studies in the dialogue between Jungian psychology and Christian theology.

Part I

Constructing a framework for critical comparison

Chapter 2

Introducing Jung and Balthasar

To set the context for a critical comparison drawn from the works of C. G. Jung and Hans Urs von Balthasar on the question of God's involvement in evil, I begin with a sketch of each man's life and work. Then I outline Jung's project in relation to Christianity and explain my focus on its first phase, his 1948 collection of essays, *Symbolik des Geistes*; and I give a summary of the main themes of Balthasar's multi-volume theological trilogy, highlighting aspects particularly relevant to a dialogue with Jung and to the question of God's involvement with evil. The chapter ends by identifying the main sources from Jung's and Balthasar's works on which I will draw.

Jung – a sketch of his life and work

It may at first glance seem obvious, for a sketch of Jung's life and work, to use his own posthumously published memoir, *Memories, Dreams, Reflections.*[1] However, the text is known to have been severely cut during the editing process, underplaying some of the difficulties of his life.[2] Further, it is avowedly no more than Jung's recollections in late old age of the inner reality of experiences that he had had up to eight decades earlier. Jung himself was aware of the problem this posed (*MDR*: 10f.).

Drawing on biographies of Jung, which have been numerous in the half-century since his death, presents another challenge. They have ranged from the appreciative, tending towards the hagiographical, through various shades of neutrality, to the critical, tending towards thoroughgoing hostility.[3] Biographies whose historiography is fully resourced will become available as the massive Jung archive is published (Shamdasani, 2005). A major challenge in writing an introductory sketch is the wealth of material and assessment from which to choose. The sketch offered here gives particular attention to Jung's developing attitude towards religion (Main, 2006a).

Jung was born in 1875 into the relatively poor household of Paul Jung (1842–96), a pastor of the Swiss Reformed Church, and into an extended family which included several other clergy. Jung's childhood was a troubled one. During his early years, he found his mother puzzling, being alternatively warm and loving and then mysteriously uncanny (McLynn, 1996: 9f.: cf. *MDR*: 65ff.). Jung's father was an Oriental and classical scholar whose faith became desiccated in the routines of church pastoral work, a problem aggravated by the constricting assumptions of scientific materialism (ibid.: 29f.; cf. *MDR*: 110ff.). Jung himself found the inner world more resourcing than the outer; he was an introvert (in the terms of his own psychological typology), finding meaning in private rituals (which he would later see as having archetypal significance (ibid.: 18f.)) and in dreams and visions (some of which he continued to reflect on for decades (*MDR*: 21–39; cf. McLynn, 1996: 13–5; Bair, 2004: 23f.)).

There were early signs of Jung's location within that stream of Christian tradition which gives priority to inner religious experience over institutional belief systems. He was critical of and saddened by his father's lack of such a faith. Jung himself experienced religious education at school as 'unspeakably dull' and churchgoing as a matter of social convention set within a conservative parochialism (ibid.: 70ff.). He came to see this as an effect of secularized scientific materialism, against which he sought to mount a defence of religion in his student Zofingia lectures (*CWA*). These lectures show that, at least in outline, Jung's scientific and metaphysical orientations were already in place before he took up his professional career and that the question of an appropriate phenomenological orientation was already exercising the young medical student. He was also at this time positively interested in the occult and in spiritual experience more generally, and saw in contemporary spiritualism evidence of the reality of these phenomena (Charet, 1993; cf. Shamdasani, 2009: 195).

Jung's early teenage vision of a defecating God shattering Basel Cathedral was not only understood by the octogenarian Jung as an experience of the 'immediate living God who stands, omnipotent and free above His Bible and His Church' but it also provided him with some of his earliest reflections on God's involvement with evil, forming 'the dim understanding that God could be something terrible' (*MDR*: 57; cf. Clark, 1998) as well as loving and gracious.

Jung attended the state authority's Gymnasium in Basel and then the medical school at Basel University (Stevens, 1990: 6). The early years of Jung's career were spent in psychiatric medicine, and then in psychoanalysis (Casement, 2001: 9–27). From 1901 he worked at the Burghölzli Mental Hospital in Zürich. He gained his doctorate in 1902 for a psychiatric study of occult phenomena, drawing on the work of the American philosopher and psychologist William James (1842–1910) and the French–Swiss psychiatrist Théodore Flournoy (1854–1920). As Jung developed his approach he found a positive response in North America (Shamdasani, 1995: 126f.; cf. Shamdasani, 1998; Taylor, 1998; Taylor, 1999: 209–34). At Burghölzli Jung contributed to the advance of the emerging discipline of psychiatry: collaborating with the hospital's director, Eugene Bleuler (1857–1939), on schizophrenia, taking forward experimental research with Wilhelm Wundt's (1832–1920) word association test, and developing ideas about the theory of feeling-toned complexes (influenced by participation in Pierre Janet's (1859–1947) seminars at the Salpêtrière Hospital in Paris).

Burghölzli was noted for its humanitarian approach and Jung proved himself to be a caring and creative psychiatrist, primarily concerned to understand the origins and meaning of his patients' symptoms (McLynn, 1996: 55–75). Before his participation in the psychoanalytical movement pioneered by Sigmund Freud (1856–1939), Jung had already developed his scientific method and his theory of complexes. The two men began a correspondence and then met, first in 1907, collaborating until 1913. They shared an interest in the origins of mental conditions and in psychotherapeutic methods (Shamdasani, 2009: 196).

Jung's 1911–12 work, *The Psychology of the Unconscious* (*CWB*), is often taken as marking the break with Freud. There were a number of important divergences between them. Jung had doubts about the exclusiveness of Freud's theory of sexuality (McGuire, 1974: 79), eventually rejecting the idea of reducing the interpretation of neurosis to a single 'root-complex' (Jung, 1913: 156). He reframed the psychoanalytical concept of libido to refer to the general life-energy of the psyche (Jung, 1928a: 17) rather than to sexuality. In his 1911–12 work, Jung also put forward a more positive, though psychological, understanding of religion. Where for Freud religious symbols were understood as products, infantile in origin, of repressed (sexual) libidinal wishes, for Jung religious symbols could be expressions of a healthy as well as a neurotically imbalanced functioning of (libidinal) psychic energy. They could also connect people with what was ancient in human experience (what he would later call archetypes) and thus could contribute to the achievements of human civilization (Main, 2006a: 299–301).

Although *The Psychology of the Unconscious* does not represent a complete parting of the ways (Stepansky, 1992: 169–99), nevertheless Jung felt that his chapter on 'The Sacrifice' (*CWB*: 369–414) foreshadowed a break with Freud, and in January 1913, with a final exchange of letters, their personal and professional collaboration came to an end (McGuire, 1974: 539, 540).

In relation to religion, and Christianity in particular, Jung described himself, when he was a medical student, as 'an educated layman who is earnestly struggling to understand Christ' (*CWA*: 106). By 1912, as he recalled many years later, he felt himself no longer identified with the Christian world view: 'In what myth does man live nowadays? In the Christian myth, the answer might be. "Do *you* live in it?" I asked myself. To be honest, the answer was no. For me, it is not what I live by' (*MDR*: 195). If there is no longer in the West a collective Christian world view, Jung went on to ask himself: '"But then what is your myth – the myth in which you do live?" At this point the dialogue with myself became uncomfortable, and I stopped thinking. I had reached a dead end' (ibid.).

During the years from 1913 to 1918 Jung underwent an intense period of 'confrontation with the unconscious' (ibid.: 194–225), a period of 'disorientation', and 'constant inner pressure' (*MDR*: 197). From one point of view, it can be seen as a 'creative illness', that is, something 'from which a person emerges with a new vision of the world or with a new philosophy'

(Ellenberger, 1970: 210; cf. ibid.: 447, 670–3). Put more provocatively, in this period Jung was 'mad … grandiose and deluded – but also … insightful' (MacKenna, 2012: 478), though such 'divine madness' can be a form of irrationality that is inspiringly creative (MacKenna, 2013). Shamdasani argues that the *Red Book*,[4] an elaboration of primary material noted from 1913–16 in Jung's *Black Books*, should be seen as fitting into a wider context of self-experimentation and was 'by no means a peculiar and idiosyncratic activity, nor the product of a psychosis' (Shamdasani, 2009: 204; cf. MacKenna, 2012: 478), even though Jung felt its threat (Storr, 1996: 89).

Jung had already discerned many of the components of his psychological theory but these years represented his own experience of what would become the central contribution of analytical psychology, the process of individuation (Shamdasani, 2012a: 367; Stein, 2012: 282). The images that welled up into Jung's consciousness were compelling, setting him a career-long task of discerning their meaning: 'the numinous beginning, which contained everything, was then' (Shamdasani, 2012a: 366 quoting Jung and Jaffé, unpublished: 177). Jung's *Collected Works* can be seen as his attempts to bring forward evidence of the generic applicability of the process he experienced, set within a theoretical map of the psyche.

The *Red Book* is also the product of a deeply religious encounter. During this period Jung reread Friedrich Nietzsche (1844–1900) but, as his *Red Book* shows, 'whereas Zarathustra proclaimed the death of God, *Liber Novus* depicts the rebirth of God in the soul' (Shamdasani, 2009: 202). In *MDR* it appears that for Jung by 1912 the traditional God of Western Christianity was already dead. The *Red Book*, however, shows Jung, in pursuit of his 'personal myth', as struggling with a continuing quest of how to live as a Christian in the modern world. For though Jung's primary material is his own inner experience and 'the rebirth of a new God-image in his soul' (Shamdasani, 2012a: 207), there is continuing engagement with the content of the 'Christian myth' as well as evidence of Jung's own Christian theological orientation. For instance, when Jung explores the theology of the ancient Orphic mysteries through the deity Phanes, he makes linking references to the Johannine view of Christ as Light of the world, to the Lucan account of the birth of Christ and to his saving, sacrificial death (Stein, 2012: 291ff.). Jung's interest in matters of the spirit (as in the structural polarity of the 'Spirit of the Times' and the 'Spirit of the Depths' (*RBLN*: 233f.)) indicates that he stands within the broad stream of German Idealism which insisted, against modern reductionism, that the everyday is not all that there is and that which is more than ordinarily real is of greater importance (Bishop, 2012: 344ff.). It also indicates that, as I will later argue, Jung can be located within certain strands of radical Protestant and 'Joachimite' theology, where spirit-filled individuals are called on to complete the work of the Son: 'the anointed of our time is not to be born in the flesh, but in the spirit' (Shamdasani, 2009: 209). Jung identifies his concept of individuation with his theological stance: 'The way is within us, … not in Gods, … Within us is the way, the truth and life' (*RBLN*: 231). Further, it is important to note for the argument that I develop in this book that the psychological process of individuation in the *Red Book* involves a descent to the realm of the dead (that is, into the unconscious (Stein, 2012: 281, Shamdasani, 2012b: 100ff.)), and that for Jung the doctrine of God already includes evil: 'God and the devil had become one' (*RBLN*: 318).[5]

Jung's analytical psychology and its associated movement emerged slowly in the decade following *The Psychology of the Unconscious*. In part this involved Jung in shifting the focus of his activities. He worked primarily with individual patients in his private practice, and formed the first Analytical Psychology Club in 1916 in Zürich. He published some important essays[6] and continued to give lectures.

The first major published work outlining his new approach, *Psychological Types* (*CW*6), did not appear until 1921. In it Jung's mature psychology of religion begins to emerge. He distinguishes God from the God-image, which he sees as an aspect of the functioning of the totality of the human psyche, conscious and unconscious. And just as part of his argument for archetypes of the unconscious is that comparable symbols appear in historically or geographically unconnected cultures, so he appeals to the *consensus gentium* (truth authenticated by consensus) for the psychological importance (though not the metaphysical reality) of God-images (ibid.: 42f.). Central to analytical psychology is the experience of the tension of opposites and the (individuation) process of coming to wholeness. This underlies Jung's ideas about symbol formation (ibid.: 473–81; cf. Franz, 1980) linked with the transcendent function (ibid.: 115, n. 86, 126, 252, n. 165, 480). I shall argue that this theoretical framework can be used to help construct a model in which Jung's reading of Christ's Cross and descent to the dead is related in critical engagement with Balthasar's.

Analytical psychology quickly became an international movement, with early reception in North America (Casement, 2001: 19–21, 138–41; Taylor, 1999; and Kirsch, 2000), involving a network of women and men from psychology and other disciplines. The pattern of Jung's own work centred on psychotherapeutic analysis of individual patients, and lectures and seminars in Zürich (*L*1: xxi–xxv; Hayman, 2002: xi–xxi) (at the Psychology Club and the Institute of Technology) and elsewhere in Europe, the UK and North America. He gained some first-hand experience of non-Western cultures in travels in the 1920s to North Africa, New Mexico and East Africa. He found inter-disciplinary stimulus among scholars, most notably at the Eranos conferences from 1933 onwards, with those interested in the study of Eastern and Western spirituality.

Jung's writings show the range of his interests, and also that he was not a systematic thinker, in relation to either the evolving practice or the theory of analytical psychology. He once said of himself: 'I can formulate my thoughts only as they break out of me. It is like a geyser. Those who come after me will have to put them in order' (Jaffé, 1986: 8 quoting Jung). Theory for Jung was a second step, an attempt to make sense of experience and observation in which he would borrow ideas from many quarters, shaping them with a primary interest in his own purposes (Shamdasani, 2003: 163–270). He should not be pictured, however, as someone wandering aimlessly through a morass of experience with no guiding orientation (*Weltanschauung* or 'attitude' (Jung, 1928/1931, *MDR*: 359 and n. 1)), though the extent of systematic coherence should not be overestimated.

A significant number of Jung's works arose in collaboration with others. Particularly relevant to Jung's psychological interest in Christianity are his work with Richard Wilhelm (1873–1930) (Wilhelm and Jung, 1962; cf. *CW*13: 1–56), the German sinologist, theologian and missionary, whose work on *The Secret of the Golden Flower* provided Jung with his first major reassurance of the cultural–historical rootedness of ideas he had garnered from work on his own fantasies (*RBLN*: 360) and on the dreams of patients; with Wolfgang Pauli (1900–58) (Gieser, 2005), a Nobel-Prize-winning theoretical quantum physicist, whose dream series opened the way for Jung's re-evaluation of the symbols of Christian theology and with whom Jung worked on synchronicity; with Father Victor White (1902–60) (Lammers, 1994; Lammers and Cunningham, 2007; Weldon, 2007), a Dominican priest–theologian, whose collaboration with Jung on a dialogue between theology and psychology eventually foundered over the question of evil; and with Rivkah Schärf (1907–87), a Jewish biblical scholar and Jungian analyst, whose monograph on Satan in the Old Testament was included by Jung in his 1948 collection of essays, *Symbolik des Geistes* (Schärf, 1948, cf. *SOT*; cf. *CW*5: 192; *CW*9(ii): 121 n. 12; Jung, 1942/1954: 242 n. 70; *CW*14: 206 n. 495, ibid.: 389 n. 46).

Jung continued publishing new material into late old age. His *magnum opus* on the psychological significance of alchemy, *Mysterium Coniunctionis* (*CW*14), was published in the year of his eightieth birthday, 1955. Ten days before his death in 1961 he finished his contribution to *Man and His Symbols* (Jung, 1978). By the time of his death recognition included honorary doctorates and fellowships from North America, the UK, India and Switzerland. The movement of Analytical Psychology was established across several continents, with the C. G. Jung Institute, founded in Zürich in 1948, providing the major focus for training and research.

Balthasar – a sketch of his life and work

In the case of Balthasar, by contrast with Jung, the difficulty is the paucity of biographical material available. Very few of the relevant archives about Balthasar's life and his theological project are open to scholars. So far there has been no full-scale, critical biography (Oakes and Moss, 2004:7 n. 4). Indeed, the one short account which was published by a relative in 1989 is the main source on which others continue to rely (Henrici 1991: 7–43; cf. Oakes, 1994: 1–12; Wigley, 2010: 3–12).

Balthasar was born in 1905 into a prosperous and distinguished Swiss Catholic family. He attended Benedictine and Jesuit schools and then undertook doctoral research in Germanic studies. His thesis, on the theme of eschatology in modern German literature, was awarded in Zürich in 1928.

From childhood Balthasar had enjoyed a 'simple and straightforward faith' (ibid.: 10). He was 'struck as by lightning' (ibid.: 11 quoting Balthasar) with a vocation (which turned out to be to the priesthood) during a thirty-day Ignatian retreat in 1927. He joined the Jesuit novitiate in 1929, was ordained as a priest in 1936 and completed his training in 1939. During this period he was deeply frustrated by the narrow neo-scholasticism in which he was being schooled. He found himself engaged in 'a grim struggle with the dreariness of theology, with what men had made out of the glory of revelation' (ibid.: 13; cf. Oakes and Moss, 2004: 3). Two people in particular were enormously significant for his development. One was the *ressourcement* theologian Henri de Lubac (1896–1991), who introduced Balthasar to the Church Fathers. One commentator argues that Lubac's reading of Irenaeus (c. 115–202) contributed to the systematic underpinning of Balthasar's theology (Mongrain, 2002). The other was Erich Przywara (1889–1972), the Jesuit philosopher theologian, who provided him with a 'way in which Catholic philosophy could engage with the contemporary world' (Wigley, 2010: 5) and the basis of his understanding of the analogy of being.

Balthasar worked in Basel as a student chaplain from 1939 until he left the Jesuit order in 1950, a separation which remained unresolved to the end of his life. Because of a formal prohibition against Jesuits in Switzerland, much of Balthasar's chaplaincy work focused on translating, editing and publishing (including the culture-preserving Klosterberg project, to which Balthasar contributed anthologies, including ones on Goethe (1749–1832) and Nietzsche (ibid.: 6)), an involvement in theatre and the arts, lecturing and pastoral work in student societies, and leading vocational Ignatian retreats.

During this time Balthasar formed a friendship with the Protestant theologian Karl Barth (1886–1968), to whose work he had originally been introduced by Przywara (ibid.: 7). Balthasar published an exposition and interpretation of Barth's theology in 1951, the first by a Roman Catholic theologian (Balthasar, 1992b). This gained qualified approval from Barth himself. Though Barth's influence on Balthasar was considerable – including his critique of nineteenth-century Liberal Protestantism, his theology of election and his thoroughgoing christocentrism – there remained 'some substantial areas of disagreement' (Wigley 2010: 8; cf. Wigley, 2007), not least over the question of analogy (ibid.: 19f.; cf. Wigley, 2007).

A major source of Balthasar's eventual estrangement from the Jesuit authorities arose from his association with Adrienne von Speyr (1902–67), who converted to Catholicism in 1940. Balthasar became her spiritual director and the amanuensis of her mystical visions and biblical commentaries (Henrici 1991:26; cf. Balthasar, 1986b: 232; Roten, 1991: 68, 71f.), for some of which he wrote prefaces. Balthasar's superiors were inclined to doubt the validity of Speyr's religious experiences. For his part Balthasar delayed his full profession as a Jesuit until they had been formally investigated. Despite their not gaining official approval, Balthasar continued to insist that '[h]er work and mine cannot be separated from one another either psychologically or theologically. They are two halves of a single whole with a single foundation at the centre' (ibid.: 28 quoting Balthasar; cf. Balthasar, 1994a).[7] Balthasar himself identified a number of key areas of agreement which some scholars have seen as enriching of and others as detrimental to his theology.

To circumvent the difficulties of obtaining the necessary imprimatur to publish her spiritual experiences, Balthasar and Speyr jointly founded a publishing house, Johannes Verlag, in 1947. They also founded, in 1945, a secular institute, *Johannesgemeinschaft* [the Community of St John], offering a lay form of consecrated life that sought to work for the sanctification of the world, whose mission could be summed up as 'the leavening of the world from within in order to make visible God's glory which still shines in this world' (ibid.: 24 referring to *RBCA*). The Jesuits would not take responsibility for this work or agree to authorize Balthasar to lead it. With considerable sadness Balthasar left the Society of Jesus in 1950, concluding that his vocation lay elsewhere (ibid.: 21).

For a number of years Balthasar was outside the mainstream of church life and worked freelance as an itinerant lecturer. At first he had only limited permission to officiate as a priest, but was able to lead retreats – so important to one who famously said he wanted to offer a kneeling not a sitting theology. In Balthasar's view, 'theology is essentially an act of adoration and prayer' to be undertaken 'on one's knees' (Balthasar, 1965: 82f.; cf. Henrici, 1991: 26; Kilby, 2004: 265; Wigley, 2010: vii), whose primary location was the church rather than the academy. This was not a matter of promoting piety over academic enquiry, but of reuniting doctrine ('theology at the desk') and spirituality ('theology at prayer' (Balthasar, 1965: 85)):

> True theology, the theology of the saints, with the central doctrines of revelation always in view, inquires, in a spirit of obedience and reverence, what processes of human thought, what modes of approach are best fitted to bring out the meaning of what has been revealed … [to bring people in] their whole existence, intellectual as well as spiritual, into close relation with God.
>
> (ibid.: 69f.)

Theological activity is, further, to be in support of Christian living:

> Only a Christian who ponders the sources (contemplation) stands a chance of attaining a genuine forward-looking attitude and the right kind of commitment (action). As we all know, the whole plan and purpose of

> the Spiritual Exercises [of Ignatius Loyola] is to provide preparation and training for apostolic, world-transforming action.
>
> (Henrici 1991:29 quoting Balthasar)

It was not until 1956 that Balthasar was incardinated, licensed to function fully, as a priest in the diocese of Chur in Switzerland. And, although he was not included in the preparations for the Second Vatican Council (1962–1965) (Lubac, 1991: 271), he was beginning to plan the multi-volume trilogy that would become his *magnum opus*. Already in 1958 he was aware of where the task would begin: 'I am trying to bring aesthetics and theology face to face' (Henrici, 1991: 27 quoting Balthasar). The first part of this work was published in 1961, with fifteen more volumes following until 1987. The trilogy deals in turn with the themes of beauty, in the seven volumes of *The Glory of the Lord*, goodness, in the five volumes of *Theo-Drama*, and truth, in the three volumes of *Theo-Logic*, with an *Epilogue* setting out why he chose to build his work on these three transcendentals of being.

Balthasar began to win official recognition in the period following the Second Vatican Council during the pontificates of Paul VI (1963–78) and John Paul II (1978–2005). It has been suggested that this was because he was an 'anti-liberal but reforming theologian, [who was] neo-patristic in his sympathies' (Nichols, 1998: xix). He was appointed as a founding member of the International Theological Commission in 1969 and in 1973, with colleagues, including Joseph Ratzinger (Pope Benedict XVI (2005–13)), he founded *Communio: International Catholic Review* as a contrasting voice to *Concilium: International Journal for Theology*, through which from 1965 Karl Rahner (1904–84) and others sought to continue theological debate in the spirit of the Council (Hitchcock, 1974: 112f.) .

Honours began to come Balthasar's way during the 1970s, culminating in the International Pope Paul VI Prize in 1984 (Henrici, 1991: 35f.). When Balthasar died in Rome in 1988, while he was preparing to be made a cardinal, he was still unable to persuade the Jesuits to take responsibility for the Community of St John. This underlines the fact that, while Balthasar had a 'conventionally Catholic upbringing and training', most of the significant influences on his work 'took place when he was consciously (and sometimes critically) on the boundaries and outside the mainstream of Catholic thought' (Wigley, 2010: 11).

Jung's project in relation to Christianity

It is recognized that Jung undertook what can be described as a project in relation to Christianity within Western civilization, which grew out of his long-term interest in religion. My contention is that this can be seen as having two different though related emphases, the first of which found expression in the under-noticed collection of essays *Symbolik des Geistes* (Jung, 1948a), with the second taking prominence from the publication of *Aion* (*CW*9(ii)) onwards. I further argue that, whilst Jung's project overall was psychotherapeutic, it also expressed his own theological stance. In *Symbolik des Geistes*, the Spirit archetype provides the primary focus for psychotherapeutic amplification but also points towards Jung's implicit theological orientation. A central theological theme of the collection is God's involvement with evil.

Jung issued *Symbolik des Geistes* in the series *Psychologische Abhandlungen* [Psychological Papers], whose aim was to make occasional publications on the key themes of analytical psychology more easily available (Jung, 1914b: 825). Unlike most of the other volumes in the series, *Symbolik des Geistes* never appeared as a whole in English translation. Most of the contents were included in the English *Collected Works*. However, the work continued to be referred to by its German title (ibid.: 649) (rather than as *Symbolism of the Spirit*[8]), and the epigraph was not included,[9] nor was the longest essay, on Satan in the Old Testament by Rivkah Schärf (Schärf, 1948). That work only appeared in English translation nearly twenty years later (Kluger, 1967). Jung's foreword (Jung, 1948b) for *Symbolik des Geistes* and four essays (on fairy tales (*PSF*), Mercurius (*SM*), the Trinity (*PADT*; cf. *PCT*) and Eastern Meditation (Jung, 1943)) appear in four separate volumes of the *Collected Works*. This incomplete publication and scattering of the collection in English-language translation may account for the relatively little notice it has attracted in Jungian studies.

Jung's project in relation to Christianity, which had been forming for some two decades before the publication of *Symbolik des Geistes*, was a development from within a larger interest in the psychology of religion. Whilst Jung repudiated the traditional Christianity of his upbringing (Homans, 1995: 115–32 *passim*), it is Aniela Jaffé's (1903–91) view that '[f]undamentally, [Jung's] entire work is to be understood as a psycho-religious statement, a progressive interpretation of the numinous by which man is consciously or unconsciously filled, surrounded, and led' (Jaffé, 1972: 184).

In *Psychological Types* Jung refers to the religious function (*CW*6:141 n. 14, 242f., 315), by which he means immediate (numinous) religious experience. This did not, however, imply a thoroughgoing positive evaluation of institutional religion. The starting position for Jung's psychology of religion within analytical psychology was that in different ways secular materialistic culture and traditional Christianity are one-sided and need to reconnect with undervalued opposites (Stein, 1985: 97f.). Jung's desire to address this question in order to be of assistance to Christianity took a considerable time to emerge.

I agree with Roderick Main's proposal that this transformational project was ushered in by Jung's 1937 Terry lectures at Yale on *Psychology and Religion* (*PRTL*) (Main, 2006a: 302), and persisted to Jung's death in 1961. In my view two overlapping emphases can be discerned in this project: one is based on the affirmative treatment of dogmas as archetypal (of which *Symbolik des Geistes* is the primary expression) rather than as the deadening outcome of the institutionalization of religious experience, the other on the identification of the God-image with the Self-image (which becomes the predominant theme from *Aion* onwards).

An archetypal understanding of Christian doctrines, which emerged explicitly in the Terry lectures, had been gestating for more than a decade. Jung had begun to gain confidence that his analytical psychology had a wider cultural rootedness from his collaboration with the sinologist Richard Wilhelm in the 1920s. Their work culminated in the publication in 1928 of commentaries on *The Secret of the Golden Flower*, a text from ancient Chinese philosophical alchemy. Jung was reassured that the structure and dynamics of the psyche which he had been exploring through his own and his patients' unconscious psychological products, mainly in visions and dreams, had already found expression in cultural history (Wilhelm and Jung, 1962; cf. *CW*13: 1–56).

Almost immediately Jung sought to open up collaboration with Christian clergy (Jung, 1928b; Jung, 1932). He proposed a practical collaboration between psychotherapists and clergy on the grounds that they engage in comparable activities. He gives a more positive assessment of what Roman Catholicism (rather than Protestantism) might offer, for instance, through its framework of rituals associated with spiritual direction (cf. *PRTL*: 43–9). A few years later in *Modern Man in Search of a Soul* Jung shows his acute awareness that traditional Christianity simply no longer engaged most modern Westerners effectively (Jung, 2001; cf. *CWA*: 45f.). And, although, among all his patients in the second half of life, Jung asserted that 'none … [was] really healed who did not [find or] regain his religious outlook,' yet, he adds, '[t]his of course has nothing to do with a particular creed or membership of a church' (Jung, 1932: 334).[10]

The Terry lectures drew on work that Jung had been doing during the 1930s, mostly presented at Eranos conferences (Jung 1940; cf. Ress: 75). The key change in Jung's stance towards traditional Christian doctrines occurs in the second lecture on 'Dogma and Natural Symbols' (*PRTL*: 34–63). At first Jung continues to refer to credal formulations in terms of his accustomed negative assessment of institutional religion. They are a 'substitute [with] the obvious purpose of replacing *immediate experience*', designed so that 'people are effectively protected against immediate religious experience' (ibid.: 43). But shortly afterwards he refers to certain dogmas ('the God-man, the Cross, the Virgin Birth, the Immaculate Conception, the Trinity') themselves as immediate experiences (ibid.: 45f.).

Clearly an explanation is needed: 'It may not be quite clear why I call certain dogmas "immediate experiences" since in itself a dogma is the very thing that precludes immediate experience'; Jung proposes that doctrinal formulations be treated as archetypal: 'Dogma is like a dream, reflecting the spontaneous and autonomous activity of the objective psyche, the unconscious. … Dogma … aptly expresses the living process of the unconscious in the form of the drama of repentance, sacrifice, and redemption' (ibid.: 46).

Jung's hope is that this psychological interpretation of Christian symbols as archetypal will provide a 'noteworthy' contribution 'for any *theologia naturalis*' (ibid.: 59). There is, however, an important caveat. These archetypal expressions do not occur exclusively in Christian theology, even if he would now say they have been helpfully elaborated in Christianity:

> [T]he Christian images I have mentioned are not peculiar to Christianity alone (although in Christianity they have undergone a development and intensification of meaning not to be found in any other religion). They occur just as often in pagan religions, and besides that they can reappear spontaneously in all sorts of variations as psychic phenomena, just as in the remote past they originated in visions, dreams or trances. Ideas like these are never invented. They came into being before man had learned to use his mind purposively.
>
> (ibid.: 46)

From this new approach flowed an effort by Jung to use the psychotherapeutic methods of dream interpretation for the benefit of Christianity (Stein, 1985: 111–78). There were a number of options to explore and issues to address. One possible option was to link the project with his work on the philosophical alchemists, whose overall aim he saw as the reuniting of the worlds (or 'natures') of spirit and matter: 'Not separation of the natures but union … was the goal of alchemy' (Jung, 1942: 161; cf. Stein, 1985: 111f.). Another option focused on an important cluster of issues relating to the question of correspondence and paradox in his 'Introduction' to *Psychology and Alchemy* (*CW*12: 1–37 *passim*). A third option was to concentrate on Christian practice and dogma. Jung gave specific attention to the Roman Catholic Mass (Jung, 1942/1954) and the doctrine of the Trinity (*PCT*, *PADT*). His interest in the Trinity for this project arose from the dream series of Wolfgang Pauli, who had been raised as a Roman Catholic. Jung found himself gripped by the puzzle of why the psyche should produce both fourfold and threefold symbols of wholeness (*PRTL*: 23f.; cf. Gieser, 2005: 141–6). Jung's view was that the Christian symbol of the Trinity suffered one-sided incompleteness in that, though spiritual, it did not include matter, though masculine it did not include the feminine, and though good it did not include evil.

The idea of a project matured slowly. First-hand contact with Eastern ideas, during his visit to India in 1938, alerted Jung not only to the magnitude of the task (requiring 'no mean *tour de force*' (Jung, 1939: 528)) but also to the imperative for him that it have a Western focus (*MDR*: 311–3). In his 'India dream,' he was being 'swept … back to the too-long neglected concerns' of the West, whose 'state is perilous' and where there is 'imminent danger of destroying all that centuries have built up' (ibid.: 313). This sense of calling was intensified in a series of visions in January 1944 following a near-fatal heart attack (ibid.: 320–9). Jung felt summoned to return to the ordinary world again, to give his attention to the European context (ibid.: 322; cf. Jung, 1948b: 650).

In an important letter to a Roman Catholic layman, Herr Irminger, in September 1944, when the tide of the Second World War was clearly running against Hitler's Germany, Jung shows that he felt that a crisis threatened the whole of European civilization including the Protestant and Catholic forms of Christianity embedded within it:

> When a crack runs through a house, the entire building is affected. ... The house is no longer trustworthy as before. A conscientious builder ... will set to work on the crack and seek ways and means to mend it. ... As a doctor I am interested only in one thing: how can the wound be healed? ... Anyone who wants to, or has to, heal this conflict [between Christ and Antichrist] is faced with a hell of a mess: he sees that the European is only half a Christian. He will become a whole one only when he can also stand on his left leg. The doctor has to treat both sides, for the whole man suffers when he is sick and not merely the half.
>
> (*L*1: 347f.; cf. *CW*9(ii): ix)

As the Second World War drew to a close, Jung became more convinced that the project to which he was called must focus on how to live in the face of evil. This was no new concern for him. Material from his 1925 seminar on *Analytical Psychology* showed that already in 1913 he had shared in a growing premonition that a destructive tide of violence would spread across Europe, as it did in the First World War (Jung, 1990: 41ff.; cf. Shamdasani, 2009: 198f.; *RBLN*: 231). In 1936 Jung signalled some of his fears about the growing threat of further barbarism, a psychotic infection arising from within the German psyche, in his essay on 'Wotan' (Jung, 1936a). In 1944 he interpreted the political evils of the century in theological terms: 'a far more terrible schism [than the Reformation] has occurred in our own day, namely the Antichristian movement which *rules* Russia and Germany. ... [I]t is a Yes or No to Christianity as such' (*L*1:347).[11]

This was an issue for civil society and churches alike: 'Every Church must beat its breast, as must every European' (ibid.: 348). His first public word, as the Second World War ended in Europe, in 'After the Catastrophe' (Jung, 1945a), was to urge on all Europeans and all Christians both a question and his proposed answer:

> How am I to live with this shadow? What attitude is required if I am to be able to live in spite of evil? In order to find valid answers to these questions a complete spiritual renewal is needed. And this cannot be given gratis, each man must strive to achieve it for himself. Neither can old formulas which once had a value be brought into force again. The eternal truths cannot be transmitted mechanically; in every epoch they must be born anew from the human psyche.
>
> (ibid.: 217)

Jung finally, in correspondence with the Protestant Pastor Wegmann at the end of 1945 (*L*1: 391–3, ibid.: 395–8, ibid.: 401–3), clarified that his project would begin with an attempt to treat the archetypal symbol of the doctrine of the Trinity psychotherapeutically. In these letters Jung clarified that his project would be for the sake of the 'catholicity' of the Church (ibid.: 392), and the 'genuine religiosity in the Catholic Church' (ibid.: 396). He sees his contribution to the Mother Church in line with the work of the Holy Spirit (intuiting perhaps that the official Church might reject his views as heretical[12]). Jung's self-characterisation is as a

> lone wanderer, the fate-marked heretic (significantly derived from αιρειν, to take, choose, decide for something!) [who] divine[s] something of that maternal foundation where he is connected with the whole of Christendom. And since the outpoured Holy Ghost is himself a great heretic, he also inflicts αιρεσις, choice and agonizing decision, on all those solitaries who disturb and loosen up the *Ecclesia* by enriching her – provided of course that they can and want to link back to a maternal Church. Whether the earthly Church recognizes this linking-back or not is perhaps a painful, personal, subsidiary question.
>
> (ibid.: 397)

He sets this task within the larger societal problem of modernity's inability to resolve, from within its narrow rationality, the conflict of the opposites of good and evil. The Second World War may have been over but the world now lived under the shadow of the atom bomb. Jung believed that what rationality cannot achieve, religion could: 'that is why the question of the Church grips [him] so urgently' (ibid.: 402).

Behind the urgency of this view lay Jung's longer-held view of why Christianity falls prey to the devastating conflict between good and evil. The problem originates within Christianity itself, insofar as it separates the spiritual from the material and ascribes superior moral value to the former. Even though in the theology of the incarnation such splitting is resisted, Jung identifies this as 'the fatality inherent in the Christian disposition itself' (*CW*9(ii): 43). Whenever there is any such one-sided overemphasis, at some stage an inevitable reversal will follow. In the context of Western European civilization this began, in Jung's view, with the Renaissance and the sixteenth-century voyages of discovery: 'The ideal of spirituality striving for the heights was doomed to clash with the materialistic earth-bound passion to conquer matter and master the world' (ibid.). The situation was exacerbated in modernity, with the 'subsequent developments that led to the Enlightenment and the French Revolution' (ibid.). There has been an exaggerated attempt to ascribe all good to the rational manipulation of the material world. But the 'centuries of reason and enlightenment' (ibid.: 35) have proved incapable of averting the disaster of two world wars and are equally unlikely, in Jung's view, to be able to avoid a third (*L*1: 402).

By the time Jung had embarked on collecting, revising and expanding the essays that were published as *Symbolik des Geistes*, his collaboration with Victor White had already begun. Their sustained attempt at a creative dialogue was eventually given up after the publication of the English translation of Jung's *Answer to Job* (Jung, 1952a; cf. White, 1952; White, 1960).

The seeds of what I refer to as a second emphasis of Jung's project in relation to Christianity, the identification of the God-image with the Self-image, were already present in the Trinity lecture in *Symbolik des Geistes.* The key feature of this emphasis is the inability inherent in Jung's phenomenological orientation towards psychological images, whether manifested in an individual's dreams or in cultural expressions such as religions, to distinguish a God-image from a Self-image. In 1948 Jung wrote:

> as one can never distinguish empirically between a symbol of the self and a God-image, the two ideas, however much we try to differentiate them, always appear blended together, so that the self appears synonymous with the inner Christ of the Johannine and Pauline writings and Christ with God ('of one substance with the Father').
>
> (*PADT*: 156; cf. ibid.: 194)

This becomes the working assumption of *Aion*, Jung's major work on the phenomenology of the Self (*CW*9(ii): 31). Jung is increasingly interested in the advent of the (third) age of the Spirit (associated with the astrological aeon of Aquarius) (*CW*9(ii): 87f, 93f.; cf. Williams, 1992: 1299, ibid.: 1304) and in exploring the interdependent relation between the divine process of becoming and the human process of individuation, with resultant changes in the God-image (Edinger, 1996; Stein, 2001). In this second emphasis, it is in the age of the Spirit that traditional Christianity's inadequate understanding of evil will be able to be addressed, for it 'will then no longer be possible to write off evil as the mere privation of good; its real existence will have to be recognized' (*CW*9(ii): 87). This second emphasis persisted for Jung until the end of his life. It appears in the first section of 'Late Thoughts' in *Memories, Dreams, Reflections* (*MDR*: 359–74). Jung comes to see the primary role, not for the Church, not even for Christian theology with a renewed pneumatology (which had been the implicit theological stance undergirding the *Symbolik des Geistes* essays), but rather for 'the individual human being, via his experience of the living spirit' to allow the 'urge of the archetype to realize itself' (*CW*9(ii): 87; cf. Jung, 1952a: 463). For reasons that will be become clear later, this aspect of Jung's interest in Christianity is probably beyond the range of a critical engagement in dialogue with Balthasar.

Balthasar's theological project

Balthasar's theological project is most fully worked out in a trilogy, written on a monumental scale, issued in sixteen volumes in English translation, comprising some ten thousand pages, written over a quarter of a century (Wigley, 2010: 1). Even so it represents a small part of a much larger output (Henrici, 1991: 31; cf. Copal, 1990). Oliver Davies, however, advises that much of Balthasar's material 'is intended to exemplify the key ideas and does not need to be scrutinized with the same attentiveness as those passages or sections which set out the governing ideas of the entire project' (Davies, 2004: 131).[13]

Introduction: Epilogue

Rather than writing his theology by dealing in turn with individual doctrines, Balthasar uses as his framework the transcendentals of being: the beautiful, the good and the true. In his *Epilogue*, Balthasar employs an architectural metaphor (of a cathedral) to illustrate how his thinking unfolds (Wigley, 2010: 143f.).

In the 'forecourt' there is a 'marketplace of religious wares' (*EP*: 9). But they have to contend with modern secularity. Balthasar is critical of the positivist, materialist science that rules out the 'unasked question' of 'the meaning of being as such' (ibid.: 21), and treats humanity rather as an object of study and improvement. He accepts that the human sciences, including psychology, try to study humanity in more suitable frameworks. He mentions psychoanalysis and the work of Freud (whose ideas he had come across while studying in Vienna in the 1920s[14]), Jung and Alfred Adler (1870–1937) as examples of this improved approach but notes that they remain 'inner-psychological sciences' (*EP*: 21). Even Jung's 'metapsychology' remains a study whose object is 'empirical man', with the shared psychoanalytical aim being 'merely the rectification of man's attitude towards his own being; in no way does it question the meaning of being as such' (ibid.).

Balthasar crosses the 'threshold' into an engagement with 'being' by means of 'a theological aesthetics, dramatics, and logic' (ibid.: 46), based on three transcendentals, beauty, goodness and truth. Transcendentals are aspects of 'commonality' (Davies, 2004: 132), 'the properties of Being that transcend every individual being' (*EP*: 46). For Balthasar, 'being' and 'Being' are linked through a paradoxical analogy, where 'similarity points to an even greater dissimilarity' (ibid.: 50). Balthasar proposes that the revelation of the fullness of Being rests on three capacities: for 'Self-Showing' (ibid.: 59–67), explored in theological aesthetics, for 'Self-Giving' (ibid.: 69–76), the goodness of the kenotic self-imparting of Being, explored in theodrama, and for 'Self-Saying' (ibid.: 77–86), the ability to articulate being as epiphany and gift, reflected on in the light of 'the creation of the world in the Word of God' (ibid.: 78) in theo-logic.

Only now is it possible to enter into the 'cathedral', the content of Christian theology, whose 'inner sanctum' is found to be 'the Christian act of salvation' (ibid.: 89; cf. *TD*4). This will be dealt with in both christological and trinitarian terms (ibid.: 89–98) (linking analogically the economic Trinity and the immanent Trinity), with the incarnation as the starting point for the exploration of the person and work of Christ (ibid.: 99–108), whose mission is continued in the mission of the Spirit, the epitome of divine fruitfulness (ibid.: 109–23).

Theological aesthetics not aesthetical theology

The seven volumes of the first part of Balthasar's trilogy, *The Glory of the Lord*, explore the beautiful as the first transcendental of being. The importance of those people who were primary influences on Balthasar is evident. He shares with Barth a commitment to the recovery of the divine glory. But in distinction from Barth he follows Przywara in stressing the analogy of being. He shows his considerable debt to Henri de Lubac in the way he draws upon the Church Fathers, not least Irenaeus, and to Adrienne von Speyr for an emphasis on the important role of religious experience in theology (Wigley, 2010:25).

Balthasar is concerned about 'the disintegration of a unified concept of being' (ibid.). He sets out the symptoms of this process of loss in *GL2* and *GL3* (Wigley, 2010: 46–53). Thomas Aquinas (*c.* 1225–74) marks the watershed. Before him it was possible for theologians to write in a so-called 'clerical' style, 'marked at its centre by the glory of God's revelation' giving 'the impact of this glory a central place in [their] vision' (*GL2*: 13). After Aquinas, theologians who sought to focus on the theme of glory had to write in a so-called 'lay' style, from the margins, as it were from exile, 'protesting against a narrowing-down of Christian theology merely to the training of pastors or to academic specialization and the timeless pursuits of the schools' (ibid.: 15).

Balthasar goes on to give his diagnosis of the problem in *GL4* and *GL5* (Wigley, 2010: 53–62). In *GL4* he sets his discussion of beauty within a broader understanding of the way that Christian theology sought to offer a reinterpretation of the ancient pagan philosophical framework. It was, in Balthasar's view, a magnificent achievement of first biblical and then early Church theologians to gather up and re-energize the three strands of pagan tradition: myth, philosophy and religion. Plotinus (c. 204–70) brought the synthesis to its most satisfactory place for ongoing development, acting as a bridge from 'Antiquity' to 'Western philosophy' (*GL4*: 296). However, there is in Plotinus an ultimate equation of divinity and being: for, although divinity's 'total revelation is for him so overwhelmingly glorious that it far outshines all the splendours of particular myths', this rests on the further assertion that 'being itself is the divine' (ibid.: 280).

Balthasar seeks to establish a fundamental distinction between his theological aesthetics (which address how created, finite human beings might apprehend manifestations of divine glory) and all forms of aesthetic theology (which rely on the trajectory of human longings for the divine, 'the fundamental yearning of the finite creature for transcendence in God' (ibid.: 321)[15]). The beauty of the world is limited by the horizon of its created finiteness, which it cannot transcend by its own effort. He makes use of Aquinas' distinction between *esse* and *essentia*. Though both these terms refer to being (and so have something in common), there is a dissimilarity between the *esse*, the existence unique to God, and the *essentia*, the existence common all creation. This is to move on from the Fathers insofar as they over-identified God and creation in the theme of 'the procession and return of creatures from God and back to God' (ibid.). Balthasar seeks 'once again to make a clear differentiation between the "glory" of God and the beauty of the world' (ibid.: 395). Although created being has a similarity to divine being, it does so without being understood as identical with it or subsumed by it. It is within this 'dissimilarity' (of the infinite freedom of God) that God provides, in creation and redemption, the horizon within which the finite can discover its true meaning.

In *GL*5 Balthasar makes substantial use of his doctoral Germanic studies and traces what he sees to be the consequences of the loss of a world view based on a Thomist analogy of being. Once the paradoxical balance is lost, Balthasar sees decline in two directions: first, the assertion that being is univocal, leading to its reduction to the scope of human rationality, and then the mystical merging of human and divine being and the subsuming of being into identity with God (*GL*5: 16–47).[16]

Balthasar begins to offer his prognosis for the way ahead (in *GL*6 and *GL*7 (Wigley, 2010: 62–72)) by reading the Old and New Testaments as witness to the divine glory (Oakes, 1994: 185). He agrees with Barth that the biblical witness as a whole must be read as 'the gracious self-communication of the totally other God' (Wigley, 2010: 63) which does not rely upon 'a dialogical plane which has been opened in advance' from the human side but rather upon a dialogue initiated by God (*GL*6: 11; cf. Nichols, 1998: 188).

Balthasar proposes ways in which human beings can engage with this divine self-communication, drawing on the two-part theological aesthetics which he proposed in *Seeing the Form* (*GL*1 (Wigley, 2010: 26–46)), involving a combined theory of vision and rapture.

Theodrama – The Saving Action

Balthasar moves into the action of the theodrama in the second part of his trilogy. He establishes his use of the dramatic metaphor, sets out his theological anthropology, develops the analogy of being as an analogy of freedoms, and then develops his theology of salvation and of eschatology.

The metaphor of drama is central to the distinctiveness of Balthasar's theology. Christian living, for Balthasar, can be summed up first and foremost as '*live performance* in solidarity with others of Christ's all-encompassing mission to the world' (Quash, 2004: 144). More than this, it is Balthasar's assertion that the very life of Godself, as revealed in Christ, is best described in dramatic categories. The limitation of 'aesthetics' is that it is, in his view, too static for the dynamic divine subject matter. He needs a theological dramatic theory to do justice 'to the singular divine action' (*TD*1: 17). This expresses itself for

Balthasar in what he wants to say both about human living in response to God and about the inner-trinitarian divine life. In terms of Christian living, for Balthasar (whether drawing on the Church Fathers' sense of God's dynamism and freedom, or on Barth's emphasis on the God who is known in his acts, or on Adrienne von Speyr's experience of God's self-disclosure to the believer, or on the European dramatic tradition or on the Ignatian tradition of spiritual practice), this is rooted in the theme of dramatic transformation, divine acts and events which call for an openness to be changed through responding on the part of the human being. But this dramatic reading of Christian living rests ultimately for Balthasar on a dramatic trinitarian reading of the Christ-event so that, when in the light of the economic Trinity he comes to speak of the immanent Trinity, his focus is not on static, formal statements of essential relations between the divine Persons but on a life which is a dynamic drama of love which holds in paradox a giving which allows for both infinite distance/distinction and also an unbroken communion.

Already in *GL6* Balthasar had signalled that fulfilling the potential of created humanity, as revealed to the world through the representative story of Israel, depended upon the ability to sustain (following Martin Buber (1878–1965)) the I–Thou relationship (*GL6 passim*) between creature and Creator on which the covenant depends. This proved not to be possible. Although the Old Testament shows attempts to find the way back to glory, fulfilment cannot be achieved. That will come only through the divine initiative in Christ, revealing the mystery of beauty, the Trinity (*GL7*: 22). Balthasar, quoting Barth, notes: 'God's beauty embraces death as well as life, fear as well as joy, that which we would call ugly, as well as that which we would call beautiful' (ibid.: 23).

Balthasar draws his metaphorical resources, in *TD*1, from the literary world of drama and also from the modern disciplines of sociology and psychology. He gives particular attention to the question of role, and the 'distinction … 'between the "I" and the allotted role', 'namely how far the actor can identify with the role to be performed in order that it may become an authentic one' (Wigley, 2010: 77 referring to *TD*1: 252; cf. *TD*1: 252–4).

But for Balthasar there is a further interest in the relationship between role and mission (*TD*1: 481–643). His intention is to argue for a theological anthropology that gives significant priority to individual uniqueness in relation to the universal. In part this is to defend the ('definitive') uniqueness of Christ (as well as of each human being) against reduction to factors derived from general principles. What for Balthasar holds the "I" and role together appropriately, as seen in Christ, is the uniqueness of vocation and mission: 'In him the "I" and the role become uniquely and ineffably one in the reality of his mission, far beyond anything attainable by earthly means' (ibid.: 645f.).

In *TD*2 (*TD*2: 11) and *TD*3 Balthasar sets out his understanding of the *dramatis personae* who are the participants in the theodrama, before going on to discuss the soteriology of the main action of the drama (in *TD*4) and the eschatology of the last act (in *TD*5).

A key question is what options will be open to the characters in this drama (*TD*2: 17–169)? In particular, given the nature of the theodrama, 'who else acts, who else *can* act, if God is on stage?' (ibid.: 17). Whatever the challenge, theodrama cannot take place unless God, 'or some accredited representative of God', is an actor, '"a person" in the action, separate from the other characters' (ibid.: 189).

It is Christianity alone that offers a way ahead. When God enters onto the world stage as Christ, as God incarnate, two dangers are avoided. The nature of the human drama, enmeshed in mortality, is not diminished, and God is not made dependent upon world processes. A 'genuine opposition of freedoms' (ibid.: 190) is essential to the drama. In Christ, God takes 'an inner, divine, absolute part … in the drama of mortal existence without threatening his absolute nature' (ibid.: 45), and the 'tragic dimension of personal existence is not softened; in fact, it is wrenched to the very limit: in the Cross' (ibid.: 49). These factors pave the way for a real dramatic encounter, which must be based on freedom to act: 'If there is to be drama, characters must face each other in freedom' (ibid.: 62). Balthasar's theory of analogy is presented as an analogy of freedom, *analogia libertatis*, based on the paradoxical interplay of infinite and finite freedom (ibid.: 189–334).

The culmination of Balthasar's theological anthropology is found in the notion of 'theological persons' (*TD*3: 261–461), by which he means 'that it is only in Christ that human beings can become real persons and act as theodramatic characters in their own right' (Wigley, 2010: 98).

Christ is the theodramatic actor *par excellence*, whose character and role are held together in mission. This is what 'makes the world drama into a theodrama' (*TD*3: 201). Balthasar has his own version of an Irenaean doctrine of recapitulation whereby '[i]n his person and mission, Christ is the "last Adam," the one who gives meaning to the whole play; as such he embodies mankind's whole dramatic situation in its relationship to itself and to God' (ibid.).

Balthasar discusses the theodramatic action in *TD*4 and unfolds his doctrine of salvation. Again, the analogy of being is central: 'the crucial paradox at the heart of human existence is our inability as finite and limited creatures to comprehend the issue of infinite and absolute being' (Wigley, 2010: 104). The infinite embraces the finite. When this embrace is refused (in humanity's No to God), there is set up a contradiction, which Balthasar distinguishes from the human experience of contrary opposites (which is central to Jung's psychology). The 'No to God' is not something human beings can put right by themselves. God does that by participating in the action of the theodrama. As Balthasar puts it:

> man's historical situation in this world is in a state of permanent tension: he is constantly on the lookout for a solution, a redemption [*Erlösung*], but can never anticipate or construct it from his own resources; nor does he even have an intimation of it.
>
> (*TD*4: 75)

Salvation relies upon a transformation of meaning. If the 'structures that govern earthly existence' (ibid.: 201), the finitude of time and death, are not merely to be swept away, how can they, rather, be given new value and meaning? It has to be (as in Anselm's (1033–1109) *Cur Deus Homo?*) by someone, namely the God-Man, Jesus Christ, entering into the theodrama, who takes on those constraints. He has taken part in the theodrama as God's representative in a trinitarian estrangement in death and beyond. Together with Adrienne von Speyr, Balthasar wants even the dereliction of the Cross and the descent into hell to be seen as 'a trinitarian event' (*TL*2: 352 drawing on Speyr (1966)) – 'in which the second Person of the Trinity is cut off from and abandoned by the first, God rejected by God' (Kilby, 2004: 264 referring to *MP* and *TD*4) – with Easter as 'the victory of the triune God over every contradiction' as even death is 'swallowed up in victory' (*TL*2: 359).

God in Christ has been victorious in the battle to redeem the situation caused by the failure of finite freedom naturally to find its fulfilment in its Creator, through the trinitarian bond of love in the Spirit. But 'this does not mean that all his work is done' (*TD*4: 427); the battle of the Logos goes on (ibid.: 425–503) with greater intensification (*TD*4: 442f.). Humanity (as well as the Church) is enmeshed in the ultimate struggle between good and evil, that is, 'the theodramatic war that has broken out between God, in his Logos, and hell's anti-logos' (ibid.: 463).

But Balthasar (in *TD*5) does not envisage '*a self-unfolding horizontal theo-drama*' (*TD*5: 48); rather, he invokes a Johannine realized eschatology (as well as drawing heavily on the mystical visions of Adrienne von Speyr). Theological primacy is again given to the Trinity as 'the last horizon of the revelation of God in himself and in his dramatic relationship with the world' (ibid.: 56). The Son's eternal procession is identical with his mission (ibid.: 80). This has consequences for earthly existence seen in the light of the divine life: 'All earthly becoming is a reflection of the eternal "happening" in God, which, we repeat, is per se identical with the eternal Being or essence' (ibid.: 67). Though, because of the paradoxical analogy of being, that is not to say that the divine life is a projection of the patterns and processes of earthly becoming. Rather, kenosis in the Godhead – 'the way in which the Persons of the Trinity "make room" ("space") for one another, granting each other freedom of being and action' (ibid.: 93) – likewise makes room for creation to find its fulfilment 'ultimately, in full participation in the life of the Trinity' (ibid.: 101).

However, the persistence of evil remains a challenge and tempers any tendency towards triumphalism in theology. This is the '*Mysterium iniquitatis* [the mystery of evil]', 'the central mystery of the theo-drama: God's heightened love provokes a heightened hatred that is as bottomless as love itself (Jn. 15.25)' (ibid.: 285). We are unable to second-guess the final judgment. Balthasar 'not without a certain fear' rests his hope on the final efficacy of grace (ibid.: 321).

Theo-logic – Divine Truth and Creaturely Truth

The first volume of *Theo-logic* (*TL*1) is the re-publication, with a new introduction, of Balthasar's 1942 *The Truth of the World*. It predates his engagement with Barth and his involvement with Adrienne von Speyr, though he had the benefits of the contributions of Przywara and Henri de Lubac to his formation as a theologian. Nevertheless, the signs of future controversies with Karl Rahner are evident in this early work. These became something of a theological *cause célèbre*, particularly after Balthasar's attack on Rahner's notion of 'anonymous Christianity' in the wake of the Second Vatican Council (Kerr, 1997; Kilby, 2004). It has been suggested that *The Truth of the World* can be seen in part as a response to Rahner's transcendental (or, in Balthasar's terms, aesthetical) theology (Dalzell, 1997: 37f.). Central to Balthasar's concern is the way that he thought Rahner's emphasis on human subjectivity threatened the primacy of 'truth's dependence on the transcendent rationality of God' (Wigley, 2010: 123). It is clear that throughout the volumes of the trilogy Balthasar's own concern is with the analogy of being, his exploration of the nature of the 'correspondence between worldly "beauty" and divine "glory"', between 'worldly, finite freedom and divine, infinite freedom' and between 'the structure of creaturely truth and the structure of divine truth' (*TL*1: 7). Reflecting the paradoxical analogy of being, Balthasar's understanding of truth is twofold: on the one hand, the truth 'of things and of man' (in *TL*1) 'ultimately points back to God the Creator'; on the other, the truth God has chosen to reveal about himself, 'in the divine, incarnate Logos and his expositor [*Ausleger*], the Pneuma' (ibid.: 13) (in *TL*2 and *TL*3) 'becomes the ultimate norm of all truth in the world' (ibid.: 30).

One of Balthasar's primary purposes, then, in the *Theo-logic* is to resolve the question of how the polarity structure of human existence (which he had taken up from Przywara) is related, through the economic trinitarian missions of the Son and the Spirit, to the eternal processions of the immanent Trinity of the God who is love, for '[t]he truth of the world is grounded in the truth of God that reveals itself in it' (ibid.: 244).

Thus, in *TL*2 and *TL*3, Balthasar unfolds his trinitarian account of how God reveals the truth about himself, first, in the Logos made flesh both *ana*-logically, through those glimpses of creaturely insight that point 'upwards' towards God, and also *kata*-logically, through the divine truth revealed in the 'coming down' of the Son to earth, and then in the Spirit, the expositor of that truth. (Wigley, 2010: 127; cf. *TL*2: 11). This is most succinctly expressed for Balthasar in the Prologue to John's Gospel (John 1:14), in that:

> Only when truth is conceived in christological–trinitarian terms can it be linked with the notion of "fullness". For it then includes, not only the other transcendentals on the ontological level ("glory", "goodness", and, in the definitiveness of the enfleshed display of the divine Word, "unity"),

> but also the Son's constitutive, indissoluble relationship to the Father and to the Spirit on the trinitarian level.
>
> (*TL*2: 21)

One of the key moves that Balthasar wishes to resist at every opportunity is the suggestion that the human experience of polarity should lead to any positing of opposition within the Godhead. G.W. F. Hegel (1770–1831) is one of those to be rejected. His ana-logical attempt to make 'the entire world an *imago Trinitatis* from below', in the triadic movement of his dialectic (from thesis to antithesis to synthesis) relies, according to Balthasar, on 'making the "other" the negation of the One and then integrating both in a higher synthesis' (ibid.: 43). Balthasar insists that the difference between the divine Persons is not to be read in this way: 'the "other" in God is … in no way the negation of the One or its "reversal"' (ibid. referring to *TD*5: 65).

Balthasar, using arguments he has already established in *The Glory of the Lord* and in *Theo-Drama*, outlines the shape of his trinitarian theology, which, arguably, could be said to envisage the intra-trinitarian life as a dualistic monism (which I shall argue later is a position held by Jung), even though Balthasar himself is always wary of views that could lead to a dualism in theology. He reiterates that the economic Trinity is the only source that reveals insight into the immanent Trinity (ibid.: 125, 138); that the Son's *mission* is the continuation of his *procession* (ibid.: 154); that the way Jesus relates to the Father and the Spirit is what indicates 'the intratrinitarian relations of life and love in the one and only God' (ibid.: 125). Thus in Jesus we discover that the divine life is constituted in an identity of unity and difference. This could be described as dualistic monism. Two truths combine dualistically, in that 'the hypostases really exist in their relative opposition' and, at the same time, monistically, since 'Father, Son and Holy Spirit are one God' (ibid.: 133).

A critical comparison based on the works of Jung and Balthasar requires some understanding of the approach towards Christian theology that Jung takes and that towards psychology which Balthasar takes. In the next chapter I set Jung's psychology and Balthasar's theology within my adaptation of a general typological framework. This will help to indicate something of the parameters within which a critical comparison of Jung and Balthasar on God's involvement with evil might be conducted. The present chapter concludes with an indication of the main sources in the works of Jung and Balthasar on which I mainly draw to explore the question of God and evil.

Evil in Jung's *Symbolik des Geistes* and in Balthasar's works

The issue of evil was of concern to Jung throughout his life. We have already noted that his early teenage vision of God shattering Basel Cathedral left him with a sense of burden concerning God's involvement with evil (*MDR*: 58f.).

In his 'Late Thoughts' written for *Memories, Dreams, Reflections* not long before his death, Jung laments that, as Western people, despite our experience of Nazism and Communism, we continue to 'stand face to face with the terrible question of evil and do not even know what is before us, let alone what to pit against it' (ibid.: 363). In the *Symbolik des Geistes* essays God's involvement with evil is a predominating theme.

The essay on fairy tales describes how the Spirit archetype manifests itself in folklore. Jung uses the fairy tale of 'The Princess in the Tree' to illustrate his theory of symbol formation, which is the primary way in which he addresses the conflict of opposites, including good and evil. The Mercurius essay draws on alchemical symbolism to describe a multifaceted figure representing the spirit archetype. A key feature of Jung's discussion is the way that this unitary symbol is composed of numerous contrary opposites. This supports Jung's dualistic monism. Rivkah Schärf's essay on Satan in the Old Testament traces the development of the emerging opposition to God from among heaven's spiritual beings. This provides a means for illustrating Jung's and Balthasar's differing theological orientations and their different understandings of analogy and polarity. The essay on the Trinity is the culmination of the first phase of Jung's project in relation to Christianity. Although it contains his suggestion that the Trinity become a Quaternity to include the Devil, Jung has several interwoven agendas: a puzzle about three- and fourfold images of wholeness, an appreciation of the Church Fathers' development of the doctrine of the Trinity and an application of his psychotherapeutic methods to the doctrine, as well as expressions of his own theological perspectives. Overall in *Symbolik des Geistes*, Jung's intention is to offer his insights into the structure and psychological dynamics of the Spirit archetype, with a particular interest in addressing the issues raised by the question of God's involvement with evil. He adds his essay on Eastern Meditation as a reminder that he sees the issues he explores as a product of European civilization and its forms of Christianity (Jung, 1948b: 650).

Further important material, in the context of the opening phase of Jung's project in relation to Christianity, is found in two more places: Jung's correspondence with Victor White which highlights the issues Jung had with the doctrine of evil as *privatio boni*; and also a chapter in his 1951 work *Aion*, where Jung seeks to bring forward evidence from early Church tradition in support of his approach to God's involvement with evil (*CW*9(ii): 36–71). Jung's aim in publishing the essays of *Symbolik des Geistes* was to initiate a project in relation to Christianity that would take the form of a dialogue: 'I have ventured to submit old dogmas … to psychological scrutiny. … If I have merely succeeded in stimulating discussion, then my purpose is more than fulfilled' (*PADT*: 199f.).

The collaboration between Jung and Victor White was initiated by White in August 1945 (Lammers and Cunningham, 2007: 3; cf. *L*1: 381), just as Jung was finally clarifying how to begin his project on Christianity. Jung's enthusiasm was evident from the start and persisted beyond the publication of *Aion* (in 1951) and White's *God and the Unconscious* (Jung, 1952d). Jung wrote that this was 'the cooperation [with a theologian] I had so long wished and hoped for' (ibid.: 302). Scholars have wondered why this venture, which started with mutual high hopes, eventually foundered. Whilst a variety of factors can be identified (Lammers and Cunningham, 2007: xxiv–xxviii), it is noteworthy that the eventual cessation of the collaboration related to the question of evil. By May 1955, after the publication in English of Jung's *Answer to Job*, the dialogue, though not the friendship, came to an end (ibid.: 272f.), since 'the challenge of seeing God as evil as well as good was more than White could embrace' (Weldon, 2007: 189).

Jung had psychotherapeutic reasons for focusing in *Symbolik des Geistes* on the character and psychological functioning of the Spirit archetype. This coincides with his own preference for an emphasis on the Spirit in Christian theology, pointing to the renewal of an original urgency: as in the early Church when the 'kerygma of the early centuries poured forth *new spirit* and it worked like fire' (*L*1: 349).

Psychotherapeutically, Jung relies on the Spirit archetype to exemplify, in the alchemical symbol Mercurius, dualistic monism, and in his fairy-tale essay he gives a working example of his (spiritual) theory of symbol formation. In the Trinity essay the Holy Spirit is given an important role in resolving towards wholeness the otherwise irresolvable conflict between good and evil, between the archetypally hostile brothers, Christ and the Devil. In the light of this, the aptness emerges of Jung's epigraph for *Symbolik des Geistes*, referring to the spirit that searches even the depths of God: *Spiritus enim omnia scrutatur, etiam profunda Dei* (1 Cor. 2:10 (Vulgate)).[17]

Balthasar, like Jung, could take a pessimistic view of the challenge of evil in the life of humanity. There is plenty of counter-evidence to set against Christianity's claim that God has resolved even in principle the question of evil:

> In the Cross, God is supposed to have reconciled the world to himself ...; but where do we discern even the beginnings or the echo of this profound upheaval or reversal? ... In fact evil, which has supposedly been overcome on the Cross, seems to have become even more virulent.
>
> (*TD*1: 64)

He echoes Jung's dismal prognosis for contemporary Western European civilization:

> now man discovers the world's dark side: aggression, the will to power, reciprocal annihilation and, in the sphere of history, the tragedy of a civilization which seems to be proceeding towards self-extinction. A light has gone out; the landscape of existence seems drear and alien.
>
> (ibid.: 49)

There is no single major source for Balthasar's theological position in relation to evil. Texts are to be found throughout his trilogy and elsewhere. Rather than being treated as a separate doctrinal subject, the question of evil is integrated as Balthasar sees that it needs to be addressed. There is an exception to this in his 'hastily written' (*TL*2: 345 n. 75) *Mysterium Paschale*, which Balthasar says he was prevailed upon to produce by a publisher who had been let down by another author (ibid.).

In the volumes of *The Glory of the Lord* there are brief discussions of the approaches to evil in Augustine (354–430) (*GL*2: 123–9) as well as Blaise Pascal (1623–62) (*GL*3: 210–15), Johann Hamann (1730–88) (ibid.: 254–61), Vladimir Soloviev (1853–1900) (ibid.: 338–52) and Charles Péguy (1873–1914) (ibid.: 435–65). There are more extended discussions in the volume on the Old Testament. That creation and humanity are made in the image of God stands for the possibility of fulfilment based on a Yes to God. Theology also has to recognize the reality of separation arising from a No to God. It is the case that

> the Bible allows for a serious and definitive development of the element of the image, for ... only in the Bible is the image something which God himself has set up with bold freedom over against himself – something which is to know God, respond to him in freedom, and welcome him with love.
>
> (*GL*6: 87)

It is in this context that the Fall and sin, the exercise of the freedom to say No to God are discussed, in sections on 'The suspension of the image', 'Sin and Malediction' and 'Sheol and God's mobility' (ibid.: 97–103, 215–9, 220–4). The theodramatic locus for the resolution of the problem that humanity's No to God has created culminates in the Cross. In Balthasar's volume on the New Testament (*GL*7) this is discussed under 'The Momentum of the Cross', with its sub-sections on 'The collision', 'Kenosis' and 'Hell' (*GL*7: 202–35).

In the volumes of *Theo-Drama*, the question of evil is highlighted as an important issue for contemporary theology (*TD*1: 48–50), and heaven and earth are discussed in terms of the world stage on which the theodrama takes place (*TD*2: 173–88). There are three further major discussions: angels and demons as *dramatis personae* (*TD*3: 463–501), the interrelation of freedom, power and evil (*TD*4: 137–201), and the 'mystery of iniquity' as an aspect of the eschatological 'Battle of the Logos' (ibid.: 442–52).

One of the distinctive features of Balthasar's theodrama, of his understanding of God's involvement with evil, is the central place he gives to Christ's *descensus*, which plays a pivotal role in his understanding of salvation. His views on the descent into hell have recently become a matter of considerable debate in his reception by Roman Catholic theologians (Pitstick, 2007; Oakes, 2006, 2007a and 2007b; D'Costa, 2009: 201–10; cf. Kilby, 2012). Aidan Nichols claims too much when he says it is in his *Mysterium Paschale* that Balthasar, in his exploration of 'the Descent, "solves" the problem of theodicy' (*MP*: 7). If one considers the sources, Balthasar's view is somewhat different: his 'Dramatic Soteriology' (*TD*4: 317–423; cf. *GL*7: 202ff., 203 n. 2) should be read before *Mysterium Paschale*, and after that the section on 'Hell and Trinity' (*TL*2: 345–61), in which he relies heavily on Adrienne von Speyr.

Notes

1 On an 'autobiography' rather than a series of biographies, see Jaffé in *MDR*: 7f. and also, for instance, Casement, 2001: 3f. and Bair, 2004: ix.
2 See Shamdasani, 1995:115–37; for the editing process, see Jaffé, 1971 and Casement, 2001: 4.
3 See Bishop, 1999: 23 n. 1.
4 The most important product of this period of intense exploration was Jung's *Red Book* (only recently published), within which, in the section called 'Scrutinies', are the *Seven Sermons to the Dead*, which were published primarily for private circulation during Jung's lifetime (*RBLN*: 346–54; cf. *CW*19: 15; Segal, 1992).
5 In the *Seven Sermons of the Dead*, the figure of Abraxas 'is the uniting of the [all good] Christian god with Satan' (*RBLN*: 367), a figure in whom the opposites are conjoined (Shamdasani, 2012a: 372).
6 See, for instance, *Collected Papers on Analytical Psychology* (Jung, 1916a), *The Structure of the Unconscious* (Jung, 1916b), and *On The Psychology of the Unconscious* (Jung, 1917/1926/1943).
7 See Mongrain, 2002: 11f. for the view that Balthasar's theology is deformed in the places where it is most obviously influenced by Speyr. Kilby argues for a 'charitable reading' without ignoring occasions where Balthasar specifically uses material from Speyr (Kilby, 2012: 9 and n. 11).
8 See Jung, 1948a: vii '*fünf Aufsätze, die sich mit der Symbolik des Geistes beschäftigen*' [five essays that are concerned with the symbolism of the spirit (Jung, 1948b: 649)].
9 Jung, 1948a: v – '*Spiritus enim omnia scrutatur, etiam profunda Dei* (I. Cor. II.10)'.
10 This approach uses Jung to promote a contemporary spirituality. See, for instance, 'We have not only outgrown the values and assumptions of mechanistic science and humanism, but we can no longer situate ourselves comfortably in the containment of the traditional religions … in their old, premodern forms' (Tacey, 2004: 2). Tacey hopes to invoke Jung and others to help to 'uncover a universal spiritual wisdom that could transform our fractured world' (ibid.: 1).
11 For Balthasar this has been the central issue throughout Christian history: 'in the post-Easter Church … everything is concentrated on man's Yes or No to the Incarnation of the Son of the Father' (*TD*4: 181).
12 See also Jung's reference to himself in the *Red Book* as 'an Anabaptist and a stranger' (*RBLN*: 304).
13 This outline draws mainly on Wigley, 2010; see also Nichols, 1998, 2000 and 2001 and Howsare, 2009.
14 From Rudolf Allers (1883–1963), a former Freudian (Henrici, 1991: 10).
15 Kerr, 1997: 159–84 and 207–9 argues against the sharpness of this distinction, as expressed in Balthasar's controversy with Karl Rahner.
16 Jung's identification of Self-image and God-image could be seen as a manifestation in modern psychology of this outcome.
17 See Balthasar on this text in *TL*3: 441–5.

Chapter 3

A framework for critical comparison

There is much debate about what Jung's aims were in relation to Christianity but relatively few studies that attempt to discern systematic themes in his work that relate to the question of the interplay between psychology and theology. Balthasar studies are at an earlier stage of development. There are no major explorations of his use of psychology, and few attempts to discern systematic frameworks within his voluminous writings (Mongrain, 2002; Howsare, 2009; Kilby, 2012) or to explore his understanding of evil (Friesenhahn, 2011). Furthermore, a framework within which to locate a critical comparison does not lie ready-made in the works of Jung or Balthasar or in the secondary literature that their work has generated. In this chapter I outline a framework, using an adaptation of a typology initially proposed by Hans Frei (1922–88) and then argue for reading Balthasar as a type 2 contextualizing theologian and Jung as a type 4 reinterpretive psychologist.

An adapted Frei/Ford typology

Frei developed a typology to provide a 'conceptual orientation' (Frei, 1992: 1) for a projected history of Christology from 1700. It is based on the interplay between two understandings of theology: first, as a specific example of a more general endeavour working within the accepted criteria of academic disciplines; and, second, as the self-description of the Christian community working with its own norms to provide the criteria for the theological enterprise. Frei proposes a fivefold typology of different versions of this interaction, each with a distinctive way of relating theology to other academic disciplines (whether philosophy or anthropology and sociology). This typology has been taken up by David Ford as a more general means of gaining perspective on the work of twentieth-century theologians (Ford and Muers, 2005: 2f., 14 n. 1).[1]

My adaptation builds on a suggestion from Frei about types 1 and 5, namely that '[o]pposite extremes sometimes tend to approach each other in circular fashion' (Frei, 1992: 5), in the sense that both deny the other any significant explanatory function and are expressed as a reflexive continuum. I propose three types of theology (type 1 traditionalist, type 2 contextualizing and type 3

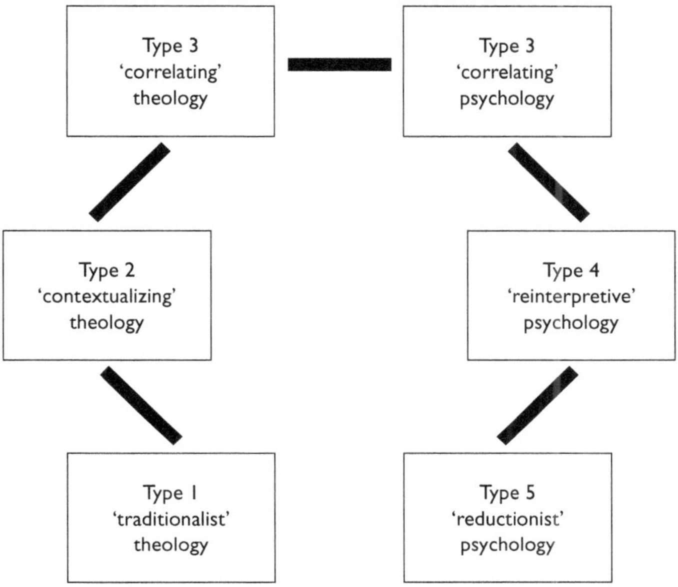

Figure 1 An adaptation of the Frei/Ford typology

correlating), relating to three types of psychology (type 5 reductionist, type 4 reinterpretive and type 3 correlating). The Frei/Ford typology, and my adaptation, does not take into account the possibility that a theologian or a psychologist may also have a personal or professional commitment to the other discipline or community of practice. Whilst Balthasar has no significant commitment to any particular school of psychology, Jung's own theological stance, I shall argue, has a significant bearing on his project in relation to Christianity.

In a type 1 traditionalist theology, complete priority is given to a version of Christianity with other disciplines having no recognized significance for that theology. For Frei, a 'Christian theology' of this traditionalist type 'is exclusively a matter of Christian self-description' (Frei, 1992: 4; cf. Ford, 1995: 537). 'There is', further, 'no formal, context-independent or independently describable set of transcendental conditions governing [its] internal logic' (ibid.). Ford comments that in modern theology this type represents an 'attempt to repeat a traditional theology or version of Christianity and see all reality in its own terms, with no recognition of the significance for it of other perspectives or of all that has happened in recent centuries' (Ford and Muers, 2005: 2; cf. Hunsinger, 1993: 261f.).

In a type 2 contextualizing theology, priority is given to a version of Christianity but with serious engagement with its present-day intellectual and cultural context. For Frei, while 'Christian self-description governs and limits the applicability of general criteria of meaning in theology'; nevertheless, theology must be open to 'restate doctrinal statements in the light of cultural and conceptual change' (Frei, 1992: 4; cf. Hunsinger, 1993: 261; Ford 1995: 537) in the service of faith in 'its quest for understanding' (Ford and Muers, 2005: 2).

In a type 3 correlating theology or correlating psychology, explanatory priority is given neither to theology nor to other disciplines. Dialogue, rather, is based on complementarity, though a theology or a psychology will give its own discipline descriptive preference. For Frei, the key point is that correlating is done on a non-systematic basis without recourse to a larger theoretical (academic) framework. Such theologies, therefore, seek correlation with other disciplines using 'ad hoc procedures' such as 'broadly pragmatic appeals to the character of human experience' (Frei, 1993: 3; cf. Hunsinger, 1993: 261). They 'propose a correlation between heterogeneous equals' (ibid.: 4; cf. Ford, 1995: 537). A key feature of a correlating psychology, in my adapted version of the typology, would thus be to see a dialogue with theology as between heterogeneous equals, giving descriptive but not explanatory priority to the psychological world view, seeking direct links with aspects of Christianity in an *ad hoc*, non-systematic way.

A type 4 reinterpretive psychology is used in my adapted form of the Frei/Ford framework to categorize psychology in its relation to theology, where priority is given to an overall psychological theoretical framework as the basis for a reinterpretation of theology. This adapts Frei's understanding of theologies of this sort, which employ a 'subsumption of theology' under the framework of general academic criteria as the basis for a revision of Christianity. Under these 'governing auspices' there is an attempt to 'correlate specifically Christian with general cultural meaning structures' (Frei, 1992: 3)[2] such as the sciences or a more general *zeitgeist*. In Ford's terms, such theologies seek to provide a 'consistent reinterpretation of Christianity in terms of some contemporary' understanding or discipline (Ford and Muers, 2005: 3).

In my adaptation of this typology, a type 5 reductionist approach gives complete priority to some modern secular philosophy or world view with no independent significance granted to theology (ibid.: 2). Frei discusses this as a theological position by relating it to philosophy (Frei, 1992: 2f.; cf. Hunsinger, 1993: 260; Ford, 1995: 536f.). Ford regards such theologies as 'hardly Christian' (Ford and Muers, 2005: 2) when 'Christianity in its own terms is only valid insofar as it fits in with' the other discipline (ibid.).[3] It is nevertheless the case that there are type 5 reductionist psychologies that allow validity to religion in general and Christianity in particular only insofar as they conform to and can be explained in terms of the criteria of that psychology.

I propose to read Balthasar's work as that of a type 2 contextualizing theologian and Jung's as that of a type 4 reinterpretive psychologist. Balthasar, like many other modern theologians (ibid.), fits within the Frei/Ford type 2 criteria in that he gives priority to Christian norms of self-description in his theology, but reworks its traditional themes in critical relation to a broader cultural and intellectual context. Unlike some other modern theologians, however, his primary location is the Church as a community of practice, rather than the academy. Although there are readings of Jung that would place him in either a type 3 correlating or a type 5 reductionist position in relation to theology, I argue that a type 4 reading is most useful in relation to Jung's intentions in the first phase of his project on Christianity, expressed in the essays in *Symbolik des Geistes.*

Balthasar as a type 2 contextualizing theologian

Central to a type 2 contextualizing theology is a stance which, whilst giving priority to a Christian self-understanding in its own terms, nevertheless shows a willingness to engage with the perspectives of other disciplines. This is in contrast both to a type 1 traditionalist theology, which gives complete priority to Christianity and no significance to other disciplines or world views, and also to a type 3 correlating theology, which seeks the complementarity of heterogeneous equals on an *ad hoc* basis. In his 'programmatic little book' (*RBCA*: 7, quoting Balthasar, 1993b: 51) *Razing the Bastions: On the Church in this Age*, Balthasar clearly locates himself in type 2 rather than either type 1 or type 3. For him the theological way ahead

> must lie in ... a path defined negatively by two solutions, neither of which can be followed. The first is the solution of an absolutism of the truth, which does not understand the new situation of solidarity, but wishes to deal with the people of our time on the same level of consciousness that characterized medieval absolutism. The other is the religious relativism of the Enlightenment ... [which] understands all forms of religion as meaningful, justified and complementary to one another on various levels of relationship to a total truth.
>
> (ibid.: 51f.)

Balthasar's type 2 contextualizing engagement is based in a general cultural openness, even whilst retaining a critical distance from culture. Such a stance, as it is expressed in Balthasar's works, is likely to mean that critical comparison with a type 4 reinterpretive psychology will be a matter of holding in tension potentially divergent views.

Openness to culture

There can be little doubt of the importance Balthasar attached to openness to the world outside the Roman Catholic Church. The depth of his musicality, evident from an early age, and his doctoral studies in German literature and the European philosophical tradition already point in that direction. Henri de

Lubac regarded Balthasar as 'perhaps the most cultivated man of our time', who offers, in Lubac's view, 'the most penetrating' 'spiritual diagnosis of our civilization' (Lubac, 1991: 272; cf. Wigley, 2010: 23). He notes Balthasar's interest in 'the diverse exploratory adventures of contemporary man' (ibid.: 273), including modern atheism. There were limits, however, even to Balthasar's range. His primary focus was on Western European civilization and within that on the humanities, with little engagement with science (Henrici, 1991: 17).

Erich Przywara, a key influence on Balthasar, himself held, as Balthasar noted with approval, 'a Catholic faith which sought not to separate and withdraw from the world but rather to engage and interact with it' (Wigley, 2010: 16 referring to Przywara, 1923). Henri de Lubac's *Catholicisme* (Lubac, 1938) encouraged a Catholic theology that was open to other perspectives. Balthasar also affirms his commitment to the view that

> the bastions of anxiety which the Church had contrived to protect herself from the world would have to be demolished; the Church had to be freed and open to the whole and undivided world for its mission. For the meaning of Christ's coming is to save the *world*.
>
> (Balthasar, 1986a: 194; cf. ibid.: 197)

This was the contemporary aspect of the *ressourcement* agenda to rediscover the wisdom of the tradition for the sake of a renewed future. Furthermore, Balthasar's formation in Ignatian spirituality meant that using the resources of the past would involve a process of re-formation of Christianity itself, 'a purification, a deepening, a centring of its idea, which alone renders us capable of representing it, radiating it, translating it believably in the world' (ibid.: 196).

Balthasar begins *Razing the Bastions* by challenging the Church to be open to the new spirit of the age that emerged after the Second World War. Even though 'the naked will to destroy sneers at' 'enthusiasm for new futures' (*RBCA*: 17), and physical ruin was accompanied by the 'intellectual collapse of beloved and trusted traditions' (ibid.: 18), yet Balthasar looked to the future in hope. Among those whom he had met during his student chaplaincy work, he discerned a new commitment, based on 'a hitherto unknown spiritual exertion', which showed 'humanity becoming aware for the first time of its unity on this planet and of the duty of stewarding itself', with an 'expansion of horizons' from regional to worldwide (ibid.: 17). Despite evidence to the contrary Balthasar envisaged that the West would have an important role to play in this process: 'Europe (dissolved as a reality) closes in upon itself, in order to become the spirit and the idea (*Geist-idee*) of future humanity as a whole' (ibid.: 20). It was in this same spirit that Balthasar had embarked on the Klosterberg project in 1940, 'designed to provide, at the end of Nazism, the cornerstones for a spiritual Europe in which an open Christian attitude could take seriously all that is affirmative in Western culture' (Balthasar, 1986a: 196).

Further, a possible pivotal role for the Church remains. Given that 'no one in today's West is older than the Church', and despite the obvious signs of the decrepitude of old age, Balthasar sees a non-Church world that is 'effectively striving toward her [the Church's] unity' (*RBCA*: 21f.). This represented, in Balthasar, a refusal to take a defeatist, self-preserving stance when so many were becoming non-practising Catholics; it is also a determination to hold on to a universalism rooted in the Gospels and the insights of the primitive Church that does not rely on numerical superiority (ibid.: 58–69 *passim*). This 'descent', in numbers and influence, like the *descensus* of Christ, is a real loss and yet, paradoxically, the spring of salvation. Such an attitude would see that the Church's 'apparent organic weakness, her decline, her division belong in reality to the mystery of a supernatural weakness corresponding, in its own time, to an exalted supernatural fruitfulness' (ibid.: 64).

If this is God's missional agenda, is the Church up to the task? Only, Balthasar suggests, if there is a recognition that a type 1 traditionalist approach, with the Catholic Church as a bastion of universality and unity in the West, is no longer appropriate.

Balthasar evokes Christianity, in an image that has Augustinian origins, as a 'fortified *civitas*', a geo-political entity concerned to extend and defend the reach of territory to be 'made accessible to the fruitful cultivation, *cultura*, of the Church' (ibid.: 48). There was a self-sufficiency about this world view in which 'Christianity and the civilized world are one' (ibid.: 47). In medieval Christianity this provided a stronghold that had little need to relate to those beyond its bastion walls: 'The Christian thought in a closed inner room, his Christian awareness emerged only weakly and vaguely *ad extra* over the boundaries' (ibid.: 48).

More or less simultaneously in the fifteenth and sixteenth centuries one external and another internal shift took place which rendered obsolescent this bastion, type 1 traditionalist model of Christianity: the European voyages of discovery of new worlds and the Protestant Reformation. These then required an interaction with the non-Christian world on a different basis. The claim to universality was shattered. The church had abandoned its obedience to the dominical injunction to unity, which soon resulted in a plethora of churches (ibid.: 49, 50f.). The claim to self-defined distinctiveness could no longer be maintained, because

> the geographical-political outer room and the spiritual-intellectual inner room of Christianity find themselves unexpectedly brought into a continuity ['a horizontal (and no longer hierarchical) solidarity' (ibid.: 50)] with the surrounding world, and this situation demanded (and still demands) that all the instincts be newly attuned and the interior organs of balance differently disposed.
>
> (ibid.: 49)

Balthasar sees that razing the bastions will involve an 'immense transformation in [Roman Catholic] Christian consciousness' (ibid.: 58). This is a matter of the Church coming out of 'a splendid isolation' and being part of 'the tumult of the age' in solidarity with humanity as a whole (ibid.: 93). In 1952 it was a task yet to be addressed, for, in Balthasar's view, the Roman Catholic Church was hampered in embracing the new task because it had remained too traditionalist, from the time of the Counter-Reformation up to the anti-modernist reassertion of neo-Thomism at the end of the nineteenth century. Balthasar uses the term 'Baroque' theology (coined by *ressourcement* theologians such as Yves Congar (1904–95)) to assert that the Church had during these centuries been overcommitted to a backward-looking attempt to perpetuate tradition for its own sake: 'its relationship to its own past leaps to the eye, but not its relation to its future' (ibid.: 18; cf. ibid.: 51 and n. 1).

This shift involves Christianity rediscovering its vocation as primarily missionary, as apostolic, rather than seeking to continue to reap the fruits of Christ's once-for-all salvation (ibid.: 58). One option would be to sweep away the Church and traditional Christianity in order to make a new start. This 'harsh grace' may take place, but Balthasar prefers to hope for the 'radiant grace' which arises from internal, theological renewal, drawing on the 'power of transcending', which is 'the lifeblood of all traditions, the vitality that knows the past and yet is able to separate itself from the past to the extent that is required by responsibility and readiness for the future' (ibid.: 22f.).

Balthasar saw this risky task as evidence of the movement of the Holy Spirit (cf. *L*1: 401–3). He notes, shortly after he had left the Jesuits, that those who are called to 'visibly radiant missions' must expect resistance and opposition from the 'forces of inertia' within the Church (*RBCA*: 24). He cites the worker priests as providing a possible model for his own calling as a praying theologian: 'a holy theologian could appear ... who would bring the holy audacity of the worker priests to the plane of meditation and doctrine' (ibid.: 26). It is the continuing mission of the Spirit which takes things forward, by means of a 'transcendence from within', that is, 'the spiritually explosive power of holiness, which is always something more than the wisdom of the tradition: [this] is the presence of the Holy Spirit for us in today's age' (ibid.: 23; cf. ibid.: 29–37 *passim*).

A distinctive response to culture

If, in *Razing the Bastions*, Balthasar is advocating a shift away from a type 1 traditionalist theology, he also wants to avoid the (type 3 correlating) relativizing complementarity which he sees as a product typical of the Enlightenment. In *Razing the Bastions*, it is clear that Balthasar engages with others primarily on the basis of the priority of the Christian world view. This emphasis remained for Balthasar when he founded the journal *Communio* as a counterbalance to those whom he thought engaged too uncritically with the non-Christian in the years following the Second Vatican Council.

Balthasar's type 2 contextualizing theology can be seen as both 'liberal' (in the sense of being open to other disciplines) and simultaneously 'conservative' (in the sense of asserting the priority of Christian truth). Edward Oakes suggests that this is not a problem, provided such labels are applied carefully (Oakes, 1994: 159–64). It is true that Balthasar was conservative in the fullness of his use of 'the sources that comprise the Great Tradition' (ibid.: 163), that is, the Scriptures and the Fathers. That is one of the marks of the *ressourcement* agenda. But unlike the conservatism of a type 1 traditionalist he criticizes the sources. On the other hand he is definitely not 'liberal', in that he was not 'willing to elevate the achievements of the Enlightenment to a governing methodological principle' (ibid). He engages with post-Enlightenment modernity in a challenging rather than an acquiescing way. Balthasar was strongly of the opinion that (type 3) 'one-sided' 'openness to the world' 'becomes exceedingly dangerous' without the challenge of a 'distinctive counterpoise' (Balthasar, 1986a: 197).[4] This wariness of using other disciplines in their own terms in a type 4 way in relation to theology indicates that dialogue with a reinterpretative psychology will be likely to involve both divergence as well as convergence.

Balthasar's (type 2 contextualizing) engagement with disciplines and world views other than Christianity is of a twofold nature: he both stresses the validity of other frameworks and also asserts the priority and the qualitative distinctiveness of Christian truth. This is a tension inherent in a type 2 theology.

Balthasar accepts as a contemporary reality for many people – 'the natural scientist ... the one engaged in the study of the humanities, ... the doctor, ... the factory worker, ... the theologian' (*RBCA*: 74) – that 'the different realms of truth demand a change of one's intellectual standpoint' (ibid.: 73). If type 1 theology can be said to envisage the realm of truth as a circle drawn around a single point, then Balthasar suggests that a type 2 theology, which accepts another realm of truth, would require a view of truth as an ellipse, drawn around two separate points. If the truth of revelation and worldly truth are to engage with one another, the Christian lay person and, by the same argument, the contextualizing theologian will find their 'own view of the world elliptic', having the character of 'a "double truth"' (ibid.: 75).

If this embodies the new task of the Church for the future, the role of the Christian lay person is of increased importance. The mission of those Christians who are engaged in a secular discipline – the typical situation of those whom Balthasar and Adrienne von Speyr's Community of St John sought to support – involves an ability to move elliptically between different standpoints.

However, without further elucidation the idea of elliptical, double truth could be taken as giving the truth of revelation and worldly truth equal status. That would tend towards reading this task in a type 3 correlating way. In this sense, Balthasar's metaphor is not a good expression of his more fundamental stance of theological priority. In Balthasar's view, rather than seeking to make the two 'coincide' (which might be a type 3 aim), the 'Christian is charged absolutely to bear this tension and extension' (ibid.), which may eventually be resolved since 'the objective truth of these secular things is not a truth closed in on itself, but a truth that is opened toward Christ, and it is a preliminary truth' (ibid.: 76f). This gives Balthasar's contextualizing approach an underlying apologetic purpose: 'the Church must go outward to the nations and teach them the Christian truth in such a way that they can understand and accept it ("inculturation")' (*TL3*: 259).

Balthasar's primary position, rather than one based on a statically described ellipse, is that divine truth is in a dynamically encompassing relation to finite, worldly truth. Balthasar envisages a process of maturation '"in motion"', between 'Christian and worldly truth, between ecclesiastical "infallibility" and human, scientific "tolerance"', which accepts 'the limited character of worldly truth' (*RBCA*: 80) whilst not endowing the truth of revelation with attributes of unchangeability. Worldly truth 'with all its plurality' tends to 'become splintered'; the Church offers to 'embrace' worldly truth within the '"pleromatic" unity' of Christian truth (*TL3*: 259).

Relating a type 2 theology to other disciplines

This raises a question about how Balthasar treats other disciplines. He argues for a shift from a type 1 traditionalist position. He would likewise look for other disciplines to move from a type 5 reductionist position. He argues that the elliptical nature of truth challenges both positions, for '[b]oth of them undergo essentially the same elliptical "double experience" even if they come from opposite poles. Both are essentially en route, … occupied with a synthesis that can never be fully achieved' (*RBCA*: 83).

The contextualizing theologian needs to be ready to be sufficiently surprised by the insights from other disciplines with their own autonomy and to be willing to co-operate with Christian lay people in order to hear 'the hour now sounding in the world' (ibid.: 85). The unending search for synthesis, however, is only finally addressed when the priority of Christian truth is acknowledged.

This leads to a second aspect of the twofold nature of Balthasar's engagement with other-than-Christian world views and truth-claims: his stress on the priority, the qualitative distinctiveness and the superiority of Christianity. Priority is held in tension with openness. Distinctiveness enables the image of an ellipse to be read in terms of analogy.

Balthasar sees that the claim to priority requires a new version of the assertion by Augustine and earlier Church Fathers that outside the Church there is no salvation. This will not be easily understood in the contemporary world (ibid.: 53ff.). It continues to make a claim for an indispensable role for the Church in the economy of salvation, for the 'grace of Christ … is universal …

it is not distributed [or, 'mediated' (ibid.: 54)] without regard for … the Church' (ibid.: 54). It will become a key theme in Balthasar's *Theo-Drama* that non-Christian horizons of meaning find their fulfilment only in the Christian revelation.

Any dialogue with another discipline by a type 2 contextualizing theology, stressing Christian priority, is likely to involve conflict, not least in conversation with a type 4 reinterpretive discipline which likewise asserts the priority of its own discipline. Balthasar understands that 'collision' is integral to the Church's mission (ibid.: 72). The bastions are evidently not razed in the sense that the Church has nothing distinctive to offer:

> The Church remains at every period what she was: the bulwark and the steward of all truth, for all the treasures of wisdom and knowledge are hidden in Christ, and no one has access to these treasures of Christ except through the Church. But when she enters into the world and becomes for the world one religion among others, one community among others, one doctrine and truth among others – just as Christ became one man among others, outwardly indistinguishable from them – her truth comes into a communism with all the forms of worldly truth: with the experiential truth of all branches of knowledge, and with the wisdom-systems of the world which attempt conclusive statements about the being of the world and of its truth.
>
> (ibid.: 71f.)

Given the new outer and inner perspectives first opened up in the sixteenth century, in Balthasar's view, the traditionalist Catholic Church has to be in (or 'enter into') the world in a different way. Christianity in relation to the world is salt. It 'must not become insipid' (Balthasar, 1986a: 201).

Balthasar held his stance, of the priority of Christianity, within a larger understanding of the ultimate priority of God, which relativizes Christian theology as well as worldly truth. It is God alone who is prior (in non-contingent infinite freedom) to the world and all its truth, for God's reality is qualitatively distinct from the world, even though the latter is made in God's image. The Christian (and presumably the Church), as well as all creation, needs to be open to re-formation through being caught up in the ongoing mission of the Holy Spirit of truth:

> The Spirit blows where he wills, Christ gives what he wills, the Father demands and takes what he wills, but the Christian stands defenceless in the midst of this billowing truth and is yielded up to every wave that breaks on him. He cannot conceal himself behind any truth that might cover him, to protect himself from a truth of God. He cannot use any known truth (to say nothing of a whole system) as a weapon against the unknown, infallible truth of God that now assaults him.
>
> (ibid.: 79)

All human attempts (theological or other) to contain the vastness of divine truth, eternally welling up out of God's infinite freedom, have in the end to acknowledge God's priority.

Underlying his approach to worldly truth and to other disciplines is his understanding of analogy and its relation to the drama of salvation. God is qualitatively, essentially distinct from and yet sufficiently similar to his creation to be known within created, existential experience: 'although God's sacred being can never be confused with one or with the totality of his creatures, nevertheless God does not wish to become visible to us other than in the context of his creatures' (ibid.: 103). This means that

> an authentic Christian experience of worldly truth [entails] the endurance of the alien character of this truth, of its inadaptability to the sacred inner room of the [inner-trinitarian] divine truth out of which Christ and the Church live and in which they are at home.
>
> (ibid.: 86)

Similarity (between the worldly and the divine) has its origins in the unity within the triune life of Godself. But in the ('essential') eternal procession of the Son within the Godhead there is also an infinite separation and distance, a kenosis which is revealed to us in the ('existential') incarnation. That brings Christ (and so also the Church) into a real involvement in human experience such that '*nil humanum mihi alienum puto* [nothing human is strange to me]' (ibid.: 87 quoting Terence (195/185–159 BCE)). And however separate from God human experience becomes, however bitter the experience of the distance and dissimilarity between divine and human truth, the infinite divine unity is always drawn in love in the direction of reconciliation.

> Thus, [the Church] drenched with the bitterest gall of the world's truth, … while in the world's night everything threatens only to break up into ever more alien and hostile parts, thus drawn into the experience of the Cross which is the self-alienation of truth (until [divine] truth and [worldly] truth no longer know each other, and find no longer any path to one another), she [the Church] matures to become the power that unites from within what has become separated.
>
> (ibid.)

Balthasar envisages that the Church will thus gather up all partial, human truths, through the reconciling forgiveness of Christ's Cross (and descent into entombment), so that 'the hard outer shells of error break open and release the captive kernel of truth' (ibid.: 88). That truth is to be embodied in a new humanity in Christ, since 'God himself broke down [all] separating walls when his Son appeared, "in order to make out of the two one new man in himself, establishing peace" (Eph. 2:15)' (ibid.: 103).

Given Balthasar's understanding of the provisional nature of all human attempts to articulate truth, of the preliminary nature of worldly (non-Christian) truth, there remains a question about the extent of his willingness to accept significant input from other modern disciplines (such as Jungian psychology) in the restatement of Christian theology.

Jung as a type 4 reinterpretive psychologist

Unlike Balthasar, Jung never wrote anything that could be called programmatic on his project in relation to Christianity. Nevertheless, Stein identifies Jung's approach as one that we can possibly identify as a type 4 reinterpretive approach. He argues that, given Jung's understanding of 'the structure and dynamics of the psyche', he 'is in a position to evaluate and to make critical-constructive observations about the completeness of doctrines about God', to offer a 'psychological interpretation of religious texts' and a 'psychological critique of theological ideas' (Stein, 1990: 18). There are, however, other readings of Jung in relation to religion and theology that suggest he could be located in other areas of the adapted typology. Even on a type 4 reading, it is important to note some of the complexities that arise from both the interlinking of Jung's theoretical orientations, scientific, phenomenological and metaphysical, and also his own theological commitments.

Other readings of Jung

Before setting out the argument for Jung as a type 4 reinterpretive psychologist, it is important to note, in terms of this typology, some other ways of reading Jung in relation to Christianity, whether as a type 3 correlating psychologist or as a type 5 reductionist psychologist.

A type 3 approach would look for a dialogue based on direct correspondence between psychological experience of God (interpreted from a Jungian perspective) and theological expressions of the reality of God. Ann Ulanov, for example, says that the contribution of Jung's psychology to theology is 'to construct a bridge … making connections between sacred images and corresponding images in our psyche' (Ulanov, 2006: 63 referring to *CW*12: 12–4) to the mutual benefit of the individual and the religious tradition, on the basis that there is a natural religious function in the psyche. Morton Kelsey seems content to elide psychology and theology when discussing Jung's ideas about 'the reality of the Self, or of God' (Kelsey, 1984: 192). Charlene Burns argues for a direct resonance between Jung's idea of the Self archetype and Schleiermacher's concept of 'feeling' (Burns, 2011). John Dourley, in a multifaceted thesis developed over five decades, explores a link between Jung's psychology and Tillich's theology (Dourley, 1981; Dourley, 2005).

In Ford's estimation Tillich is a type 3 correlating theologian because he seeks in Christian symbols the answers to basic questions raised in contemporary life

(Ford and Muers, 2005: 2). Jung, seen as a type 3 correlating psychologist, in response to the questions raised by life experience, offers a psychological account of the Christian symbols that the theologian invokes. Dourley argues that this complementarity relies, in the case of both Tillich and Jung, on an appeal to the religious nature of humanity, namely that 'the reality of religion is embedded in the fabric of the human soul, and that it finds its inevitable expression in the consciousness that arises from such depths' (Dourley, 1981: 7). Dourley suggests that, for both men, reconnection with the true wellsprings of religion might revalidate the institutional forms of Christianity and statements of its doctrine which have lost their efficacy for modern people. Traditional theology is a thing of the past, best left behind since it dangerously severs people and cultures from 'authentic religion'. A new spirituality, it is alleged, is more likely to emerge than a revivification of the traditional, and to better effect. According to Dourley:

> Both Tillich and Jung were convinced that their culture was severed from authentic religion. Throughout their lifetimes and especially in their seniority each devoted their energies to the recovery of the roots of religion in the human. This recovery for both was in the interests of the restoration of a valid sense of religion to their culture. The hoped-for revalidation of religion could occur in institutional religion but probably through a new mythic consciousness alive in the wider societal mind beyond institutionally identifiable religion.
>
> (Dourley, 2008: 192; cf. Stein, 1987: 3f.)

Once Jung, from his Terry lectures onward, begins to treat Christianity's doctrines as archetypal in their own right, there is more scope for the entirety of Christianity to be brought into a (type 4) reinterpretive engagement with the entire framework of Jung's analytical psychology and the process of individuation. It is possible in the phase of Jung's project expressed in the *Symbolik des Geistes* essays to maintain not only a connection but also a critical distance between a type 4 psychology and a type 2 contextualizing theology.

This breaks down, however, as Jung's project in relation to Christianity progresses, and particularly from *Aion* onwards. He came to rely increasingly on the idea of the empirical indistinguishability of Self- and God-images. Interest centres upon the changing God-image as a function of evolving human consciousness. Dourley (following Jung), however, extends the benefit to Godself. God needs the human psychological process. Only in humanity can God become conscious, enabling the education and redemption of God in history. This view has themes in common with the proposals of Edward Edinger (1922–98) (Edinger, 1996) and Murray Stein (Stein, 2001).

These authors are careful not to reduce God to a function of human consciousness, for, with Jung, they give priority to the role of the collective unconscious in the process of a changing God-image. Nevertheless, since the psychological is assumed to have a direct correspondence to divine process, it is hard to escape the conclusion that God is in some way contingently dependent on the human psyche and its processes. Stein's explicit view is, 'there is no difference between … the evolution of a God-image … [and] evolution in God in and of [God]self' (ibid.: 20). This is a type 3 position which in the end, I suggest, also offers very limited options for dialogue between Balthasarian theology and Jungian psychology.

A different response, during Jung's lifetime, to the possibility of dialogue between his psychology and Christian theology was to insist that (as suggested in the opposition of types 1 and 5) the two disciplines should not seek to impinge on each other. Raymond Hostie (1920–99), who had some sympathy with Jung's psychological ideas, eventually concluded: 'The religious function is rooted in man, but revealed truths have their source in God; and whenever these two realities come together, any confusion of them is fatal' (Hostie, 1957: 222). Less forcefully, John de Gruchy implies that Jung would be better keeping to his psychological researches rather than offering 'speculations' in theological disciplines in which he has no expertise (Gruchy, 1984: 203). One positive outcome of a type 1 / type 5 stand-off is that it avoids the issue of reductionism. Jung always protested that he was misunderstood when he was charged with psychologism. But the drawback is that it also offers almost no options for dialogue between theology and psychology.

James Hillman (1926–2011) and more recently Wolfgang Giegerich have been more critical of Jung's interest in Christianity. Hillman emphasizes the archetypal aspects of the human psyche and is critical of Jung's persisting interest in monotheistic Christianity, insisting that the workings of the psyche more naturally map on to a polytheistic world view (Hillman, 1975; cf. Casement, 2001: 130). More radically (in type 5 terms), Wolfgang Giegerich argues that Jung was mistaken in hanging on to any engagement with God or God-images in his psychology and that the only way forward for humanity, by a thoroughgoing process of demythologization, is to allow God to die (Giegerich, 2010).

My proposal is that, for the first phase of Jung's project in relation to Christianity, he is read as a type 4 reinterpretive psychologist who enters into dialogue with Christian theology in its own terms, understood in the light of his analytical psychology. However, this type 4 reading needs to take account both of the interrelation of three theoretical orientations (scientific, phenomenological and metaphysical (Chapman, 1988)) and also of his own theological commitments.

Jung's scientific orientation

Jung always thought of himself as an empirical scientist. His early work on the word association test broadly conforms to a materialist, experimental approach.

However, the more crucial aspect of Jung's scientific orientation is that it differs from the generally prevailing academic criteria (Tacey, 1997; Ulanov, 1997; Casement, 2001: 155 and Bulkeley and Weldon, 2011) by being vitalist and energic rather than materialist, and for giving priority of interest to final rather than historical causes (Main, 2004: 177).

From the start of his intellectual career Jung's scientific stance was that of a vitalist rather than a materialist. In his first Zofingia lecture, on 'The Border Zones of Exact Science' (*CWA*: 1–19), he asserts that materialism in science is an 'absurd colossus with feet of clay' (ibid.: 6) and mocks 'the dogma that [such] science actually explains some things' (ibid.: 11). He argues rather that 'a pre-existent vital principle is necessary to explain the world of organic phenomena' (ibid.: 18); it 'constitutes, so to speak, the scaffolding on which matter is built up' (ibid.: 30). If in this sense the vital principle has ontological priority, in the realm of psychology it provides the basis for the epistemic priority of psychic phenomena: 'The vital principle … is the enduring factor in the phenomenal realm' (ibid).

Jung saw several dangers lurking in the prevailing materialism of modernity: hubris, in claiming that in principle 'all aspects of life have been fully explored'; stagnation, 'intellectual death' (ibid.: 19), and 'moral instability'; a technologically based society which leads to 'the brutalization of the working man' (ibid.: 36); the educationalist castigating all that resists such a narrow stance as 'medieval nonsense which is threatening to extinguish the lamp of his enlightenment' (ibid.).

Jung is also wary at this stage of contemporary forms of institutional Christianity that confine themselves within modern rationality. In the Zofingia lectures, he argues that clergy, for instance, who oppose what they see as 'the sin of spiritualism' are unwittingly, with other rationalist moderns, 'encouraging the general moral debacle' (ibid). In youthful enthusiasm Jung looked forward to the day he hoped would quickly arrive, when 'bells [would be] ringing out to proclaim the disgrace of a Germany overcome by materialism' (ibid.: 44).

Two world wars would convince Jung that an immense effort would be needed to address the catastrophic shattering of modernity's materialist optimism and belief in progress. Jung's *Red Book* contains a number of premonitions of the horror of war overwhelming Europe (*RBLN*: 231). This problem is exacerbated if people rely entirely on conscious rationality and, seeing themselves as in the right, do not know how to get free of their enmity against those who carry their 'shadow' projections. This was Jung's reading of both the First and the Second World Wars. He wrote in 1916:

> The psychological concomitants of the present war … are uniquely fitted to force upon the attention of every thinking person the problem of the chaotic unconscious which slumbers beneath the ordered world of consciousness. This war has pitilessly revealed to civilized man that he is still a

> barbarian, and has at the same time shown what an iron scourge lies in store for him if ever again he should be tempted to make his neighbour responsible for his own evil qualities.
>
> (Jung, 1917/1926/1943: 4; cf. Jung, 1936a)

The ruinous end of the Second World War in 1945 was one of the spurs towards undertaking his project in relation to Christianity, in which addressing the question of evil would be central (Jung, 1945a).

Materialist science struggles to see a place for the non-rational in religion. Jung's vitalism at first led him to be critical of Christianity in thrall to modern materialism. Later it allowed for an empirical approach to religion which valued the phenomenological reality of the spiritual. This preference is already evident in the Zofingia lectures. He does not gainsay that in the material world there is an essential place for discovering through empirical science 'the operation of causality in the realm of concrete phenomena' (*CWA*: 18). But this does not address the questions that are the realm of final causation, and which must not be ignored despite the element of mystery: 'The "Why?" lingers in the background: it is and remains inexplicable' (ibid.).

For a period, however, Jung seems to have been content to work in Freudian terms with reductionist explanations. There are examples of determinist and reductionist views in Jung's essays on 'The Significance of the Father in the Destiny of the Individual' (Jung, 1909/1949) and on *The Psychology of the Unconscious* (*CWB*). This had a particular effect during this period on Jung's psychology of religion. In the 1909 essay Jung espouses a Freudian aim of identifying historical causes, namely 'to gain a deeper insight into the driving forces that determine the individual's fate' (Jung, 1909/1949: 320 n. 21[5]) and in the 1911–12 essay he sees God in reductionist terms:

> Since, psychologically understood, the divinity is nothing else than a projected complex of representation which is accentuated in feeling according to the degree of religiousness of the individual, so God is to be considered as the representative of a certain sum of energy (libido).
>
> (*CWB*: 61)

There is a hint of special pleading by Jung when, in a 1945 letter to Victor White, he claimed to have written in this way only in order to win a hearing from psychoanalytical colleagues (*L*1: 383f. and nn. 1–3).

Nevertheless, Jung's settled view within his analytical psychology is that both understandings of causation are needed for a satisfactory scientific orientation: 'no explanation of nature can be mechanistic only', where a 'mechanistic', 'causal' view 'conceives an event as the effect of a cause'. In addition the 'energic' view is also needed, which 'is in essence final' in the sense of moving in 'a definite direction (goal)' with the actual end not yet known (Jung, 1928a: 3–6 *passim*).

In his scientific orientation Jung shows a preference for final rather than historical causes, but he also distances himself from an a priori view of purpose. In the way that Jung talks of purpose and of final causes, it seems reasonable to conclude that his orientation is teleological. But Jung makes a distinction between final purpose and teleological (in the sense of predetermined) purpose.[6] In an essay on dream psychology he writes:

> When a psychological fact has to be explained, it must be remembered that psychological data necessitate a twofold point of view, namely that of *causality* and that of *finality*. I use the word finality intentionally, in order to avoid confusion with the concept of teleology. By finality I mean the immanent psychological striving for a goal. Instead of 'striving for a goal' one could also say 'sense of purpose'. All psychological phenomena have some such sense of purpose inherent in them.
>
> (Jung, 1916/1948: 241)

In the 1966 revision of the essay on 'The Structure of the Unconscious', Jung notes that in eschewing teleology he wants to stay closer to the immediacy of psychological phenomena. The end is not yet known. He rejects 'an end given a priori', and nor is there a 'pre-existent fixation of a final end'; rather: 'All one can say is that things happen as if there were a fixed final aim. In psychology one ought to be as wary of believing absolutely in causality as of an absolute belief in teleology' (Jung, 1916/1966: 294 n.19). In this way Jung holds fast to an emergentist rather than an a priori understanding of final causes.

Jung's phenomenological orientation

Jung's student Zofingia lectures provide evidence of his early interest in the inner life of the psyche and that he hoped to find in a phenomenological orientation a means of connecting his scientific and metaphysical interests (*CWA*: 21–47 *passim*). On the one hand Jung is attracted to real, direct encounter with the divine, as exemplified by 'the "pietist" [who] holds that Christ consoles him, actually and directly, through the power of the Holy Spirit which Christ promised once to send to his own people' (ibid.: 102). On the other hand, however, Jung was concerned that espousing such a pre-modern world view would involve 'social and scientific indifference' and threaten 'the further progress of civilization' (ibid.: 110; cf. ibid.: 108f.).

Insofar as the norms of reductive, materialist science held sway in the academy in the context in which Jung was working, he would eventually seek to establish the practice of analytical psychology on a vitalist understanding of science with primacy given to a phenomenological orientation (as already noted): 'The vital principle ... is the enduring factor in the phenomenal realm' (ibid.: 30). The claim that the phenomena of psychological experience have epistemological priority (that is, that mental phenomena are not merely epiphenomena, reductively explicable in terms of physiology) is based on an idealist ontology which invokes vitalism as the prior foundation of all reality: 'the *principium vitae* constitutes, so to speak, the scaffolding on which matter is built up' (ibid.). And, although his understanding of the structure and dynamics of the psyche was still to be articulated, Jung, in the Zofingia lectures, is already aware that the full story of the phenomenal psyche will not be confined to consciousness: 'we ought not to seek for the principle of life within the consciousness' (ibid.: 31). Following Schopenhauer (1788–1860), he speculates that the life force, 'the soul', will be understood as a 'transcendental' entity (a '*Ding an sich*', borrowing a phrase from Kant). It will have characteristics of being 'intelligent' (that is, having 'purposefulness in its acts'), 'independen[ce] of space and time' and 'immortality' (ibid.: 31f.; cf. ibid.: 38–43). These student fraternity lectures already hint at things he would say about the transgressivity of archetypes in his essays on synchronicity written in collaboration with Wolfgang Pauli more than half a century later (Jung, 1951, Jung, 1952b). The phenomenological orientation provides a unitary locus, holding together the duality of physical and metaphysical:

> [W]e are living at the boundary between two worlds. Our body formed from matter, our soul gazing toward the heights, are joined into a single living organism. We see our lives coming into contact with a higher order of being. The laws governing our mental universe grow pale before that light, emanating from the metaphysical order, which it is granted us to dimly divine. Man lives at the boundary between two worlds. He steps forth from the darkness of metaphysical being, shoots like a blazing meteor through the phenomenal world, and then leaves it again to pursue his course into infinity.
>
> (*CWA*: 47)

Harley Chapman argues that Jung's phenomenological orientation is an aspect of his methodology rather than a philosophical commitment (Chapman, 1988: 63–7). Roger Brooke, on the other hand, seeks to argue that Jung makes some significant contributions to the existential phenomenology agenda by asserting the complexity and depth of experience (Brooke, 1991; Brooke, 2000).

Brooke argues that Jung 'shows an understanding of human being that lies at the heart of existential phenomenology' (Brooke, 1991: 2). In a rationalistic world, which follows Nietzsche in declaring the death of God, thinking about being requires, as Heidegger (1889–1976) argues, imaginative *poesis* to continue to see being as Being: 'To be a poet in a destitute time means to attend ... to the trace of the fugitive gods' (ibid.: 8 quoting Heidegger). For Jung, recovering wholeness from the neurotically one-sided rationalism of modernity involved recovering the 'religious outlook' (Jung, 1932: 334).

Some of the key points of Jung's phenomenological orientation are expressed in his hermeneutical method (Brooke, 1991: 28–51), his understanding of the ontological priority of experience (ibid.: 63–94), and his theory of archetypes (ibid.: 136–60).

Jung's hermeneutic approach begins with the description of psychological phenomena before engaging with their explanation. In *Psychology and Religion* he advocates this empirically descriptive approach – 'the mere classification and accumulation of experience' – so that he can look at the fact of, for instance, a theological doctrine and avoid 'metaphysical … considerations' (*PRTL*: 5f.). He treats many sorts of phenomena (including patients' dreams and the credal formulations of Christian doctrines) equally as empirical texts whose symbolic meaning is then to be explored by two sorts of interpretation, association and amplification. Thus:

> The essence of hermeneutics … consists in adding further analogies to the one already supplied by the symbol: in the first place subjective [associative] analogies produced at random by the patient, then objective [amplificatory] analogies provided by the analyst out of his general knowledge. This procedure widens and enriches the initial symbol.
>
> (Jung, 1916/1966: 291)

By this means Brooke argues that Jung hopes to reconnect 'experience to its authentic ground' (Brooke, 1991: 49). This itself is future-oriented and makes use of Jung's concern for finality, not predetermined but emerging, the coming-into-being of a possible future, greater wholeness.

The ontological priority of experience can be illustrated by Jung's understanding of the psyche. It is radically subjective. There is no other, Archimedean point from which to look at the psyche from outside. Part of psychological experience is the sense that archetypal images come from outside consciousness. Even though Jung borrows the Kantian phrase *Ding an sich* to allude to their otherness, with their origin in the objective (collective) unconscious, they remain intrapsychic. Apart from the criticism that Jung uses the Kantian idea without sufficient attention to its intended meaning (Nagy, 1991, Voogd, 1984), his phenomenological orientation can be seen to collapse into psychologism, as Martin Buber thought (Buber, 1952; Jung, 1952c).

Archetypes, which Jung saw could not be directly encountered, were, as Brooke summarizes, 'the primordial roots of those complexes which structure behaviour, images, affects, and thoughts as these emerge in the typical situations of human life' (Brooke, 1991: 159). Although Brooke would like to rework Jung to fit consistently within an existential phenomenology, he has to admit that for Jung himself 'phenomenology was not a consistent methodological home' (ibid.: 50), nor is it a simple matter to fit a Jungian interpretation of religious experience without remainder into a phenomenological concept such as 'depth' (Brooke, 2000: 104).

Jung's type 4 reinterpretive approach to Christian theology is based on criteria he developed in analytical psychology, with a scientific orientation that is vitalist, with an emergentist understanding of final causes, and with a phenomenological orientation which gives priority to the subjective, empirical study of subjective experience. This would be a straightforwardly, if distinctive, modern psychological approach from within which to offer a reinterpretation of Christian theology. But, further, account must be taken of Jung's metaphysical orientation.

Jung's metaphysical orientation

If a type 2 contextualizing theology has to accord at least initially some measure of validity to the insights of other disciplines, a type 4 reinterpretive psychology needs a comparable stance. Jung, however, as a scientist and as a phenomenologist, disavows metaphysical assertions. Nevertheless, there is evidence not only that Jung had metaphysical views of his own, but also that he brings his own theological commitments to his project in relation to Christianity.

In her introduction to Jung's *Memories, Dreams, Reflections*, Jaffé asserts that 'Jung explicitly declared his allegiance to Christianity' but notes that he approached questions about Christianity 'from the standpoint of psychology, deliberately setting a ['bound[7]] between it and the theological approach' (*MDR*: 13). Perhaps Jung was to some extent a victim of a wider problem, a gap between the criteria of the Christian community (enabling him to share aspects of his metaphysical and theological views with Christian clergy and lay people) and those of academic theology (distancing his scientific and phenomenological psychology from metaphysical claims).

Jung asserted that metaphysics is the province of philosophers and theologians and is off limits for the empirical scientist. In establishing his analytical psychology as a valid aspect of medical science, Jung insists that the phenomenological reality of psychological subjectivity is a proper field of study in its own right. Psychological experience is to be neither reduced to an epiphenomenal function of some other biological cause nor mistaken (in the case of experience of God) as evidence for an objective metaphysical reality. Jung argues, for instance, that the scientific orientation can be an important safeguard against straying on to theological territory. Doctrinal statements 'can – and for scientific reasons, must – be reduced to man and his psychology, since they are mental products which cannot be presumed to have any metaphysical validity' (*PADT*: 180).

In relation to his scientific orientation, once he has passed through the reductionism of his Freudian period, Jung does not deny metaphysical realities but rather, as a scientist, has nothing positive to assert. In his 1911–12 essay, as already noted, Jung's reductionist view is that God 'is nothing else than a projected complex ... the representat[ion] of a certain sum of energy (libido)'

(*CWB*: 61). In the 1952 revision of this text, Jung removes the 'nothing else than', but he now sees God in psychological terms as a 'collective archetype', that is 'a psychic existent which should not in itself be confused with the idea of a metaphysical God. The existence of the archetype neither postulates a God, nor does it deny that he exists' (*CW*5: 56; cf. ibid. n. 29).

Again, in his foreword to the *Symbolik des Geistes* essays, Jung separates the scientific from the metaphysical:

> It goes without saying that in any such discussion [of the Trinity], metaphysical views cannot be considered, because, within the confines of a scientific psychology and its tasks, an idea characterized as 'metaphysical' can claim the significance only of a psychic phenomenon. Equally the psychologist does not presume to say anything 'metaphysical', i.e. transcending his proper province, about his subject-matter – that lies outside his competence. In so far – and only in so far – as the Trinity is not merely an object of belief but, over and above that, a human concept falling within the purview of psychology, can it be subjected to scientific observation.
>
> (Jung, 1948b: 649f.; cf. Jung, 1939/1954: 478; *L*1: 384; and Jung, 1929a: 49)

Given that assertions about God are also made within the self-description of the Christian community, Jung's disavowal of metaphysics (in the arena of debate with science) is not necessarily inconsistent with his also stoutly protesting that 'nowhere and never have I denied God' (*L*1: 349). Jung was not professionally involved in academic theology, but as a layman he retained contact with the Christian community and with theologians and had an active interest in theological issues.

Chapman proposes that 'Jung was a scientist by choice but a metaphysician *malgré lui*' (Chapman, 1988: 143). He struggles to find direct evidence of Jung's metaphysical orientation, except in letters in the last decade of his life (ibid.: 123–51), where, although God, for Jung, 'is a mystery that cannot be unveiled' (*L*2: 254), 'the Unfathomable itself' (*L*1: 125), he is nevertheless self-evident: '[t]he existence of a transcendental reality is evident in itself' even though 'it is uncommonly difficult for our consciousness to construct intellectual models which would give a graphic description of the reality we have perceived' (*CW*14: 551). Just occasionally Jung allowed himself to 'indulge in transcendental speculation …: God has indeed made an inconceivably sublime and mysteriously contradictory image of himself [the Trinity], without the help of man, and has implanted it in man's unconscious' (Jung, 1952c: 667).

It is perhaps more significant for our purposes to note Jung's persisting interest in the Christian community of practice, the Protestant and Roman Catholic Churches, embedded within Western European civilization. It is to

Christianity in this sense that he eventually seeks to offer the assistance of his analytical psychology. In this regard it is important to register not only Jung's metaphysical orientation, but also his own theological stance. Buber is among those who felt the need to unmask Jung as a heretical (Gnostic) theologian because he valued knowledge above faith (Stein, 1985: 8f.). In my view he is best characterized as a radical Protestant.

In his student Zofingia lectures Jung evidently still stood within the ambit of Christianity and the Swiss Reformed theological tradition. Although it is clear from the *Red Book* that Jung's own theological explorations remained linked to key features of Christianity, he spoke very rarely about his own theological commitments. However, in a lecture to Protestant clergy in 1932 he not only referred to himself as a Protestant (Jung, 1932: 340; cf. *L1*: 346), but added: 'My own position is on the extreme left wing in the parliament of Protestant opinion' (ibid.: 347). This seems to be a reference to what until recently has gone under the generic title of Anabaptism,[8] but which is now usually referred to as radical Protestantism. It seems to me that, as regards theoretical orientation, Jung best fits the characterization of what George Williams, in his magisterial study (Williams, 1992), has called a 'prophetic or revolutionary spiritualist'.[9]

There were a number of emphases shared by most sixteenth-century radical Protestants: a direct relation with God, enthusiasm (which was used as term of abuse by their opponents), individuality and the contribution of lay people, inner divine inspiration and prophetic utterance and action. The credibility of leadership often rested on spiritual gifts (ibid.: xxxiv–xxxv). It could also include a spiritual primacy which could suggest 'in veiled language, deification' (ibid.: xxx).

Jung lays great stress on direct religious experience. Religion, in his Zofingia lectures, must have 'vivacity, … energy, … enthusiasm' (*CWA*: 47). He came to see enthusiasm as two-edged – 'a veritable gift of the gods or a monster from hell' (Jung, 1944: 583; cf. Jung, 1920/1948: 315) – not least in the political and social conditions of the mid-twentieth century. Although for Jung individuality involves deep connection with the universal aspects of what it is to be fully human, nevertheless the individual has prior value for him over the institutional in religion or the mass-mindedness of '-isms' in twentieth-century society. When he was engaging with the theological aspects of Christianity Jung called upon his layman's perspective. For the youthful Jung, prophetic leadership is required to counteract the desiccated Christianity of modernity: '*Deeds* are needed to wake up religion, miracles are needed, and men endowed with miraculous powers. Prophets, men sent by God!' (*CWA*: 46). Although one factor in Jung's procrastination over whether to publish his *Red Book* may have been because 'it sounded like prophecy' (Shamdasani, 2009: 214; cf. ibid. n. 188), yet at the start of the work Jung linked texts from the prophet Isaiah, which Christianity has interpreted messianically, with the Johannine text asserting that Christ is God's only-begotten Son (*RBLN*: 229).

In the sixteenth-century Reformation the emphases found in radical Protestants who are classifiable as prophetic or revolutionary spiritualists can be seen in part as a re-expression of aspects of medieval mysticism (Williams, 1992: 1298). There are positive references in Jung's Zofingia lectures to medieval mysticism – as well as to seventeenth-century pietism, which can be seen as another flowering of the emphasis on direct spiritual experience (*CWA*: 98ff., 102, 105, 110). Sixteenth-century radical Protestants, stressing 'the divine immediacy' often through 'Spirit-infusion' (Williams, 1992: 1299), usually rejected any church alliance with secular authority and were often suspicious of any form of institutionalization of religion (ibid.: 1299). From the point of view of their theoretical orientation, there was often a preference for an *ecclesia spiritualis*, a restoration of the true church, since the Catholic and Protestant Churches were thought to be irreformable (ibid.: xxxiii).

When Jung came finally to clarify his project in relation to Christianity, in his 1945 correspondence with Pastor Wegmann, he noted how unusual it was for someone with such views as his to want to offer them for the benefit of the institutional church (*L*1: 397). I set out in chapter four a claim that Jung's version of a radical Protestant 'spiritual' theology has a 'Joachimite' shape, and I shall argue later that this theological orientation is as integral to his project in relation to Christianity as his psychotherapeutic interpretations.

Locating Jung as a type 4 reinterpretive psychologist requires us to bear in mind that 'Jung's positions on religion were complex, with seemingly opposed or disparate currents of interest flowing into and out of one another' (Main, 2006a: 297). Consideration of Jung's three theoretical orientations illustrates the perceptiveness of that observation.

Since Jung held a vitalist understanding of science, he evinced a deep suspicion of materialist science, the technology based on it, and a belief in progress and the rational resolution of humanity's problems. Jung also held a metaphysical orientation which gave theological primacy to the spiritual. He had a deep suspicion of institutional Christianity not least in forms that sought to ally themselves with secular modernity. Since his vitalist science claimed to be empirical, he tended to draw a sharp line to keep his psychology separate from philosophical and theological metaphysics. His emphasis on direct religious experience was consonant with the phenomenological orientation underlying his analytical psychology. But whereas on the one hand he sought to escape from radical subjectivism, asserting both a real physical world and an objective unconscious aspect of the psyche, yet on the other, given his understanding of the unknowability of the archetype in itself, he was unable in the end to distinguish empirically between Self- and God-images.

However, we can locate Jung within a type 4 reinterpretive psychology on two grounds. The first is his adoption, in the Terry lectures, of the idea that some Christian doctrines are archetypal. It can be argued that Jung's phenomenological orientation provides him with a linking middle ground between science and religion. This is consistent with Main's conclusion that 'out of the tension between religion and science Jung forged a psychology that partakes of both religion and science and yet is fully identifiable with neither (Main, 2006b: 166 n. 6; cf. Main, 2004: 91–114). However, the basis on which Jung's analytical psychology relates to Christianity and its doctrines has to take account of the fact that his analytical psychology arises primarily out of the self-description of the practice of a psychotherapeutic community. The relationship of the norms of that community to those of materialist science, or philosophical metaphysics, or existential phenomenology, is always on Jung's terms. Within the adapted Frei/Ford typology this is a valid stance, even if proponents of those academic disciplines are often critical of what they take as Jung's misusage of the sources of support on which he draws.

The second ground for reading Jung as a type 4 reinterpretive psychologist, at least in the first phase of his project in relation to Christianity, is that he wishes to use his psychological insights for the benefit of the institutional (Roman Catholic) Church. However, in this regard, we have to bear in mind the complication, not explicitly envisaged in the Frei/Ford typology, that Jung held theological views of his own which (as we shall see) affect the psychotherapeutic aspects of his project.

As his correspondence with Victor White got under way in 1945, Jung summed up his understanding of a dialogue between psychology and theology which is consonant with the type 2 / type 4 approach outlined in this chapter. Jung is grateful that a theologian has understood his scientific ('empirical') and phenomenological ('practical') orientations. He restates his usual public disavowal of metaphysics. However, his assertion, that this is the proper business of the theologian (to which the scientist might make a modest contribution), keeps his own personal theological commitments largely out of view:

> You have rendered justice to my empirical and practical standpoint throughout. … I never allow myself to make statements about the divine entity, since that would be a transgression beyond the limit of science. … My personal view in this matter is that man's vital energy or libido is the divine pneuma all right … When you talk to scientists … you cannot say that man's goal is actually realized in God. … What you can show … is the symbol of the self, a well-defined scientific phenomenon, which anybody may call God, but the scientist cannot prove it to be God. … But it is precisely what the theologian has to say, namely that the dogma is the hitherto most perfect answer to and formulation of the most relevant items in the objective psyche and that God has worked all these things in man's soul. The scientist however cannot prove such an assertion, he can only try his best in his limited sphere.
>
> (*L*1: 384f.)

If we read Balthasar as a type 2 contextualizing theologian and Jung, at least in the *Symbolik des Geistes* phase of his project on Christianity, as a type 4 reinterpretive psychologist, then, in continuing to build the framework for a critical comparison, there are four areas that present themselves for consideration: namely each author's understanding of the human being (Jung's map of the psyche and Balthasar's theological anthropology); of overall theological orientation; of analogy; and of polarity. I explore these in the next two chapters and argue that Jung and Balthasar, despite some interesting convergence, differ in ways that are important for a critical comparison of their understanding of God's involvement with evil.

Notes

1 I follow Ford's rather than Frei's enumeration.
2 On balance Hunsinger (1993: 260) prefers to stress correlating in type 4 and subsuming in type 5 (cf. Ford, 1995: 537).
3 Kilby tends in this direction when she argues that, for instance, social theologies of the Trinity cannot give 'a picture of what God is like *in se*' but rather, in terms of a philosophical understanding of grammar, only an account of how, for the Christian community of practice, 'various aspects of the Christian faith hang together' (Kilby, 2000: 444).
4 See Balthasar's opposition to Rahner's idea of the 'anonymous Christian' (Balthasar, 1986a: 198ff.).
5 Omitted in the 1949 revision.
6 Chapman, 1988: 81–3; Main, 2004: 177; Huskinson, 2006: 204. Lucy Huskinson describes Jung's individuation process as a 'pre-designated teleological scheme' heading toward the realization of its 'goal or culmination' in the Self (ibid.; cf. Casement, 2001: 41). It is true that Jung does not always use terms precisely or consistently. On one occasion he goes as far as to say: 'Life is teleology par excellence; it is the intrinsic striving towards a goal, and the living organism is a system of directed aims which seek to fulfil themselves' (Jung, 1934a: 406; cf. Jung, 1917/1926/1943: 40 and Jung, 1952b: 493). And while he can distinguish between a 'causal' and a 'teleological' understanding of psychological phenomena (Jung, 1917/1926/1943: 59; cf. Jung, 1928c: 131, 151f.), nevertheless he also insists on drawing a distinction between 'finality' and 'teleology' and that his psychology is built on the former and not on the latter (Jung, 1928a: 3–6, 23–5).
7 The American edition ('bound') makes more sense than 'bond' (in the English edition) in the light of Jung's emphasis on 'understanding and reflecting, as against the Christian demand for faith' (*MDR*: 13).
8 Jung has only a few passing references to those generically referred to as 'Anabaptists', repeating the magisterial Protestant estimation of them as diabolical fanatics (*PRTL*: 10 n. 12), and his own socio-psychological assessment of the movement as an example of a 'psychic epidemic' (Jung, 1945b: 593; cf. Jung, 1970b: 362).
9 This summary draws primarily on Williams (1992: xxviii–xxxvi, 1–21, and 1289–1311). Williams' researches are confined to a sixty-year period from about 1520, when a plethora of small groups sprang up, mostly in northern Switzerland, southern Germany and the Netherlands, nearly all of which shunned the link of Christianity to the state found in magisterial Protestantism and counter-reform Catholicism and within which Williams identifies three broad strands (each with a number of subdivisions): Anabaptists, Spiritualizers and Evangelical Rationalists.

Part II

Bases for critical comparison

Chapter 4

Anthropology and theological orientation

Balthasar and Jung both thought that modernity suffered from debilitating defects. For Jung, modernity's one-sided overemphasis on a narrow, conscious rationality meant that, in Western civilization in general and also in the Christianity embedded within it, there was a reduced ability to access the symbolic life of archetypal images within a living Christian doctrinal world view. This (neurotic) dissociation was what his process of individuation was intended to heal. Balthasar believed there was a comparable loss of appreciation of the divine glory, together with an 'assertion of the independence of human rationality from divine revelation' (Wigley, 2010: 58), which was made apparent in the separation of theology as an academic discipline from the spirituality of the lived experience of faith. Through his 'kneeling theology' Balthasar attempted to reposition Christian faith and practice so that it could enable a modern seeking after God, an aesthetical theology, to go beyond the limitations of its own resources and reinhabit a world view giving priority to divine revelatory initiative, a theological aesthetics.

This common concern about modernity might provide a general shared field of interest within which to compare Jung's and Balthasar's understandings of God's involvement with evil. More particularly, there are specific areas that will prove to be important. The first of these, which is pertinent to a critical comparison of the work of any psychologist and theologian, is each author's anthropology. And in the case of Jung and Balthasar a second is each author's underlying theological orientation. In the first of these, there is a measure of convergence. In the second they are clearly divergent. With regard to anthropology, Jung's map of the psyche focuses on the process of individuation; Balthasar's on salvation understood theodramatically. Although Balthasar discusses Jung's psychology in relation to the concept of role, the extent of their convergence is limited insofar as he thinks all psychologies are trapped within the confines of a modern world view. I argue that Jung's radical Protestant theological orientation can be described as 'Joachimite' and I follow Mongrain in his claim that Balthasar's is a *corpus triforme* stance. These are both strands within the range of Christian theological tradition, though they have not been comfortable in each other's company. In chapter five, I discuss two further differing understandings, of analogy and polarity, which are highly significant for a comparison of their views on God's involvement with evil. I illustrate these divergencies through a discussion of Schärf's essay on Satan in the Old Testament, which Jung included in his *Symbolik des Geistes* collection of essays. Jung's approach is one specifically rejected by Balthasar.

Comparable anthropologies?

Jung's map of the psyche

Jung's theoretical framework was formulated from his empirical approach to the psyche, his practice of psychotherapy, and many strands of philosophical thought about human psychology which had informed the European tradition for centuries and had by the late nineteenth century evolved the philosophical concept of the unconscious (Ellenberger, 1970; Samuels *et al.*, 1986: 155–7; Shamdasani, 2003). His map of the psyche comprises a number of structural components: persona, the ego complex, the personal unconscious, the collective unconscious, and the Self.

The persona is that aspect of the psyche through which a person manages relations with their external world and, in relation to the personal shadow, addresses some important aspects of the tension between good and evil (*CW*6: 465–7; Samuels *et al.*, 1986: 107f.; Stein, 1998: 105–124). The term 'persona' is taken by Jung from the Latin word for an actor's mask. In a positive sense it is 'the face we wear to meet the social world around us' (Stein, 1998: 106; cf. Casement, 2001: 142): 'the individual's system of adaptation to ... the world' (*MDR*: 416). The personal unconscious, the shadow, and the persona are 'complementary structures' (Stein, 1998: 105). Jung describes the shadow as 'the "negative" side of the personality, the sum of all those unpleasant qualities we like to hide, together with the insufficiently developed functions and the contents of the personal unconscious' (Jung, 1917/1926/1943: 65 n. 5). There is a strong tendency for another person, who carries the unconscious projection of aspects of an individual's shadow, to be perceived as evil in comparison with that individual's persona understood as good. The recognition and withdrawal of such projections is an important first step towards social and psychic well-being (*MDR*: 273).

The ego complex is the centre of consciousness, which, despite the inevitable limitations of subjectivity, is essential not only to psychology as a discipline but to the evolution of civilization and culture (*CW*6: 425; Stein, 1998: 13–34). Jung's framework of psychological types proposes that energy moves either outwards (as extraversion[1]) or inwards (as introversion), using one or more of four functions which are paired in mutual tension (the thinking and the feeling evaluating functions, the sensing and the intuiting perceiving functions). This typology offers a means for understanding how we process information and experience (*CW*6: 482f., 414–7, 436f., 481f., 433–6, 461–3, 453f., 447f., 458f., 454f., 452f., 427; cf. Samuels *et al.*, 1986: 153–5; Casement, 2001: 67–78).

The personal unconscious 'compris[es] all the acquisitions of personal life, everything forgotten, repressed, subliminally perceived, thought, felt' (*CW*6: 485). The collective or objective unconscious ('whose contents have never been in consciousness, and therefore have never been individually acquired, but owe their existence exclusively to heredity' (Jung, 1936b: 42)) and its archetypes (ibid.: 42f.; Stein, 1998: 85–103) are age-old patterns of mental activity, 'the ground principles' (Jung, 1934/1954: 38) of the unconscious, 'the inherited part of the psyche that gives rise to patterned tendencies of thought' (Casement, 2001: 142). The collective unconscious is 'the precondition of each individual psyche, just as the sea is the carrier of the individual wave' (Jung, 1946: 169). The archetypes include the contra-sexual sub-personalities, anima/animus, which as 'soul-images' connect the conscious psyche to the unconscious (*CW*9(ii): 11–22; Stein, 1998: 125–49).[2] The universal archetypes produce a vast variety of symbols in the dreams of individuals and, in the collective, in folklore, mythologies and religions.

The Self[3] is the culmination of the archetypes, the meta-psychological or 'transcendent' basis of subjectivity which also 'forms the ground for the subject's commonality with the world, with the structures of Being' (Stein, 1998: 152; cf. ibid.: 151–69; *CW*9(ii)). For Jung, '[t]he self is not only the centre [of the psyche] but also the whole circumference which embraces both conscious and unconscious; it is the centre of this totality, just as the ego is the centre of the consciousness' (*CW*12: 41).

These structural components of the psyche are in dynamic interrelation, which Jung elaborates in terms of key features such as libido and symbol. Central to analytical psychology is the idea of libido understood as psychic energy (*CW*6: 455; *CWB*: 125–67; Jung, 1928a: 14–8; Samuels *et al.*, 1986: 53f.; Stein, 1998: 59–83). Jung was interested primarily in exploring the meaning of the 'symbols of transformation that accompany changes in the direction of flow of energy' (Casement, 2001: 67; ibid.: 64–7). He used the Greek philosopher Heraclitus' (fl. *c.*500 BCE) notion of *enantiodromia* [running contrariwise] to express his view that these changes of the direction of flow of psychic energy represent a 'principle which governs all cycles of natural life' (*CW*6: 426).

Jung understands a symbol as 'the best possible description or formulation of a relatively unknown fact, which is none the less known to exist or is postulated as existing'; he distinguishes this from a sign, 'an abbreviated designation for a *known* thing' (*CW*6: 474), which he takes to be Freud's usage (ibid.: 477). The symbol is thus 'pregnant with meaning', 'living', coming into consciousness from the unconscious, as yet 'only divined and not yet clearly conscious': 'It is, therefore, quite impossible to create a living symbol … from known associations' (*CW*6: 475 and Stein, 1998: 82). On the one hand the symbol is subjective, appearing significant to one person but not to another; yet on the other hand it is objective, arising from within the collective unconscious: '[t]he living symbol formulates an essential unconscious factor … for it touches a corresponding chord in every psyche' (*CW*6: 477).[4] Living symbols are thus likely to be experienced as archetypal images and find expression in cultural and spiritual forms.

Jung made a distinction between the archetypal image, the experienced phenomenon, and the archetype, unknowable in itself, which Jung saw as, using a Kantian phrase, a *Ding an sich*. For Kant this phrase referred not only to something unknowable but also to incommunicability. Jung was aware that he was reinterpreting Kant,[5] using the concept in a way that 'enables us to get an unexpected glimpse of the superb purposefulness of the animate universe' (*CW*A: 72). In terms of the phenomenology of archetypal images Jung drew somewhat more straightforwardly on a concept from theology to express his understanding of the numinosity of archetypes. The German Lutheran theologian, Rudolph Otto (1869–1937) published *The Idea of the Holy* in 1917, using the concept of numinosity to promote the importance of the non-rational aspect of religious experience (Otto, 1958: 6; cf. Chapman, 1988: 86–98; Schlamm, 1994; Main, 2006b; Huskinson, 2006).

For Jung an archetypal symbol is a mystery, the unknown coming into conscious knowing, and he employed Otto's concept to describe the non-rational aspects of the psychological experience of archetypal symbols, that is, 'all that is uncontrollable in man – the *numinosum*,[6] to use an apt expression of Rudolph Otto's' (Jung, 1934c: 104). For both Jung and Otto the numinous is on the one hand subjectively experienced but at the same time comes from beyond us. For Otto, it is 'subjective', yet it is 'felt as objective and outside the self' (Otto, 1958: 10f.). For Jung, it is from the objective collective unconscious that 'numina [which] are psychic *entia* … force themselves upon consciousness' (*CW*12: 183). But whereas Otto uses the phrase 'wholly other' to indicate the nature of the *mysterium* as 'that which is quite beyond the sphere of the usual, the intelligible and the familiar' (Otto, 1958: 26), Jung is concerned that reference to something wholly other risks severing the analogical link between the metaphysical and the phenomenological realms (*CW*12: 11 n. 6). This would make futile the human, psychological searching after God.

Otto's concept – *mysterium tremendum et fascinans*[7] – refers to a mystery that is both repelling and attracting. That which is *tremendum* has three further characteristics, awesomeness, overpoweringness and urgency, all of which are used by Jung. The awesomeness of numinosity produces, for Otto, 'a terror fraught with an inward shuddering such as not even the most menacing and overpowering created thing can instil' (Otto, 1958: 14). Jung speaks of the '"holy dread" of the numinous' (*PADT*: 150). Overpoweringness, for Otto, highlights our sense of creatureliness, producing a feeling of 'being but "dust and ashes" and nothingness' (Otto, 1958: 20). For Jung, '[t]he numinous character of these experiences is proved by the fact that they are *overwhelming*' (*PADT*: 184). Urgency, for Otto, in phenomenological terms, is 'vitality, passion, emotional temper, will, force, movement, excitement, activity, impetus', and, in theological terms, 'a genuine aspect of the divine nature – its non-rational aspect', pointing to a 'living' as opposed to a 'philosophic' God (Otto, 1958: 23). Likewise Jung sees that religion depends on a 'vital link' between 'the regulating [*sc.* God-] images' and 'the instinctual powers of the unconscious' through 'the relation of the individual to God'. In such circumstances, 'religious ideas' retain 'their numinosity, i.e. their thrilling power' (Jung, 1945/1954: 301).

The numinous mystery not only repels but also attracts. For Otto, its non-rational quality of *fascinans* 'allures with a potent charm' (Otto, 1958: 31), leading to 'a bliss which embraces all those blessings that are indicated or suggested in positive fashion by any "doctrine of salvation"' (ibid.: 33). Similarly, for Jung, 'Numinosity … is wholly outside conscious volition, for it transports the subject into the state of rapture, which is a state of will-less surrender' (Jung, 1947/1954: 186). But, whereas Otto stresses that either an acceptance of creature consciousness or religious exaltation results in there being 'no consciousness … separate from the deity' (Schlamm, 1994: 27; cf. ibid.: 31 n. 38), Jung insists on the need of an element of conscious independence in relation to the numinous. An example of this is found in the dream Jung had in which he was with his long-dead father. Paul Jung bowed his head to the ground before 'the highest presence'. Carl Jung followed suit, but with a 'millimetre' to spare (*MDR*: 245, 247; cf. Schlamm, 1994: 27).

The most important process in Jung's anthropology, and the overall purpose of analytical psychotherapy, is the developmental transformation which he calls individuation. It can be described in terms of the emergence of the Self and the integration of its symbols of greater wholeness into consciousness (*CW*6: 448–50; Stein, 1998: 171–97). The interrelation of Self and ego is of crucial significance. Unless they remain distinct there is a danger of inflation and psychosis, with the ego possessed by or identified with the Self. Unless ego and Self are linked the person will be prey to dissociative neuroses. Individuation is not the promotion of a self-centred individualism; rather, it is a process in which a person becomes authentically integrated, both distinctively in relation to others and also more deeply in relation to what is (archetypally) universal about being human.

Given that the unconscious acts in a compensatory manner, archetypes can appear to function as paired opposites. If any cultural embodiment of the Self archetype, such as Christ in the Christian world view, becomes, as in that case (so Jung argues), too one-sidedly good, then another opposing archetype is likely to emerge. Jung sees that Christ and the Devil epitomize what he calls the archetype of hostile brothers (*CW*9(ii): 72–94). However, more fundamentally, all archetypes, and supremely the Self, contain opposites and also the deep impulse towards union. The Self is '*the* organizing principle of the unconscious' (ibid.: 204) and it, out of its own nature as a monistic *complexio oppositorum* and, in a process of symbol formation, provides the 'archetypal urge to co-ordinate, relativize and mediate the tension of the opposites' within conscious experience (Casement, 2001: 146). Key features of Jung's psychological anthropology which relate to comparable concerns for Balthasar are numinosity, persona, the ego and the Self.

Balthasar's theological anthropology

There are some hints in *Razing the Bastions* that Balthasar is likely eventually to find the insights of psychology as preliminary as those of all other versions of worldly truth, even if initially a renewed theological anthropology finds twentieth-century developments in psychology relevant. For a theological anthropology needs to go beyond its tradition of an over-individualistic Augustinian model of human maturation, which envisages moving 'from a dust-carrying contact with "you" to the bliss of solitude with the "I" – … [then] turn[ing] its attention to the marvel and the mystery of God' (*RBCA*: 101). Modern psychology is in tune in principle with a contemporary emphasis on the solidarity of humanity. The theologian sees this in terms of engagement with God, who is One, which involves the integration of the spiritual and the profane, the inner and the outer, the individual and the collective; in the present time,

> the one who seeks God in the inner room encounters once again the outer realm of the 'you', the arena of the profane, and it is only together with all the brethren and all the creatures that he can come before the one God: Father, Son and Spirit.
>
> (ibid.: 101f.)

However, in the end, if Jung were to hope to argue for a restatement of Christian doctrine based on psychological insights, Balthasar would be wary, since human truth does not correlate directly with divine truth. Balthasar seeks a better path than one which follows 'Augustine's psychological speculation', since 'the solitary structure of the soul cannot supply the supreme image for the living exchange of love in the eternal God' (ibid.: 29).

Balthasar also seeks to exempt the Church (and at least those spiritually alive Christians) from the worldly laws of secular human sciences, particularly if they are applied by other disciplines in a type 5 reductionist manner:

> The Church and the Christians in her do not fit any categories of the history of philosophy, psychology or sociology, such that they could be definitively described on the basis of these categories. A Christian transcends these laws precisely to the extent that he believes. He does not owe it to the flesh to live according to the flesh, nor does he owe it to

> the laws of historical sociology to conform to them. But … the majority, the mass in the Church obey these laws … And the consequence is the great defections which in turn, as new 'failures', introduce new uncertainty among the masses, bringing in their turn, in a vicious circle, yet more defections.
>
> (ibid.: 45)

Balthasar's approach depends on the idea that worldly truth, including modern psychology, is limited to its own horizons and that it needs saving from itself and from beyond itself by divine truth as revealed in Christ. In a summarizing essay he writes, 'where the tension between being a Christian and being a man like other men is… so strong that it must appear to the natural man as lacerating and "psychologically" unbearable by every standard of closed and harmonious humanity' there is offered in Christ a 'sign' and a 'reality' of true humanity (Balthasar, 1986a: 201f.). In terms of anthropology this proposes an interplay between two connected but different realities, conscious human experience and a greater divine reality, which is in part revealed and in part remains unknowable. Balthasar argues that depth psychologies, Jung's as well as those of Freud and Adler, can do no more than offer the 'acceptance of limitation' (*TD*1: 493; cf. *TD*1: 505–531), 'with the ultimate goal of therapy as that of integrating man into the totality that embraces him' (*TD*1: 505).

Jung's use of Otto's concept of the numinous is not taken up directly by Balthasar.[8] Nevertheless, there is some comparability between the interplay, in Jung's analytical psychology, of the archetype and the experience of numinous archetypal symbols and the relatedness, in Balthasar's theology, of the divine glory and the human experience of beauty, set within his understanding of 'seeing the form' (*GL*1: 117–27).

Balthasar, like Jung following Otto, found it important to challenge the modern confining of experiential reality to conscious rationality. For Balthasar the theological consequence was that the Western world view 'no longer permits space for an experience of worldly Being as an epiphany of God's glory' (*GL*5: 483). Mystery is as central to Balthasar's theory of experience as it was to Jung in his use of numinosity. Images of transcendental beauty have irreducible mystery: 'Those words which attempt to convey the beautiful gravitate, first of all, toward the mystery of form (*Gestalt*) or of figure (*Gebilde*)' (*GL*1: 19). He also speaks of an 'indissolubility of form', which is killed by dissection: 'we can never again recapture the living totality of form once it has been dissected and sawn into pieces, no matter how informative the conclusions this anatomy may bring to light' (ibid.: 31).

Form, for Balthasar, has similarities with the idea of numinosity, particularly in the links between the *mysterium* and splendour, aspects of *tremendum*, and also between *fascinans* and rapture. Jung connects the archetype in itself with the archetypal image. Balthasar, likewise, in his theory of aesthetics, holds together the mystery of the splendour[9] of transcendental beauty and its representational form: 'The beautiful does not live on splendour alone; it also needs figure (*Gestalt*) and image (*Bild*), … even if image (*Ge-bild*) is beautiful only as the imaging forth of that splendour which is beyond all images (*überbildlich*)' (*GL*6: 87).

Although Balthasar does not stress the repelling aspect of the *tremendum* found in the concept of numinosity, he nevertheless sees that transcendental beauty is the aspect of that which is overwhelming in transcendental truth: 'For the name of this radiant property of truth, which overwhelms by its splendour, its indivisible integrity, and its perfect expressive power, is, in fact, none other than beauty' (*TL*1: 141f.).

In Balthasar the primary emphasis is on the attractiveness of beauty, which, occasionally he acknowledges includes the ugly. Apprehending transcendental beauty, which always appears to us in an empirical form, involves both being 'enraptured' (*GL*1: 119) by the attractive power of the form and also being drawn towards the deeper reality beneath the form (ibid.: 118). What is important about transcendental beauty, and the forms in which it is revealed, is its power to attract and transform. We can call God beautiful because he is 'the one who arouses *pleasure* (*Wohlgefallen*), creates *desire* (*Begehren*) for himself, and rewards with *delight* (*Genuss*) … [he is] both *lovely* and *love-worthy* [*liebenswürdig*]' (ibid.: 53 n. 6).

The *tremendum* aspect of this understanding of beauty is not to be detached from the content of the revelation, culminating in Christ crucified. Here transcendental beauty evokes an awe-filled as well as a joyous response: 'In this self-revelation, God's beauty embraces death as well as life, fear as well as joy, what we call "ugly" as well as what we call "beautiful"' (ibid.: 56 quoting Barth). Balthasar hints at how this will work out in his doctrine of salvation, for God's 'beauty' 'embraces the most abysmal ugliness of sin and hell by virtue of the condescension of divine love' (ibid.: 124).

Although Balthasar's understanding of how the divine glory is manifested in the forms of worldly beauty and Jung's of how archetypal reality is expressed in the numinosity of the symbolic, archetypal image are in some respects comparable, nevertheless there is a difference which points towards the issue of good and evil. When Jung (and Otto) hold together the repelling and the attracting aspects of numinosity, they give greater stress to the *tremendum*. Jung (and Otto) give greater weight to the 'darker' side of the numinous and Balthasar to the 'lighter' side of the beautiful.

On matters relating to persona and ego, Balthasar is concerned with the question of the disjunction, the 'dualism … between what I represent and what I am in reality' (*TD*1: 481), 'the disparity between [the] "I" and [the] social role' (ibid.: 505). Jung is aware of the problems that arise if the ego (Balthasar's 'I') is over-identified with or disconnected from the persona (Balthasar's social role). Balthasar is further concerned with how the unique, though necessarily limited, ego can 'find himself by finding the whole', suggesting that the relevant question is whether the 'vanishing point' of the 'I' is 'within or above the empirical world, whether it can be attained by the subject's own efforts or can only be received as a gift in the process of striving for it' (ibid.: 482). Balthasar's view is that psychology is limited to the empirical world (cf. Block, 2005: 191) and that true wholeness of identity comes only when understood theologically, as a divine gift.

Jung's psychological anthropology cuts across Balthasar's options. He proposes a larger view of the empirical world, to include the collective unconscious as well as individual ego consciousness, so that wholeness comes from interaction with the Self, which is admittedly this-worldly – that is, intra-psychic or (if we grant its psychoid transgressivity) intra-cosmic. Nevertheless wholeness, for Jung too, comes as a gift within the process of striving for it.

Although Balthasar acknowledges Jung's 'reverence in the face of the mystery of being' (*TD*1: 516; cf. ibid. n. 11), and that his position is that 'man is far more than his consciousness' (ibid.: 517), Balthasar's view seems to be that Jungian wholeness (related to the Self) is an achievement of the ego. Jung's 'Self' is 'that synthesis of all vital forces that is attainable by the "I" in its self-transcendence into the universal plane' (ibid.: 504). Balthasar also notes Jung's disavowal of metaphysics when he ('like Kant') 'renounces recourse to anything lying outside the psyche' (ibid.: 515; cf. ibid. n. 4). Balthasar then regards it as 'completely paradoxical' that Jung replaces the stability of a unique individual with something that emerges through an ongoing process of individuation, 'the result of which (if it were fully realized) is the "self"' (ibid.: 517).

It is, however, a misreading of Jung to suggest that for him through individuation the ego becomes the Self. In Jung's dynamic map of the psyche the connection between the social role (the persona) and the person living in the conscious world (the ego) will only function healthily insofar as a mutual connection between the ego and the archetypal Self of the collective unconscious is made and maintained. It mischaracterizes Jung to say that he 'ultimately leads the individual, having laid aside his "persona", to acceptance' of the underlying priority of the Self, 'a vital substratum that governs and sustains' 'the "I"' (ibid.: 505).[10] It is going too far to say that the ego in Jung's theory is nothing more than 'the "resultant" of a particular configuration of numerous collective elements of the stream of life', an 'extruded consciousness' which then has the (individuating task) of bringing itself 'into a correct relationship' with 'the whole world of the archetypes' (ibid.: 517). This underplays the real, though limited, autonomy of the ego.

For Balthasar, there is a primary value to individual uniqueness, which is a given rather than the outcome of a process. It makes little sense that, as he understands Jung's proposals, uniqueness means different things at the beginning and at the end of individuation. As the ego complex first emerges in the developing person, '[w]hat is "new" in the individual psyche is an infinitely varied recombination of ancient constituents' (ibid. n. 20 quoting *MDR*);

whereas, at the end, 'uniqueness will be the mode in which the elements are integrated into the totality' (ibid.: 517).

Balthasar compounds his limited reading of Jung when he says that the aim of Jung's process of individuation is not only to leave the persona behind but for the self to have priority over the ego. He says, correctly, that Jung 'is acquainted with a transcendence of the empirical ego (in the process of individuation) toward the superordinate self, a totality that can only be reached in an approximate manner' (ibid.: 520). But he goes too far in saying that for Jung individuation is 'the process of becoming a "self"' (ibid.: 521), identifying more and more fully with symbols of wholeness (such as Christ and Buddha), becoming 'an incarnation of that totality into which he has transcended himself and to which he has surrendered himself' (ibid.). Although Balthasar correctly acknowledges the a priori aspect of Jung's idea of the Self (ibid.: 520), he goes further than Jung would in claiming an ability of conscious willing to achieve wholeness and an undue passivity of the conscious ego in relation to unconscious archetypes, rather than, as Jung insists, struggling with unconscious contents.

What Balthasar does not perhaps give sufficient allowance for in Jung is the measure of independence of the ego. He chooses, for instance, to stress as ontological Jung's decision for therapeutic and self-experimenting purposes 'to allow himself "to be carried along with the stream [of libido]" for years in order to be receptive to the utterances of the unconscious' (ibid.: 517, quoting *MDR*). Balthasar could have read Jung in the light of his own views about humanity's finite freedom in relation to God. Finite freedom exists only because of the entirely non-contingent creating decision of God's infinite freedom and at the same time this finite freedom gives humanity a real measure of independence, which Balthasar calls *autexousion*, in relation to the divine, the true source and goal of its life and meaning.

In Balthasar's anthropology the conscious "I" is simultaneously self- and other-aware. In Jung's terms the life energy of ego consciousness is simultaneously introverted, inwardly directed, and extraverted, other-directed. Balthasar relates his concept of 'self-possession' to individual uniqueness held within the acknowledgement of other(s). But more important than the issue of the one and the many is that openness to other beings means that we are open to the reality of Being. That is,

> finite freedom, as *autexousion*, as consent to oneself in the freedom of self-possession, is by no means alienated but rather inwardly fulfilled by consenting to that Being-in-its-totality which has now [in Christ] unveiled itself as that which freely grounds all things, as that which, in infinite freedom, creates finite freedom.
>
> (*TD*2: 242)

A Jungian approach would say something comparable about the relation of the ego and the Self.

Balthasar's anthropology is always theologically grounded. It is an area in which he drew on Barth, seeing 'humanity as God's co-respondent partner in creation' (Wigley, 2010: 65). As well as the priority of grace, there is, for Balthasar, an important role for human choice and responsibility:

> What is a person without a life-form, that is to say without a form which he has chosen for his life, a form into which and through which to pour out his life, so that his life becomes the soul of the form and the form becomes the expression of his soul?
>
> (*GL*1: 24)

In Jung's terms this will involve conscious acceptance of persona (role), but for Jung as well as for Balthasar something more profoundly constitutive is involved. In Jung, the choice to participate in the process of individuation, to strive for wholeness, requires not only the pursuit of personal fulfilment but also the ethical integration of the process into the person's life in the world.

For Balthasar, the concept of mission functions in a similar way to the process of individuation in Jung's psychology. It is through discerning and taking up whatever is called for in one's mission that, for Balthasar, the person fulfils his or her humanity and becomes a 'theological person' (*TD*3: 261–461). That this mission is, for Balthasar, only discernible 'in Christ' means that there is interplay between individual uniqueness in mission and its ecclesial rootedness: 'only in Jesus Christ does it become clear how profoundly this definitive "I"-name signifies vocation, mission. In him the "I" and the role become uniquely and ineffably one in the reality of his mission' (*TD*1: 645f.). For Jung, too, the ego and persona enable lived wholeness, but only when held in dynamic integration with the Self (of which, in the West, Christ is the symbol *par excellence*).

Beyond anything Jung envisaged, for Balthasar the ultimate theological ground for his anthropology is the inner-trinitarian life: 'in Christ the *processio* within the godhead, which constitutes the Son as the Father's dialogue partner, is identical, in God's going-out-from-himself toward the world, with the *missio*, the sending of the Son to mankind' (ibid.: 646). Balthasar's anthropology is, thus, intended to serve his theodramatic reading of salvation. Outlining what it means to be a theological person 'establish[es] the preconditions for human participation in the divine drama' (Wigley, 2010: 93). Though each person has a unique calling, 'their mission', each, also, 'is left … to play their part well or ill' (*TD*3: 38). Christ is unique and has a 'normative, archetypal quality' (ibid.: 258) because in him both person and mission are one (ibid.: 201), because he 'possessed a sense of mission that was eschatological and universal' (ibid.: 149), and because he gathers up, recapitulates, the entirety of the human relatedness to God: 'In his person and mission, Christ is the "last Adam", the one who gives meaning to the entire play; as such he embodies mankind's whole dramatic situation in its relationship to itself and to God' (ibid.: 201). Thus it is 'only in Christ that human beings can become real persons and act as theo-dramatic characters in their own right' (Wigley, 2010: 98).

It is clear that a Balthasarian approach to anthropology has considerable convergence with that of Jung, even though we have to admit that Balthasar's discussion of Jung's psychology is to some extent partial and occasionally strays into misreading. But if a measure of convergence about anthropology points in the direction of a fruitful critical comparison of Balthasar's theology and Jung's psychology concerning the question of God's involvement with evil, what turn out to be more important are three areas of divergence: theological orientation, analogy and polarity. Consideration of the first of these takes up the remainder of the present chapter.

Differing theological orientations

Jung and Balthasar have differing orientations to their overall theological frameworks, particularly in relation to the Trinity. Jung's framework can be characterized as 'Joachimite'. He gives priority to the work of the Spirit and also envisages three successive theological ages, with each one going beyond an aspect of the incompleteness of its predecessor. Balthasar holds a view which relates to the patristic notion of the *corpus triforme*, in which each phase, though with its own distinct features, represents the unity of trinitarian life christologically understood.

Jung's 'Joachimite' theological orientation

In *Symbolik des Geistes*, as throughout his published writings, Jung's own theological position often remains implicit, emerging only partially from time to time. More explicit references come when he addresses or corresponds with clergy. The 1932 reference to his radical Protestantism came in a lecture to German Protestant pastors. It was to a Roman Catholic in a 1944 letter that he said: 'Though I know little of Catholic doctrine, that little is enough to make it an inalienable possession for me. And I know so much about Protestantism that I could never give it up' (*L*1: 346). Fuller accounts of his theological orientation are rare.

However, there is such a statement in a 1954 letter to a Roman Catholic priest, Père Lachat, which, as the following extended excerpt shows, draws together succinctly the themes of good and evil, the Holy Spirit and the Trinity:

> [The Holy Spirit's] dwelling in a certain number of human individuals and their transformation into υιϖ [*sic*] του θεου [sons of God] signifies a very important step forward beyond 'Christocentrism'. Anyone who takes up the question of the Holy Spirit seriously is faced with the question whether Christ is identical with the Holy Spirit or different from him. With dogma, I prefer the independence of the Holy Spirit. The Holy Spirit is *one*, a *complexio*

> *oppositorum*, in contrast to YHWH after the separation of the divine opposites symbolized by God's two sons, Christ and Satan. On the level of the Son there is no answer to the question of good and evil; there is only an incurable separation of the opposites. The annulling of evil by the *privatio boni* (declaring [it] to be μη ον) is a *petitio principii* [begging of the question] of the most flagrant kind and no solution whatever. It seems to me to be the Holy Spirit's task and charge to reconcile and reunite the opposites in the human individual through a special development of the human soul. The soul is paradoxical like the Father; it is black and white, divine and demon-like, in its primitive and natural state. By the discriminative function of its conscious side it separates opposites of every kind, and specially those of the moral order personified in Christ and Devil. Thereby the soul's spiritual development creates an enormous tension, from which man can only suffer. Christ promised him redemption. But in what exactly does this consist? The *imitatio Christi* [following of Christ] leads us to Calvary and to the annihilation of the 'body', that is, of biological life, and if we take this death as symbolic it is a state of suspension between the opposites, that is to say, an unresolved conflict. That is exactly what Przywara has named the 'rift', the gulf separating good from evil, the latent and apparently incurable dualism of Christianity, the enmity of the devil and of damnation. (Inasmuch as good is real so also is evil.)
>
> (Jung, 1954a: 689f.)

Within Jung's theological position there lies a version of the three-eras theology of Joachim of Fiore (*c*.1105–1202). Jung makes a number of references to the Cistercian theologian and mystic, who proposed a trinity of epochs, summarized (by Balthasar) thus:

> the age of the Father, the Old Covenant, is succeeded by the age of the Son (yielding a deeper revelation of the Father); next we can expect an age of the Spirit, in which, finally, the true spiritual essence of the entire Godhead [no longer obscured by ecclesial and clerical prescriptions (*TL*3: 415)] is to emerge.
>
> (*TD*3: 512; cf. *TL*2: 207f.)

The third age, according to Joachim, due to start in 1260, would be one of radical Christian freedom, realizing the 'eternal Gospel'. Though Joachim received the support of several Popes, Aquinas argued against him (*TL*2: 208) and eventually his views on the Trinity were condemned by the Fourth Lateran Council in 1215 (*TD*4: 380). The extension of his views, among some Spiritual Franciscans – that since about 1200 the spirit of life was no longer to be found in the epochs of the two testaments, so that the age of the 'eternal Gospel' would supersede the gospel of Christ – was declared heretical in 1256.

Jung gives an outline, in *Aion*, of the story of Joachim, his advocacy of the advent of the 'everlasting gospel' and the reign of the age of the Holy Spirit (*CW*9(ii): 82–9). He acknowledges that Joachim's views were taken further by others in ways that were bound to be seen as heretical. He explicitly links his own psychological (and theological) reading of Joachim with sections of his essays in *Symbolik des Geistes* (ibid.: 85 n. 58 and ibid.: 86 n. 59).

Jung proposes that Joachim was 'probably … seized by the archetype of the spirit' (which Joachim understandably identified with the 'third Person of the Godhead' (ibid.: 85)). Jung links this to his own discussion, in the fairy tale essay, of the spirit archetype (ibid.: 85 n. 58 referring to *PSF*: 214–7), manifesting as 'an ambivalent dualistic figure', which he sees as 'engendering the most contradictory manifestations within the Holy Ghost movement' (ibid.: 86). The psychological (and theological) purpose of the emergence of the age of the Spirit is to produce 'a religious attitude that was destined to bridge and compensate for the frightful gulf that had opened out between Christ and Antichrist in the eleventh century' (ibid.). For Jung this leads directly to the contemporary world:

> The antichristian era [of Joachim's time] is to blame that the spirit became non-spiritual and that the vitalizing archetype gradually degenerated into rationalism, intellectualism, and doctrinairism, all of which leads straight to the tragedy of modern times now hanging over our heads like a sword of Damocles.
>
> (ibid.)[11]

Jung thinks that the theological problem is that in 'the old formula for the Trinity … the dogmatic figure of the devil is lacking' (ibid.). Jung's solution is twofold: 'first, the present age must come to terms drastically with … the absolute opposition that is not only tearing the world asunder politically but has planted a schism in the human heart' (ibid.); secondly (with Jung's help), it must rediscover 'the original, living spirit', which, 'because of its ambivalence', as he sets out in the Mercury and the Trinity essays (ibid. n.59 referring to *SM*: 237–50 and *PADT*: 174–80), 'is also a mediator and uniter of opposites' (ibid.). In the case of the alchemical symbol of Mercurius: 'The paradoxical nature of Mercurius reflects an important aspect of the self – the fact, namely, that it is essentially a *complexio oppositorum*, and indeed can be nothing else if it is to represent any kind of totality' (*SM*: 241). In the case of the Trinity, the Spirit takes God's purpose further than the Son was able to, for

> [a]fter he had experienced the world's suffering, this God who became man left behind him a Comforter, the Third Person of the Trinity, who would make his dwelling in many individuals … In the Paraclete, therefore, God is closer to the real man and his darkness than he is in the Son.
>
> (*PADT*: 179)

Further, God himself emerges immanently from the collaboration between the Spirit and humanity: for '[j]ust as man was once revealed out of God, so, when the circle closes, God may be revealed out of man' (ibid.).

In Balthasar's view, Joachim 'unsuspectingly opened the door to all those who have since sought a Church of the Spirit to supersede the Church of Christ' (*TL2*: 208). He would number Jung among them.

Balthasar's corpus triforme theological orientation

Balthasar was critical of Joachim's theology, even though he recognized in it an important emphasis on the 'engagement of the Spirit of God with the spirit of man in the Spirit of Christ' (*GL2*: 23). However, when Joachim proposes that the eschatological age of the Spirit is about to dawn in the twelfth century, he breaks up the integrated framework of the *corpus triforme*:

> If the Old Covenant is the period of the Father and the New Covenant the period of the Son, then out of the parallelism of these periods, which are read into each other and each interpreted by the other, springs the understanding of the Spirit, because in the dispensation of salvation the Spirit also proceeds from both the Father and the Son.
>
> (*GL2*: 262)

It is antithetical to this integrated approach to envisage 'a division of salvation history into periods' as Joachim did. Balthasar sees that Joachim's emphasis on the gospel of the Spirit makes the third era theologically superior to the first two, which by comparison are seen as manifestation of the 'letter' (*TD3*: 400 referring to Lubac; cf. *TD4* : 446 and ibid. n. 2 referring to Lubac, 1979–1981 and *TL2*: 206f.).

Balthasar's *corpus triforme* response to Joachim (and Jung) is based on the view that the 'age' of the Spirit has begun with the Resurrection of Jesus (or, more properly, with Pentecost). No event that is significant in trinitarian terms can cut Church history in two. The Spirit will lead us into 'all truth', and this is none other than the truth of Jesus, which, in turn, in his own words, is none other than the truth of the Father (John 16:13–15). Since the Spirit 'who searches the depths of God' (1 Cor. 2:10) has already been given to believers by Jesus, resulting in the most intimate relationship conceivable between God and the world, it is impossible for the future to bring any qualitative leap forward. Furthermore, the notion of a successive revelation of the three divine Persons is nonsensical, since essentially they interpenetrate. In the relationship with God prior to Christ, only the living (triune) God can have been revealed, even if not formally in his triunity. This is affirmed by the Fathers of the Church:

> [T]he Word had not yet stepped over definitively to man's side, to be recognizable as a divine Person, and the Spirit that rested on man had not yet finally penetrated his heart … What has taken place in the Christ event cannot eschatologically be superseded.
>
> (*TD3*: 512f.)

The use of the term *corpus triforme* is found first in Origen (*c*. 185–*c*. 254), though Balthasar (who, Mongrain suggests, follows Henri de Lubac at this point (Mongrain, 2002: 37–45 and ibid.: 48 n. 46) sees it as implicit in the Church Fathers from Irenaeus onwards. This orientation is christocentric in the sense that the entire history of humanity is seen through the perspective of the incarnation. By way of Origen, Balthasar makes use of a version of Alexandrian *corpus triforme* christology (*GL*1: 528–30; *TD*2: 111–2) in which the body of Christ has three forms: a body of Scripture including the Old Testament, the incarnate body of the Logos of the Father, and an ecclesial body. The first and third, because people are involved in their 'communication and formation', have something 'opaque' about them – unlike 'the testimony borne to the Son by the Father and the Holy Spirit' (*GL*1: 531). Nevertheless, 'they are both still perceptible expressions of the Christ-form (*corpora Christi*)' (ibid.). For Balthasar, 'Christ's mediating form is multiple …, and yet this multiplicity can ever give expression only to the one form', for which the phrase *corpus triforme* is appropriate (*GL*1: 528f.). There is both difference and continuity between the first and second phases, creation and redemption, and between the second and third phases, redemption and the ongoing mission of the Spirit and life of the Church.[12]

An important feature of Balthasar's version of a *corpus triforme* orientation is divine pedagogy, based on the Irenaean idea of 'becoming accustomed' (*GL*2: 79). For instance,

> Man becomes accustomed to obey God, to bear his Spirit, to be a pilgrim in the world, to follow his word. … But God too has to become accustomed to mankind: … dwelling among men. … This process of accustoming takes place in the whole order of salvation, [but] especially in the Old Testament which is a … preliminary training … of mankind for the coming of Christ.
>
> (ibid.: 79f. referring to Irenaeus)

This pedagogical process of becoming accustomed is, as Balthasar summarizes Irenaeus, 'gentle, easy, quiet, patient' (ibid.: 77), for humanity 'behaves like a child and acquires wisdom only slowly by experience' (ibid.: 78). This must not, however, be over-idealized. For just as the child learns 'through injury', so humanity's training comes 'through … experience of the opposite, of the loss of God's grace' – 'the whole dispensation of salvation … allows of the fall', indeed it has a 'profound necessity within God's free order of salvation' (ibid.: 78f.). Though he has no specific Irenaean references, Balthasar is clear for himself that God also has to undergo a process of becoming accustomed to the humanity he has created.

It could be said that Balthasar missed an opportunity to explore aspects of convergence between Jung's map of the psyche and his own theological anthropology. It is divergence, however, which predominates when their theological orientations are considered. The issues of analogy and polarity are important for both Balthasar and Jung. They are further important bases for a critical comparison of their works, in that they are markedly divergent. They are the focus of the next chapter.

Notes

1 Jung's spelling.
2 Jung's views on gender have been a significant area of debate within and beyond analytical psychology (Casement, 2001: 124–6).
3 In this book 'Self' is spelled with an initial capital letter to distinguish Jung's use of this concept from the ordinary usage where self is synonymous with the conscious ego. Note, however, that in *Collected Works* 'self' is uncapitalized.
4 Balthasar likewise gives greater priority to the image which is understood as an epiphany of divine glory (in his theological aesthetics) rather than a human perception of beauty (in theological aesthetics), which is taken to point to the divine.
5 Nagy, 1991: 63–74 argues that Jung is using Schopenhauer's interpretation of Kant.
6 The Latin term was coined by Jung (Main, 2006b: 166 n. 10). For a possible personal connection with Otto through the Eranos Conferences, see Main, 2006b: 166 n. 9; Bair, 2004: 413.
7 *Fascinans* and not, as in Jung, 1959: 458, 463, *fascinosum* (Main, 2006b: 166 n. 10).
8 In his trilogy Balthasar makes only passing reference to Otto (*GL*4: 37; *GL*7: 169 n. 14; *TD*1: 556ff.; *TD*3: 72), with one mention of his idea of 'the Holy' (*TD*4: 303), but none to the concept of the numinous.
9 Balthasar works with a Thomist distinction between 'splendour' (*Glanz*, *lumen* or *splendor*) and 'form' (*Gestalt*, *species* or *forma*) (*GL*1: 118).
10 Balthasar is correct in noting that Jung stresses persona problems at the outset of analysis (*TD*1: 517–8 and ibid.: 517–8 nn. 21–3 referring to Jung 1928c), but wrong to say that Jung thinks it can be dispensed with since it, for Jung, 'is a function for adapting the individual to the real world' (Jung, 1916b: 298).
11 However, Balthasar notes 'how multifariously Joachim's vision [of the Spirit ruling the Third Age of the world] underpinned the Enlightenment' and 'the development of modern rationalism' (*TD*4: 458 and ibid. n. 2; cf. Lubac, 1979–81).
12 It is these continuities, rather than the phrase *corpus triforme*, that Balthasar finds in Irenaeus (Mongrain, 2002: 38f.).

Chapter 5

Analogy and polarity

Balthasar held a paradoxical view of analogy. Jung usually relied on direct correspondence between the human and the divine. However, Jung identified but did not develop a question about the relation of similarity and paradox, which might have allowed for a psychological reinterpretation more compatible with Balthasar. Balthasar acknowledges the importance of polarity in human experience. Nevertheless, he was strongly suspicious of any hint of dualism in relation to God. I term Jung's understanding of polarity as dualistic monism. Balthasar's overriding interest is not in polarity as a feature of the human condition but rather in the polarity between God and creation. For this he develops a dialectic of contradiction. The interplay of Jung's and Balthasar's use of analogy and polarity will be important for understanding some of the complexities of carrying through a critical comparison of their understanding of God's involvement with evil. I seek to argue (in chapter nine) that a Balthasarian approach to analogy and a Jungian approach to polarity might take us beyond the difficulties with which a type 2 / type 4 engagement between them would find itself confronted. The essay on Satan in the Old Testament provides, at the end of this chapter, a case study of Jung's and Balthasar's differing theological orientations and their divergent use of analogy and polarity.

Differing views on analogy

On the question of analogy Balthasar holds a paradoxically dynamic balance between an assertion of similarity between God and humanity and a simultaneous assertion of an ever-greater dissimilarity. In the introduction to *Psychology and Alchemy*, Jung shows that he was aware of the importance of both correspondence and paradox in religious ideas. In practice, however, his working theory of analogy relies on a correspondence of similarity as the basis for connecting psychological insights with Christian doctrines.

Analogy is a significant theme throughout Balthasar's trilogy, that is (as already noted), the 'correspondence between worldly "beauty" and divine "glory"', between 'worldly, finite freedom and divine, infinite freedom' and 'the structure of creaturely truth and the structure of divine truth' (*TL*1: 7).

Balthasar's view of the analogy of being can be summarized as a 'similitude in "greater dissimilitude"' (*TL*2: 82).

Przywara had introduced Balthasar to this concept, drawn from the canons of the Fourth Lateran Council of 1215 (*TL*2: 94 n. 16). As Balthasar expresses it,

> the creature, no matter how high grace may lift it, can never overtake the divine aseity. Nevertheless, there must already be something in God that enables him to plan and to posit in existence a creature that in its being and essence is an image of, and so is similar to the triune God.
>
> (ibid.: 82)

Similarity is based in the view that humanity, as part of creation, is in the image of God, for 'if God's will to give form really aims at man as God truly wants to shape him,' Balthasar argues, 'then it appears impossible to deny that there exists an analogy between God's work of formation and the shaping forces of nature and of man as they generate and give birth' (*GL*1: 36). For his simultaneous emphasis on the dissimilarity Balthasar uses Aquinas' 'real distinction between *esse* and *essentia* … [which] … enables us once again to make a clear distinction between the "glory" of God and the beauty of the world' (*GL*4: 395). It is the dissimilarity of the *esse*, the existence unique to God, from the *essentia*, the existence common to all creation, which, although it shares a similarity with divine being, does so without being understood as identical with it or subsumed by it. It is a paradox that the similarity of created being with Absolute Being must be held within their ever-greater dissimilarity.

This philosophical principle of analogy is used by Balthasar to serve primarily theological ends, whereby the *analogia entis* [analogy of being] is reworked as the *analogia libertatis* [analogy of freedom]: 'if there is finite being and truth at all, it is only because of a free creative deed and utterance of God' (*TL*1: 229). Human being and truth exist because of the choice of the infinitely free God to reveal himself in an act of loving self-communication, first, in a creation which enables creatures to know something of worldly and divine truth, and ultimately in the incarnation. Just as Balthasar rejected, in his anthropology, the idea of stand-alone self-sufficient autonomy, so for him the cosmos, in its being and truth, has a real but contingent measure of freedom: 'the world as it concretely exists is one that is always already related either positively or negatively to the God of grace and supernatural revelation. There are no neutral points or surfaces in this relationship' (ibid.: 30).

Balthasar's theology of analogy is revealed supremely in Christ, who embodies in the theodramatic unfolding of his mission the ultimate likeness to and difference from God, which itself expresses God's choice to live out in the world this aspect of the inner-trinitarian life of love. In *GL*6, anticipating the fulfilment that would be revealed in Christ, who is 'the archetype of all creaturely participation in the glory of God' (*GL*7: 21 quoting Barth), Balthasar writes:

> The full light of revelation [in the New Testament] will show that such a feat of daring on God's part [freely making a creation with sufficient finite freedom to respond to God or not] is possible only because in God himself there exists an eternal reciprocity of living love: in the final analysis the biblical doctrine of the image can be understood only in the light of the divine Trinity. … [This] provid[es] a final … justification for worldly beauty, since it is only here that the image, which finite worldly reality is of necessity, can be taken up and secured in the eternal Image, which is the archetypal image (*Urbild*) even as it is the image that transcends all images (*Überbild*).
>
> (*GL*6: 87)

The divine christological initiative, though occurring as an event in post-creation history, is not to be understood as a second step, entirely distinct from creation:

> The perception of God, who is imperceivable in himself and yet has become perceivable through his free grace, is realized when God comes into the world [in Christ], and yes, *becomes world*. His allowing us to participate in his Godhead, which is above the world, precisely in this and no other way, occurs not in a second process, but in the one and only process. This is the *admirabile commercium et conubium* [wondrous exchange and marriage]. In God's condescension lies man's exaltation.
>
> (*GL*1: 302)

By contrast, Jung, it could be said, struggles to establish the basis of a comparable theory of analogy. His primary appeal is to similarity. He sees a direct parallel, for instance, between the (transcendental) universality of the collective unconscious and the *imago Dei*. On this basis, he argues that in the collective unconscious the archetypes

> are the prior conditions or patterns of psychic formation in general. … They are in themselves non-perceptible, irrepresentable (since they precede all representation), everywhere and 'eternally' the same. Hence there is only one collective unconscious, which is everywhere identical with itself, from which everything psychic takes shape before it is personalized, modified, assimilated, etc. by external influences. … The theological parallel is the idea of the *likeness of God*. There is only *one imago Dei*, which belongs to the existential ground of all men. I cannot speak of 'my' *imago Dei* but only of 'the' *imago Dei*. It is the principle by which man is shaped, one and the same, immutable, eternal.
>
> (*L*1: 408f)

An implicit appeal to similarity underlies Jung's use of a version of the causal argument to assert the existence of God. If, he argues, the word 'archetype' is, etymologically, an imprint, there must be an imprinter: 'The word "type" is, as we know, derived from τυπος, "blow" or "imprint"; thus an archetype presupposes an imprinter' (*CW*12: 14).[1] An underlying reliance on direct similarity allows him to invoke the comparison between the human workman and God, when he refers to archetypes as 'so to speak, organs (tools) of God' (*L*2: 130; cf. ibid.: 606).

In *Psychology and Alchemy*, Jung comes closest to recognizing that the relation of human and divine needs something in addition to direct correspondence. Similarity is Jung's starting position. He asserts that there are 'psychological factors which correspond to divine figures' (*CW*12: 9). In answer to those who say that this amounts to psychologism, reducing religion to psychology, Jung retorts rather sharply:

> I have been accused of 'deifying the soul'. Not I but God himself has deified it! *I* did not attribute a religious function to the soul, I merely produced the facts which prove that the soul is *naturaliter religiosa*, i.e. possesses a religious function.
>
> (ibid.: 13)

The focus of Jung's approach to analogy is psychological. The soul 'has the dignity of an entity endowed with consciousness of a relationship to Deity' (ibid.: 10), that is to say, 'a correspondence' (ibid.: 11). The basis of the connection is the 'psychological factor', '*the archetype of the God-image*' in the collective unconscious of humanity (ibid.). Given that Jung is working with a simple notion of similarity, he has two concerns. He wants to avoid suggesting on the one hand an identity ('affinity' (ibid.)) between God and the soul and, on the other, an idea of God that allows for no connection. Thus: 'It is ... psychologically quite unthinkable for God to be simply the "wholly other", for a "wholly other" could never be one of the soul's deepest and closest intimacies – which is precisely what God is' (ibid.: 11 n. 6). But the focus of Jung's interest is always on direct correspondence between psychological truths and religious affirmations, for the 'archetypes of the unconscious can be shown empirically to be the equivalents of religious dogmas' (ibid.: 17).

Jung does not manage, in *Psychology and Alchemy*, to bring into his theory of analogy his insight about the importance of paradox in attempting to articulate religious truth. Elsewhere Jung was able to acknowledge the dissimilarity which Balthasar relates to God's infinite freedom. Humanity should not presume to 'trespass against God's freedom and omnipotence' (*CW*9(ii): 46). It is also clear, in the *Red Book*, when Jung is writing in an explicitly religious vein, that paradox is a significant factor, as he wrestles with the idea that God is both loving and terrible. If, as he believed the 'image of God throws a shadow that is just as great as itself', does that mean that God has two 'essences' (*RBLN*: 230)? How could that be true of the one God?

In *Psychology and Alchemy*, Jung emphasizes that for him as a psychologist the religious affirmations that most deserve his attention are those which are expressed paradoxically: 'The only statements that have psychological validity concerning the God-image are either paradoxes or antinomies' (*CW*12: 11 n. 6; cf. *MDR*: 384). He gives examples of what he means:

> Does one equal three? How can three be one? Can a mother be a virgin? ... Has it not been observed that all religious statements contain logical contradictions and assertions that are impossible in principle, that this is in fact the very essence of religious assertion? As witness to this we have Tertullian's avowal: 'And the Son of God is dead, which is worthy of belief because it is absurd. And when buried, He rose again, which is certain because it is impossible.' ... [T]he paradox is one of our most valuable spiritual possessions, ... [and] their multiplication enriches [religion] because only the paradox comes anywhere near to comprehending the fullness of life.
>
> (ibid.: 15f.)

However, Jung makes use of this insight, in *Psychology and Alchemy*, not in the service of a theory of analogy but so that the psychologist might help to 'increase the number of persons who have at least some inkling of the scope of paradoxical truth', and that they might understand again 'what is meant by the paradoxes contained in dogma' (ibid.: 16). Further, the theologian who knows about (psychological) paradox will better 'trust God to speak in the soul' (ibid.: 17).

Jung's primary insight about paradox, in *Psychology and Alchemy*, goes not to inform his theory of analogy but to underscore the dualistic monism of his theory of archetypes, including the psychological symbol of wholeness, the Self, as a 'union of opposites'. It is here, however, that he finds the (archetypal) Christian dogmatic symbol of wholeness, Christ, wanting. This will have particular significance for Jung's use of his psychology in a reinterpretation of Christian theology, particularly in relation to God's involvement with evil. This is evident when Jung says:

> The self is a union of opposites *par excellence*, and this is where it differs essentially from the Christ-symbol. ... The opposition between light and good on the one hand and darkness and evil on the other is left in a state of open conflict, since Christ simply represents good, and his counterpart the devil, evil. This opposition is the real world problem, which at present is still unresolved.
>
> (ibid.: 19)

There are ample grounds to suspect that Jung's reliance on analogy as direct correspondence means that he would have found it difficult to relish the

Balthasarian challenge of 'the constant vigilance required to keep the transcendental beauty of revelation from slipping into equality with an inner-worldly natural beauty' (*GL*1: 41) of archetypal images in psychological experience. Indeed, eventually Jung had no means for distinguishing God-images from Self-images.

Differing understandings of polarity

A third area of divergence between Balthasar and Jung is that of polarity. Balthasar and Jung both grant the importance of polarity in the human experience of contrary opposites. Balthasar, however, is very concerned lest this dualistic understanding of polarity be taken into the doctrine of God. As we would expect from Jung's approach to analogy he is not troubled by the prospect of a theology that accepts a dark as well as a light side in God. However, he is also, in psychology and theology, concerned to avoid dualism. Balthasar's approach is to focus on the divine–human relatedness, developing a dialectic of contradiction. Jung draws on resources such as the alchemical figure of Mercurius to support what I term his dualistic monism. These two approaches are outlined here. They have a major influence on the construction of a critical comparison between Jung and Balthasar on God's involvement with evil.

Balthasar's dialectic of contradiction

Balthasar fully accepts the experience of polarity in the ambivalence of creaturely existence and that in practice this involves a struggle with the tension of contrary opposites. But he resists all attempts to see the theodrama (and therefore the Christian way of life) and, much less, the inner-trinitarian life, in these terms. In part this is to defend against theological dualism. In this he stands within the mainstream of Christian tradition. In the history of theological approaches to the problem of evil, it is evident that a most important issue for Christianity has been that raised by 'the threats and temptations of dualism – in Manichee, Gnostic, and other forms' (Larrimore, 2001: xxiii). Balthasar is particularly suspicious of those who

> [f]aced with man's ambivalence and all the suffering in the world, … apprehend the abyss which the Cross opens up between sheer divine love and sheer God-forsakenness, [and] … attempt to trace it back to a source in the Absolute, so rendering it accessible to reason.
>
> (*TD*2: 419)

In Balthasar's terms this suppresses the Christian revelation in favour of 'speculation', which has deeply infected Christian theology from second-century Gnosticism, flowering into Manichaeism, through late-Augustinian views about predestination on into the Middle Ages, the Protestant Reformation and Catholic Jansenism.

It runs counter to Balthasar's theory of analogy to extrapolate human experience understood as a tension of opposites into the inner-divine life. Drawing on the New Testament writings of both John and Paul, Balthasar develops a christological and trinitarian dialectic expressed as theological contradiction rather than anthropological contrariety. He prioritizes the tension between the light and truth of the Logos and intra-cosmic darkness:

> In his self-exposition in the flesh, the Logos expresses himself to the uttermost extreme. ... The darkness ... does not *want* to know [the light]. Jesus is the witness to the truth that he is; ... not to believe that he shows God is to contradict [*Wider-spruch*] him ... so that contradiction ... [or] dialectic means the yawning abyss of sheer irreconcilability and enmity.
>
> (*TL*2: 317)

Balthasar holds his position over against an intra-cosmic, anthropological dialectic based on the tension of contrary opposites within humanity, with Martin Luther (1483–1546) as a prime example of the attempt to work with this anthropological dialectic theologically, 'by declaring that man simultaneously yea-says and gainsays, believes and disbelieves, hates and loves, is *justus et peccator* [righteous and sinner]' (ibid.; cf. ibid.: 335–45).

In the human realm Balthasar accepts the reality of contrariety and the consequences of an overemphasis on one pole of a pair of opposites: 'Partial truths can and must be supplemented by their contraries – this is the truth of Hegel's logic' (ibid.: 321). Balthasar was aware that Jung's analytical psychology stood within this tradition. He noted that Jung's 'doctrine of types develops according to the governing categories of tension, polarity and complementarity' – 'the problem of opposing features', including 'good and evil' (*TD*1: 518 and ibid.: 518 n. 24 referring to *MDR* and *CW*14). He further sees that Jung has both a psychological and a theological agenda. On the one hand, Balthasar acknowledges that Jung keeps the question of evil in the human sphere: 'The good-and-evil polarity must not be extrapolated from the weft and woof of the psyche' because 'it is only in the field of human willing and acting that the opposition between them is brought to a head morally' (ibid.: 518f. quoting *CW*9(ii)). On the other hand, however, Jung links psychology and theology by direct analogy. Balthasar notes that for Jung the Self is 'the horizon onto which the ego projects itself' (*TD*1: 519). It is 'quaternary', and its 'symbols are not distinct from those of the divine' (ibid. and ibid. n. 27 referring to Jung, 1928c, *CW*9(ii) and *CW*11). Thus he sees that for Jung theological judgements are based on the tenets of his psychology:

> The Christian Trinity is ... exclusively light, it lacks the shadow, evil; beside Christ, the good Son, it needs the devil, the son who has gone

> astray. For, confronted with the world as it is, who can take refuge in the excuse that God did not will the evil in it?
>
> (ibid.: 519)

This becomes the basis on which Jung can read, for instance, the book of Job, where Job is said to have 'discerned the opposites in the divine nature' (ibid. and ibid. n. 30 referring to Jung, 1952a, *MDR*, *PRTL*, and *CW*12).

If an anthropological dialectic, based on the experience of polarity, is made into a theological principle, then Balthasar is concerned that God will have a necessary involvement with evil, compromising his absolute love and infinite freedom: 'Interpreted in Christian terms, what Hegel understands as "truth" would be a God who gains himself only through the principle of the demonic, understood as the "awful power of the negative"' (*TL*2: 321).

Thus it is for its theological consequences that Balthasar is wary of an anthropology based on the tension of opposites. In part this is to ensure that his christology retains the ability to be a manifestation of the (ever-greater) divine infinite freedom rather than be defined by the limitations of creation's finite freedom. Balthasar does not typically portray his Christ as participating in the anthropological dialectic, bearing the tension of opposites of human experience. He thinks it is a false hope that a psychological or a world process (such as Jung's individuation or Hegel's synthesis) could finally resolve the tension of opposites, much less resolve the ever-greater dissimilarity (and dialectical contradiction) between Creator and creature.

If Balthasar relies on the assertion that Christ was tempted like other human beings yet without committing actual sin, then Jung questions whether this does not diminish the humanity in Christ by denying him a dark side, a shadow. But for Balthasar the Logos addresses the primary agenda, the contradictory dialectic between God and humanity. To focus on the contrary dialectic within human experience starts in the wrong place. The point of departure must be the contradiction opened by the human choice of saying No to God, in relation to which God takes action through Christ's obedient suffering. Christ, rather than addressing the problem through the experience of contrariety, 'withstands in himself the contradiction of sin', and he 'overcomes it from below' because he 'remains and endures in obedience' (ibid.: 326) to death and beyond.

One of Balthasar's key criticisms of Luther is that he makes christology and anthropology coincide completely, each 'founded' upon the other (ibid.: 339). Just as the human being 'can be simultaneously *justus* (*et peccator*)' (ibid.), so Christ is 'simultaneously "supremely righteous and supremely sinful, … supremely blessed and supremely damned"' (ibid.: 337 quoting Luther). He participated in the Cross as a sinner would, so that 'he "withstood the most terrible reality of all, God's wrath"' (ibid.: 338 quoting Luther). This leads to the view that God's Being contains the contrary opposites of love and wrath. This is the ultimate consequence, as Balthasar sees it, of 'a thoroughgoing contradiction dialectic' (ibid.: 344) grounded in anthropology, namely a 'God of majesty [who] revealed himself in the wrath–love contradiction of the Cross …the nakedness of whose terrifying majesty man cannot bear' (ibid.: 342).

Balthasar sees a comparable problem in Hegel's attempt to make 'the entire world an *imago Trinitatis* from below' (ibid.: 43 referring to *TD*5: 65), based on the thesis-antithesis-synthesis of his dialectic. Eventually, human contrariety is imputed into the Godhead. For this reason, Balthasar resists Hegel's general strategy of 'making the "other" the negation of the One and then integrating both in a higher synthesis' (ibid). He insists that the human experience is not to be extrapolated into an opposition within the Godhead: 'the "other" in God is pure … positivity, and in no way the negation of the One or its "reversal"' (ibid.).[2]

Mongrain argues that Balthasar's position is a reworking of the theology of Irenaeus (*c.*120–*c.*200), with the dialectic between Creator and creature being summed up as 'unity-in-difference' (Mongrain, 2002; cf. Balthasar 1990a: 4–11; *GL*2: 31–94 and *TD*2: 140–9). Put positively, the Christian revelation (following Irenaeus's 'doxological paradox') affirms 'the mutual glorification of God and humanity in Christ' (ibid.: 30 quoting Irenaeus), namely, the glory of God is the human being fully alive, the glory of humanity is the vision of God. When this is spoken against, contra-dicted, by humanity, the dialectic that calls for resolution through divine initiative is set in train. When the Christian revelation is welcomed with a Yes to God, there is, as seen by Irenaeus, a 'mutually affirming yet ontologically asymmetrical relationship between God and the creation' (ibid.: 32).

Rather than accept Luther's God, whose hidden majesty breaks out in wrath and love, Balthasar, following Irenaeus, maintains the unknowable mystery of the glory of God and affirms that love alone (available through the visible form of Christ) is the key to the relationship with God that is on offer. Balthasar quotes Irenaeus to this effect: 'According to his splendour it is impossible to know God … [yet] as regards His love [as seen in the Word] we constantly learn the ever-greater immense splendour of God'; and: '[a]ccording to his splendour he is unknown to all who have been made by him … but as regards his love, he can always be known in the one through whom he created all things' (ibid.: 31).

Jung's dualistic monism

The question of opposites was a major preoccupation for Jung and a central component of his psychology. There are at least six hundred references to opposites in the General Index to his *Collected Works* (Forryan and Glover, 1979: 495–9). A brief sketch of Jung's understanding of opposites, of their tension and union, in anthropology and in theology, will be sufficient to highlight ways in which he diverged from Balthasar. For theological reasons, Balthasar chose to highlight problems he saw in Luther's view of contrary opposites. Jung – a 'psychologized Protestant', as he has been called (Casement, 2001: 47) – asserts the foundational importance of opposites in human experience and also challenges an entirely pessimistic view of the fluctuation between opposing contrary poles. Such a fluctuation, following Heraclitus, Jung calls *enantiodromia*. For Jung a dualistic process is founded upon an underlying monism.

Opposites play a central role in Jung's map of the psyche and in his understanding of the process of individuation. As early as his university years he was already espousing the view (which has been dubbed his 'pessimistic dualism' (*CWA*: xxii)) that the world and God are composed of opposites. In the Zofingia lectures Jung says of the created world, '"This is the way to view all the works of the Most High; they go in pairs, by opposites"' (*CWA*: 79 quoting Ecclesiasticus). A major theme of Jung's *Red Book* is that unconscious contents split into opposites as they emerge into consciousness. Jung speaks of the 'spirit of the depths' (whose contents are 'the inexplicable and the paradoxical' (*RBLN*: 229)), which is in structurally polar opposition to 'the spirit of this time' (whose realm is that of understanding, knowledge). On the basis of direct analogy with the human psyche, in his essay 'On Psychic Energy' he holds a doctrine of God in which the 'God-concept' is 'not only the essence of spiritual light, ... not only the spiritual goal of salvation in which all creation culminates, but also the darkest, nethermost cause of Nature's blackest deeps' (Jung, 1928a: 55).[3]

Libido, psychic energy, the vital life force, which is central to analytical psychology, is 'a living balance between opposites' (ibid). Jung uses the metaphor of the psyche as a 'steady stream' of libido (*CWB*: 170; cf. Chapman, 1988: 6 and 13–62 *passim*), 'a continuous flow or current of life', like 'a watercourse that flows from a mountain into a valley' (Jung, 1928a: 37, 38). Jung envisages the libidinal flow going (progressively) forwards, and then, in response to blockages, (regressively) backwards, eventually seeking other channels to allow the forward flow to resume. There is an inherent duality in this model of psychic energy, comparable to a current of electricity alternating between positive and negative poles: 'I see in all that happens the play of opposites, and derive from this conception my idea of psychic energy ... in much the same way as physical energy involves a difference of potential ... [between] opposites' (Jung, 1929b: 337). On numerous occasions Jung asserts that without a tension of opposites there is no life energy (Jung 1917/1926/1943: 29, 53, 75, 80; *CW*6: 202; Jung 1942: 112, 118; *PADT*: 197; *CW*14: 418, 497; Jung, 1958a: 727; *MDR*: 383).

It is clear that for Jung psychic energy is both a monistic entity and also a conjunction of (dualistic) opposites. He asserted, for instance against White who detected in his work a 'Manichaean streak' (Lammers and Cunningham, 2007: 142 n. 38), that everything in his psychology is opposed to simple dualism: 'my critic [Victor White] should know how very much I stress the unity of the self, this central archetype which is a *complexio oppositorum* par excellence, and that my leanings are therefore towards the very reverse of dualism' (*CW*9(ii): 61 n. 74). I refer to Jung's position, therefore, as a paradoxical dualistic monism.

Jung's position is not best understood statically but rather in relation to the dynamic process of individuation. The energic unity holds together during a period of libidinal progression, but it breaks down (in neurotic dissociation) into conflict during a period of regression, with the unconscious producing transformations of libido (through the 'transcendent function' (Jung, 1917/1926/1943: 80)) in the form of symbols of greater wholeness, healing the dividedness and producing individuation. It is the archetypes of the collective unconscious that produce symbols of wholeness. This process of symbol-formation is central to Jung's project in relation to Christianity and will be dealt with in detail in chapter eight. For now, we need note only that archetypes also are understood in terms of paradoxical dualistic monism – monistic entities made up of the conjunction of opposites. The Self, for instance, 'as a symbol of wholeness, is *coincidentia oppositorum*, and therefore contains light and darkness simultaneously' (*CW*5: 368).

For Jung this is not only his answer to the charge of dualism but also the antidote to a simple monism in Christianity: 'For the Christian neither God nor Christ could be a paradox: they have to have a single meaning, and this holds true to the present day' (*CW*9(ii): 46). One of Jung's chief complaints against Christianity is that Christ, who for Jung functions in Western civilization as the foremost symbol of the Self (*PADT*: 152–7; *CW*9(ii): 36–71), contains only the light, and 'lacks the nocturnal side of the psyche's nature, the darkness of the spirit, and is also without sin' (*PADT*: 156), and thus his repressed psychological shadow manifests in projection as the prince of this world, the devil (*CW*9(ii): 41 n. 23).

Jung's doctrine of God is likewise based on dualistic monism. He has, however, often been accused of Gnosticism, most notably by Martin Buber (Segal, 1992). Jung thought of his *Seven Sermons to the Dead*, within his *Red Book*, as a 'poem' 'in "Gnostic" style' (Jung, 1952c: 663f.), but debate with Buber quickly fell into the gap Jung liked to open up between metaphysics and psychology. Jung thought the Gnostics important because they addressed the issue of the reality of evil robustly, but he realized they were not a good basis for debate with Christian theology since we have fragmentary knowledge of their views, mainly available to us through their opponents (cf. Casement, 2001: 49–52 and 116–24).

Balthasar is aware that Jung is concerned with 'the problem of evil in God' (*TD*1: 519 n. 30)[4] and he thinks there is evidence of dualism, when Jung draws on Jakob Böhme's (1575–1624) 'split Divinity' (ibid.: 520), that is, a God who can be wrathful as well as loving, as experienced by the ascetic hermit and patron saint of Switzerland, Brother Klaus (Nicholas of Flüe, 1417–87) (Jung, 1934/1954: 11).

But it is clear that Jung is primarily interested in thinkers (such as philosophical alchemists) who illustrate the individuating process whereby opposing forces are joined into a greater wholeness, the outworking of a dualistic monism rather than a Gnostic dualism (cf. Jung, 1934/1950: 312f.). Further, this was probably part of the appeal of Rudolph Otto for Jung, as a theologian who affirmed a monistic God who had to be experienced (non-rationally) in his duality, as both *tremendum* and *fascinans*: 'These two qualities, the daunting and the fascinating, now combine in a strange harmony of contrasts', resulting in the 'dual character of the numinous consciousness' (Otto, 1958: 31).

Jung thought that his approach through the principle of dualistic monism helped to provide a psychological solution to a problem raised in Hegel's philosophical system. The criticism is that Hegel provides no resolution to the thesis-antithesis-synthesis process because syntheses are always the start of another phase of the process initiated by one-sidedness. Jung's view was that the dualistic monism of archetypes in principle at least provides the possibility of closure: 'The self ... is absolutely paradoxical in that it represents in every respect thesis and antithesis, and at the same time synthesis' (*CW*12: 19).

Jung, however, remains vulnerable to Balthasar's further criticism that Hegel's contrariety between 'one' and an 'other' is extrapolated into the Godhead. Jung holds a comparable view, though he draws it from ideas in ancient number symbolism and late medieval alchemical texts (cf. *PADT*: 117ff.). 'One' and 'two' are associated with the 'One' and the 'Other':

> The 'other' can have a 'sinister' significance ... as something opposite and alien. Therefore, argues the medieval alchemist, God did not praise the second day of creation, because on this day ... the *binarius*, alias the devil, came into existence. ... The 'One' and the 'Other' form an opposition.
> (ibid.: 118)

It was clearly a struggle for Jung to keep a consistent focus on an understanding of polarity in human experience as dualistic monism. His psychology contains dualistic principles and he understood God to have dual aspects. But the vision and possibility of wholeness rested on a view of the archetype (and God) as a monistic *complexio oppositorum*, a view for which he argues in his Mercurius essay in the *Symbolik des Geistes* collection.

It is also important to affirm that although Balthasar's primary focus was on the polarity between God and humanity (arising from both the dissimilarity within analogy and the dialectic of contradiction) – and that this made him theologically wary of the human experience of the polarity of contrary opposites – nevertheless Balthasar recognizes the play of opposites within human experience.

Balthasar follows Przywara in the way he discusses three fundamental polarities in created life: spirit and body (*TD*2: 355–64), man and woman (ibid.:

365–82),[5] individual and community (ibid.: 382–94; cf. Przywara, 1935; Przywara, 1938).

The body–spirit polarity is the most relevant here, not least because in some of the Fathers this was linked to 'the freedom to embrace good or evil' (ibid.: 362). There is an initial sense that contrariety is at play: 'The tension between body and spirit is manifested in the contrary pull of the two poles' (ibid.: 355f.). However, 'anthropology [and *pari passu* psychology] must accept the idea that there is an ambiguity to be taken into account here: what seems like a natural polarity is also an unnatural dichotomy' (ibid.: 358).

The human realm, however, provides too limited a horizon for the sought-for resolution. The riddle of this tension of opposites, highlighted by the boundary of death, seems to have no more than endless *enantiodromia* to offer: 'In all three dimensions, man seems to be built according to a polarity, obliged to engage in reciprocity, always seeking complementarity and peace in the other pole' (ibid.: 355). Balthasar sees that the challenge relates to maintaining a spirit–body connectedness. Not only does the spirit need to keep its connection with the bodily, being dependent upon 'the physical-spiritual infrastructure', but also it must transcend the bodily 'in order to perform its specific operation, reflection' (ibid.: 359).

Balthasar sees two options, both of which for him are unsatisfactory. Humanity can (presumably consciously) create and mediate 'a kind of natural synthesis' of the worlds of matter and spirit (ibid.: 360). This position of an 'Aristotelian "middle"' (which Jung also sought to avoid) lacks liveliness (ibid.: 364). The other option is to accept that body and spirit are 'utterly contrary to each other', and, accepting the duality, to choose to relate to one of them (ibid.: 360). This is theologically unacceptable as fundamentally dualistic.

Consequently, for Balthasar, humanity must be 'pointed beyond [its] whole polar structure' (ibid.: 355). Since these polarities need to be understood in terms of a decline in what humanity was created to be, as a consequence of humanity's No to God, it is only through the addressing of this more fundamental dialectic of contradiction that the situation of polar contrariety can be adequately addressed. This will be in the action of the theodrama: 'the unity of the contrary movements [of the spirit 'downwards' and the body 'upwards'] can only arise out of a dramatic engagement' (*TD*2: 364), whereby Christ must

> execute fully both movements without hubris and without degeneration: [he] would have to come down into flesh 'from above' … plumbing the dimensions of 'world' and 'flesh' to the very bottom. … [He] must undergird and embrace every possible declension from God. And from below, on the basis of a perfect fleshly being, [he] must go beyond the realm of the 'world' so as to bring both world and flesh with it, in its transcendence, up to God, 'transfiguring' it, not 'spiritualizing' it in some incorporeal manner. (ibid.)

Independently of Balthasar, Jung also made use of Przywara's *Deus Semper Maior* in his seminars on the Ignatian *Spiritual Exercises* (Becker, 2001: 62–4), and he refers to him in his 'Introduction' to *Psychology and Alchemy* (*CW*12: 27 n. 14 referring to Przywara, 1938) .

Jung thinks that Przywara has put his finger on the problem with the idea of a 'rift', 'the gulf separating good from evil, the latent and apparently incurable dualism of Christianity, the eternity of the devil and damnation' (*CW*18: 689f. referring to Przywara 1938: I, 71ff.; cf. Becker, 2001: 63f.). The line of Jung's argument is that a christocentric Christianity cannot resolve the problem of the tension of contrary opposites: 'Christianity has made the antinomy of good and evil into a world problem and ... an absolute principle'; worse, 'Christian symbolism ... leaves the conflict open. ... [T]here is a rift running through the world' (*CW*12: 22). Jung, however, remains hopeful. Despite the 'gaping "rift" in the Christian order of things', 'Christian symbolism is particularly concerned with healing, or attempting to heal, this very wound' (ibid.: 27).

Balthasar and Jung have different ways of suggesting that humanity can move beyond the *impasse* of polarity. For Jung it is a combination of the processes of analytical psychology and the work of the Holy Spirit ('Psychology has no proof that this process does not unfold itself at the instigation of God's will' (*CW*18: 690)). Balthasar is sure that the way ahead lies in a theology based on a theological aesthetics which enables us to see the glory of the Lord, on the divine initiative in Christ to enter into the world drama, underpinned by a thoroughgoing theo-logic. That is his answer to an apparently open question: 'whether this projection [that he sees in Jung] onto God of a polarity structure that is typical of the creature ... can lead conditioned man beyond himself to the unconditioned, to that which conditions him' (*TD*1: 520). For '[t]he truth of the world is grounded in the truth of God that reveals itself in it' (*TL*1: 244). Balthasar looks to God to redeem humanity; Jung sees humanity as necessary for the redemption of God.

There is, however, a further distinction to be drawn between two aspects of polarity, namely the qualitative dissimilarity between God and creation and the experience of contrary opposites as constitutive of humanity. In chapter nine, I argue that, following Balthasar's view of analogy, they must not be conflated but that nevertheless they can be brought together, continuing to respect the tension of their difference. But I conclude these chapters, in which I have been exploring the bases for a critical comparison of Jung's and Balthasar's understanding of God's involvement with evil, with a case study, which illustrates aspects of their differing theological orientations and understanding of analogy and polarity.

Satan in the Old Testament – a case study

Rivkah Schärf's essay on Satan in the Old Testament in *Symbolik des Geistes*[6] 'describes the historical development of the ungodly spirit, Satan, as depicted in the texts of the Old Testament' (Jung, 1948b: 649; cf. *CW*18: 711 n. 8). Initially it would seem that some aspects of Schärf's essay point to convergence with Balthasar's double view of divine pedagogy in the Old Testament and of a proleptic reading of it. But different understandings of incarnation are evident and the question of the mutuality of pedagogy remains to be explored. More typically of Jung's 'Joachimite' theological orientation, Schärf's essay relies on a notion of an unfolding deity rather than on a Balthasarian, *corpus triforme*, three-phase trinitarian drama. Further, Schärf's essay provides examples of themes that are at the heart of divergence in the dialogue between Jung and Balthasar: the nature of analogy and the issue of dualistic monism. Whilst Jungian thinking comes very close to reductive psychologism by arguing that God needs humanity in order to individuate, Schärf uses this to make a case for mutuality of learning, particularly in the book of Job, which Balthasar discusses in terms of theodrama. Finally, Schärf's essay helps to illustrate how, for both Balthasar and Jung, the understanding of evil, in the shift from the Old to the New Testament, is both historically conditioned and represents a step change in response to the advent of Christ. Balthasar sees this in theodramatic terms. Jung relates it to the constellation of the archetype of hostile brothers and seeks to make a case (going beyond Schärf) for Satan to be seen as a Son of God.

Theological orientation

Part of Balthasar's reading of the Old Testament is that it offers an example in the first phase of the *corpus triforme* of divine pedagogy in which God and humanity learn to become accustomed to each other. In the story of Balaam's ass (Num. 22:22–40), the word 'Satan' is only an adjectival means of describing an action of an angel of the Lord, who is an 'adversary' [*le-satan-lo*] by standing in Balaam's way (*SOT*: 38). Schärf sees this as God using his opposing angel to create human consciousness:

> The human will becomes conscious through its collision with the divine will, by coming up against the adversary. Thus, behind the deadly threat of the divine opposition there is also a hidden positive, purposeful aspect; the adversary, as such, is at the same time the creator of individual consciousness.
>
> (ibid.: 76)

This is an example of divine pedagogy.

In the Chronicler's version of David's census of Israel, 'Satan stood up against Israel and incited David to count the people' (1 Chr. 21:1–6; cf. 2 Sam. 24:1–9). Schärf refers to Gerhard von Rad (1901–71) in seeing this Satan as 'a "demonic-destructive principle firmly anchored in the plan of salvation"' (ibid.: 161). She argues that it was Satan's prompting action which produced consciousness of the guilt of transgressing, which in turn 'create[d] room in David for the will of God and makes David the carrier of revelation' (ibid). Equally, as 2 Samuel shows, 'it is clearly Yahweh who himself provokes the man David to sin against him'; 'as *Satan*, Yahweh himself leads man into this sin' (ibid.: 160). Her conclusion is that we may 'also justifiably surmise a divine purpose in the temptation of David into sin' (ibid.: 161). Such purposive action is pedagogical (though for Jung, perhaps, evidence of God's direct involvement with evil). For the moment, the question of the mutuality of learning is reserved.

For Balthasar a key aspect of reading the Old Testament as part of the *corpus triforme* is that it is proleptic, pointing towards the incarnation. Schärf notes that Philo (20BCE–50CE), Justin Martyr (103–65) and other patristic authors saw in the Old Testament figure of the angel of the Lord a prototype of the Logos (ibid.: 71 n. 33). For her it is Yahweh's 'manifestation … turned toward man as a hypostasis, as it were [Yahweh's] function of relationship' (ibid.: 59). She sees particular significance in the angel of the Lord appearing in human form (to Abraham and Sarah at Mamre, to Lot in Sodom, to Joshua at Jericho, at the call of Gideon, and in helping Daniel interpret a vision (cf. ibid.: 71 n. 33 referring to Gen. 18:2ff., Gen. 19:1, Josh. 5:13, Judg. 6:11, Dan. 8:16)). Further, since, as she argues, angels in the Old Testament (and Satan, too) emerge originally as functional aspects of Yahweh, from among his heavenly host, they 'have much to do with the mythologem of God becoming man' (ibid.: 71 n. 33). However, whereas for Balthasar the incarnation is God's infinitely free decision to enter onto the world stage as the God-man for the sake of the theodrama, for Schärf it is an expression of a divine need for self-realization.

Schärf and Balthasar agree that in the Old Testament God's primary realm is heaven. God is not alone there, as illustrated by numerous examples in Genesis – including the mysterious 'our' of Genesis 1:26, the 'sons of God' (in 6:2), the Lord appearing as a trio of angels (in 18:1f.) (*TD*3: 473, 474 and n. 3) and Jacob's ladder dream, and in the prophets, at Isaiah's election and Elijah's transportation (*TD*3: 473f.). For Balthasar, heaven 'is inhabited and … its denizens are God's messengers, in contact with the earth', 'execut[ing] the divine commands or … watch[ing] over the earth' (*TD*3: 473f. and ibid.: 474 n. 3 referring to von Rad). Schärf concurs: 'angel of the Lord' means '"the emissary of God"' (*SOT*: 58). But Balthasar links all this to the second phase of the *corpus triforme*, the human context of the incarnation. These passages are reliably revelatory since they give us 'direct access' 'to the world of angels with which Jesus is acquainted' (*TD*3: 474 citing Matt. 18:10, 26:53; Mark 1:13)[7] and which, in the case of Jacob's dream, was applied christologically in the tradition.

Schärf's emphasis is rather on angels arising from within God, in the first instance carrying out divine functions: 'It is important … that [the angel of the Lord] carries out functions which in other passages, often even in the same story, are assumed by Yahweh himself' (*SOT*: 58). She cites, among others, the promise to Hagar of a multitude of descendants by an angel (in Gen. 16:10) and the same promise to Abram by the Lord (in Gen. 15:5) (ibid).[8]

Balthasar opposes all such emanationist views as at root gnostic. Agreeing with Barth, he asserts that angels are 'not emanations of God or aspects or ideas of God' (*TD*3: 479) and he opposes the idea that angelic and demonic powers are 'aspects of God in the act of revealing himself' (ibid.: 465). The function of angels, even in the book of Job, is to highlight the difference of God in comparison with his creation: 'One of his angels may be permitted to appear before him as an "accuser" (Satan), but this is only in order to bring his righteousness into even higher relief' (ibid.: 475). Even given the hosts of heaven, God is pre-eminent in 'the process in which Yahweh becomes the Lord and centre of a "divine company" of angels, the commander of a heavenly army, and is borne up on cherubs' wings and transported in Ezekiel's chariot of glory' (ibid.: 474 referring to Eichrodt). God's monotheistic independence is primary: 'in contradistinction to the proliferating belief in demons everywhere else, even in Israel – Yahweh stands alone: he alone is to be worshipped and feared' (ibid.: 475).

Analogy and polarity

Schärf's essay has running through it two sets of assumptions central to Jung's thinking – on analogy and polarity resolved within dualistic monism – which have already been identified as major areas of divergence from Balthasar. The case of Satan in the Old Testament provides an illustration of that divergence.

In relation to the theory of analogy as direct correspondence, not only does the story of 'how the image of Satan goes through a development' link to Jungian insights about the 'development of consciousness' but it further associates 'that demonic … process … with the Godhead' (*SOT*: x).[9] Schärf argues that Old Testament monotheism arose out of 'the concept of an ambivalent god, the mingling of light and dark, of good and evil … not unity against multiplicity [polytheism and many cacodemons] as its absolute opposite; it is rather the *unity of multiplicity*' (ibid.: 10).[10] She sees this in terms of psychological processes, such as the 'unconscious identification' of Yahweh and his angel when 'one is and can be taken for the other' (ibid.: 64). In her view, this process of divine development reached only relatively low levels in terms of the development of consciousness in the Old Testament period. God develops what Jung called a 'mana' personality (Jung, 1928c: 227–41). At this stage of human development 'the elements of a personality can detach themselves from it without ceasing to be connected with it. They can even constitute its life principle without the personality itself ceasing to exist' (*SOT*: 66). In Exodus (Exod. 23:20f.) the angel of the Lord is the 'exterior soul' of Yahweh (*SOT*: 67). Schärf sees this 'differentiation process in the divine personality' take place when, in 2 Samuel 24:16, 'it is as if there arose a conflict in God, which is followed by an inner change: he repents his stern judgment' (ibid.: 70) – an example based on the assumption of direct correspondence between human psychology and the life of God.

In relation to the question of evil, Schärf sees the emergence, in the book of Job, of a process which Jung sees as typifying the age of the Son, that of conflict which cannot find resolution. The divine process is described in Jungian archetypal terms where the 'archetypes are the expressions of primal human experiences, which can occur everywhere on earth' (ibid.: 91). The book of Job opens with a divine wager, 'a test of strength between divine and demonic potencies' (ibid). She relates the meaning of this motif to stages in the development of human consciousness:

> It seems to correspond to a phase in the development of human consciousness in which the opposites have separated and become apparent but in which there is as yet no stability. It still is *uncertain* who is stronger. The good must still *prove* itself stronger than the powerful evil, cleverness stronger than stupidity, and consciousness struggling out of unconsciousness must maintain itself against the darkness of the unconscious
>
> (ibid.: 92)

The second Jungian assumption that underlies Schärf's essay is that of dualistic monism. Schärf does not identify this explicitly as the doctrine of God with which she works, nor does she refer to Jung's phrase for God as a *complexio oppositorum*. Yet her entire thesis rests on the view that the angels and Satan (ibid.: 107ff. referring to 1 Kgs. 22:19ff., Job 1:6 and 2:1), who emerge from among the 'heavenly host' or 'sons of God', are 'divine beings ... parts of the God-substance' (ibid.: 100). By implication the one God contains positive and negative elements. The emergence, in Micaiah ben Imlah's vision (1 Kgs. 22:19–23), of a spirit exercising a will of its own is seen by Schärf as indicative of 'an inner conflict in the deity, which is most enlightening in regard to the development of the God concept in the Old Testament' (*SOT*: 109f.). That is to say: 'The dark, demonic side of God begins to emerge from the ambivalent mixture with his light side and shows itself as a distinctly dark "spirit"' (ibid.: 110). Jung himself seems to confirm this when he says that her essay shows that already in the Old Testament there was 'a differentiation in the God-image' (*CW* 9(ii): 192).[11]

Balthasar accepts (as part of the pedagogical process) that in 'the pristine world of the Old Testament, ... the *satán* (of the books of Job and Zechariah) is an embodiment of a heavenly and ultimately divine quality' (*TD*3: 485). Nevertheless, by contrast, he sees the dangerous possibility that Old Testament angelology and demonology will be linked to a dualistic doctrine of God. He is opposed to using Old Testament texts to argue for the existence of 'an independent "Satan" (as is evident from a comparison of 2 Samuel 24 and 1 Chronicles 21)' by combining 'the "evil spirit" (Judg. 9:23; 1 Sam. 16:15; 1 Kgs. 22:19ff.) and the "accusing angel" (Zech. 3:1; Job 1:6, 2:1)' (ibid.: 472).

Balthasar is suspicious of exploring the 'theological development of the "angel of Yahweh"' as an expression of the positive aspect of God, on the grounds that 'originally this "angel" was … a manifestation of God himself' (ibid.: 471 and ibid. n. 21 referring to Haag), since he suspects that Old Testament demonology would be used as a 'theological defence' of the negative aspect of God: 'God's negative action or attitude (his "wrath")' (ibid.: 472). Finally, Balthasar rejects such theologizing as 'speculative', on *corpus triforme* grounds. We should judge the Old Testament in the light of the New, which shows us that the true (biblical) theology of Satan is as the tester and opponent of the mission of Christ.

One of the most challenging parts of Schärf's essay relates to her reading of the book of Job in relation to the question of God's involvement in evil. Her hope was that, in her survey of all the texts about Satan in the Old Testament, 'insofar as these texts depict a development in the concept of God, one may, in this sense, speak also of God's fate in the human soul, without this being misinterpreted as a blasphemy [of psychologism]' (*SOT*: 5).

She certainly refutes the suggestion that Satan and God in the book of Job represent a dualism, even though there is now 'a contest between Satan and Yahweh, and it is a pointed dialectical encounter, a real speech by God and counterspeech by the adversary' (ibid.: 110). The origins of this adversary are nevertheless from within the host of heaven, 'in the inner realm of the godhead' (ibid.: 136), which retains its unitary nature (though for Schärf this is an achievement forged from an earlier polytheism).

More importantly, Schärf rests her monism on the nature of the interaction between God and Job. The heavenly and earthly dramas intertwine in such a way that they must be adjudged to be differing aspects of a single phenomenon. On this reading, God and Satan represent the good and evil aspects of God and the correspondence between the heavenly and the earthly realms is reflexively direct. Each mirrors the other. Job

> experiences the falling-apart of the two sides of God. *God splits apart in him.* Satan does not appear to Job as such; all the events having to do with Satan take place in heaven, in the circle of the *bene ha'elohim* [host of heaven]. It is an issue between divine beings, between God and Satan. But the *reflex*, as it were, in the human realm is the split of the God image in Job. … Job becomes conscious of it, just as God, on the heavenly plane, becomes conscious of his own doubt when it opposes him. It is really one identical process, in its divine and human manifestations.
>
> (ibid.: 126)

On the one hand, Schärf finds it difficult to avoid reductionist psychologism, given her (Jungian) understanding of analogy as direct correspondence, yet, on the other hand, she proposes that the God–Job encounter, by means of doubt, opens up a space within which mutual learning can take place. Not only, as she sees it, does Job learn the depths of the reality of the two aspects of God, but God learns that he needs man to reveal to himself the consequences of his twofold nature: 'So Satan is the destructive doubt within God's personality; yet it has a mysterious existential necessity for God and man and their relation to each other' (ibid.: 123). This all happens 'because God needs man'; Job has 'a deep presentiment' of this when he says to God: 'you would long for the work of your hands' (Job 14:15b) (ibid). Her conclusion is that, in the book of Job, 'a new plane of inner happenings has been reached within God and thus also within man' (ibid.: 124).

She goes even further and makes God dependent on humanity to enable him to attain self-realization. What is shown in the book of Job is 'the final, urgent goal of the activity manifested in Satan: the human soul as "dwelling-place" of the God becoming conscious of himself' (ibid.: 162). Jung reiterated this in a letter to Erich Neumann (1905–60) in 1952: 'God is a contradiction in terms, therefore he needs man in order to be made One' (*L2*: 33). Schärf presses her case: God needs Job for the sake of God's own search for wisdom.

> One must therefore assume that it was this being comprehended, this having room in man, which was important for God. He obviously wants man to be the carrier of his (divine) self-knowledge. … The paradoxical depth of God's speech in chapter 38[:1 – 40:1] becomes fully evident only when it is seen that this God, who is so passionately wooing man, does so by describing to man his worldwide superiority as the power of nature. Man is nothing over against this tremendous divine force, yet God needs him in order to *know* this power. God needs man for the sake of insight.
>
> (*SOT*: 130f.)

As Balthasar might have suspected would happen, she arrives at a position resembling a form of gnostic dualism. God's insight, as Schärf sees it, when he engages with Job, is that he is both the one who makes a covenant with his creation and also 'the dark nature god who can destroy what he has created' (ibid.: 127). But as a personal communication to Schärf illustrates, Jung's reading of this text is that it is one God who holds together these two opposing aspects, reasserting his dualistic monism:

> In his great final speech God reveals himself to Job in all his frightfulness. It is as if he said to Job: 'Look, that's what I'm like. That is why I treated you like this.' Through the suffering which he inflicted upon Job out of his own nature, God has come to this self-knowledge and admits, as it were, this knowledge of his frightfulness to Job. *And that is what redeems the man Job.* This is really the solution to the enigma of Job, that is, a true

> justification for Job's fate, which, without this background, would, in its cruelty and injustice, remain an open problem. Job appears here clearly as a sacrifice, but also as the carrier of the divine fate, and that gives meaning to his suffering and liberation to his soul.
>
> (ibid.: 129)

Following Irenaeus, Balthasar accepts that, in the human learning process of becoming accustomed to God, the testing of 'trials and temptations' is a necessity (*GL2*: 80). Indeed, 'whoever flees the double knowledge and the double spiritual sensation is secretly destroying himself as a human being' (*GL2*: 79 quoting Irenaeus[12]). This resonates with Schärf's suggestion that Satan's role in the Old Testament is best seen as part of God's preparation of humanity through suffering for his saving initiative. Given the usual Balthasarian caveats, the comparable understanding of a pedagogical role is clear.

In Schärf's view, Satan can be seen (like the Old Testament Law) to be a necessary part of the pedagogical process: 'The Law was to some extent a necessary prior stage before man could become a vessel for God' (*SOT*: 132 and ibid. n. 95). Satan's role, particularly in the book of Job, is properly understood, in Luciferian terms (ibid.), as bringing the light of insight, though suffering. On God's side, it was Satan, as an aspect of the divine being, who catalysed for God the learning about how God relates to humanity by doubting the straightforwardness of human praise of God. Before Job, God, who contains both creative and destructive forces, was simply unpredictable. Since Satan's role in the book of Job, God now 'knows about it' (ibid.: 127). For humanity, Satan 'brings man the knowledge of God, but through the suffering he inflicts on him' (ibid.: 132). Further, 'Satan is the misery of the world which alone drives man inward, into the "other world". It is Satan who drives man beyond himself as animal being, as mere creature of nature' (ibid.). Schärf's conclusion is that Satan, '[b]y means of [voicing God's inner lurking] doubt about Job [Job 1:9f. and 2:4], is the *spiritus agens* of this change; but he is also the destructive activity of God arising out of God's doubt about man [Job 1:12 and 2:6f.] (ibid.: 130).

But for Balthasar, given his paradoxical understanding of analogy, the human agenda for learning would not apply in the same way to God. Balthasar would not countenance the idea that God is contingently dependent upon humanity in order to learn about himself, even if he has to accustom himself to relating to the finitude of humanity. The dissimilarity of the analogy of being must be maintained. Nevertheless, Balthasar thought, in line with a *corpus triforme* orientation, that in the book of Job the learning for God lay within an experience that would be at the heart of the theodrama in Christ. Job experienced abandonment by God and yet appealed to God against God for the right to receive care as God's creature (Job 16:20b–21). The challenge for God in the theodrama is likewise to bring together into 'unity … the glory of God and uttermost abandonment by God, Heaven and Hell' (*GL6*: 290).

On this Jung and Balthasar could agree. The heart of the theological drama in the New Testament for Jung is that in the conflict between Christ and Satan 'we gaze for the first time into the luminous realm of divinity on the one hand and into the abyss of hell on the other' (*PADT*: 173).

In both Balthasar's and Jung's theological orientations, it is important to note that shifts take place in the transition from the Old to the New Testament. From a Jungian point of view it is a shift from a position of dualistic monism, most evident in the book of Job, to Christ and Antichrist as contrary opposites. As Schärf expresses it, there is a move away from a doctrine of God as containing opposites: 'the *coincidentia oppositorum*' (*SOT*: 146), 'the unity which embraces and resolves the opposites' (ibid.: 157; cf. ibid.: 16, 73, 97, 126, 129, 134). At its point of greatest profundity in Job, 'in the sharpest paradox, … Job experiences the duality of God in his unity', and yet this enables Job (16:20f.) to plead with God to vindicate him against God (ibid.: 126). The move towards the New Testament is in the direction of 'the detachment of Satan from God' which 'formed the premise for the New Testament development of Satan into the contrapersonality of God' (ibid.: 159). Jung sees this as caused primarily by the constellating of another archetype, that of the hostile brothers. For Balthasar, Antichrist arises in the theodrama in response to God in Christ entering upon the world stage. This is a point on which Balthasar and Jung agree. Jung notes that a 'glance at the Scriptures … is enough to show us the importance of the devil in the divine drama of redemption' (*PADT*: 172). Indeed, 'the real devil first appears as the adversary of Christ' (ibid.: 173). Both Jung and Balthasar acknowledge a contextual influence from dualistic sources in the inter-testamental period, but the advent of Christ is the significant new factor.

Balthasar recognized the influence of non-biblical sources on beliefs that appeared in the inter-testamental period, which would be central to the theodrama revealed in Christ, such as the atoning value of a righteous man's suffering and resurrection (*TD*3: 476). He also acknowledges that dualisms, such as that in Qumran between Michael and Belial (ibid. n. 13), 'pass over without modification into the New Testament' (ibid). He was cautious, however, of the danger of historical reductionism, of the sort he perceived in Bultmann's (1884–1976) programme. If we accept the view that 'the belief in spirits and demons has been superseded as a result of our knowledge of the powers and laws of nature' (ibid.: 469 quoting Bultmann), then Christ becomes 'trapped in an environmentally determined superstition' (ibid.: 470).

Jung recognized the historical influence of Persian and Jewish ideas on theological themes in the New Testament 'about the beginning and end of time' and that these presaged 'a kind of enantiodromian reversal of dominants … [namely] the dilemma of Christ and Antichrist' (*CW*9(ii): ix). Schärf locates the origin of this transition of Satan to what she takes to be historically later books of the Old Testament. In 1 Chronicles 21:1, *satan* finally becomes a proper name and 'Satan is an independent personality' (*SOT*: 39; cf. ibid.: 155). For the first time this figure is not defined in relation to God:

> Satan is divested of his character as a *divine* function. He no longer appears, as in the book of Job, as part of the divine court; he is an independent figure, apparently separated from God, who no longer stands in dialectical confrontation with God or his angel, as in Job and Zechariah.
>
> (ibid.: 155)

Even so, this is not full-blown dualism, since Satan in 1 Chronicles does 'exactly what Yahweh himself does' in 2 Samuel (ibid.: 160; cf. *TD*3: 472). Satan has not yet become 'the rebellious angel of high rank who seeks to supplant God as the ruler of the universe' (ibid.: 117). In her view, at the end of the Old Testament the figure of Satan was susceptible to dualistic influence: 'Only when the Satan figure was ripe enough to detach itself from the personality of God could traits of similar figures in the religious environment become associated with it' (ibid.: 52). In Persian dualism 'there exists a primary opposition' between 'Spenta Mainyu [the good spirit] and Angra Mainyu [the evil spirit]' (ibid.: 156), which, Schärf argues, paves the way for 'Satan as the adversary of the Messiah' (ibid.: 157) in Jewish apocalyptic writings and in the New Testament. Schärf identifies the Jungian perspective on the theological consequences of these influences when she notes:

> The detachment of Satan from God, who is then 'cleansed' from his darkness, carried tremendous consequences. It formed the premise for the New Testament development of Satan into the contrapersonality of God and for his complete splitting-off, as this is expressed in the mythologem of the 'bound' dragon of the Apocalypse.
>
> (ibid.: 159)

As we shall see in chapter six, Balthasar seems to be straightforwardly clear that evil has its origin in choice exercised within the measure of independence provided by God for creatures with finite freedom. Jung seeks to keep alive the rumour that in some mysterious way God is involved in the setting in which the original act of disobedience took place. In the first (Old Testament) phase of both a *corpus triforme* and a 'Joachimite' theology, there is important mutual accustoming between God and his creation. What the case study of Satan in the Old Testament shows is that, in any critical comparison, account needs to be taken of the importance of Jung's dualistic monism in face of the tendency towards a gnostic dualism and at the same time of the ever-present spectre of psychologism arising from Jung's theory of analogy based on direct correspondence. But it is worth noting that Balthasar's recognition of the importance of learning between God and humanity in the Old Testament is an implicit acknowledgement that, even if God is not to be seen as involved in the origin of evil, yet he, from the start (and in preparation for the New Testament phase of the theodrama), is involved in learning what the consequences are of the presence of evil in a fallen world for the divine–human relationship. Both Jung and Balthasar were convinced of the contemporary as well as the perennial importance of evil. Both men sought to address the question of the reality of evil: Jung did this primarily through his correspondence with Victor White, centred on a discussion of the doctrine of *privatio boni*; Balthasar through his theological use of the metaphor of drama. This provides the theme and material for the next chapter.

But I conclude this chapter with some reflections for basing a critical comparison of Jung and Balthasar on reading them respectively as a type 4 reinterpretive psychologist and a type 2 contextualizing theologian.

In relation to the understanding of humanity, Balthasar's stance, as a type 2 contextualizing theologian, was, on the one hand, open to engagement with modern depth psychologies, but, on the other, he gives more than descriptive preference to his theological anthropology. It has normative priority. He views Jung's psychology as a secondary enterprise since its horizon of meaning has to be limited to the world of finite creation. At least in the first phase of his project in relation to Christianity, Jung was prepared to put his psychology to the service of theology. In this sense his type 4 reinterpretive approach was amenable to collaborative dialogue rather than a conflictual one focusing on assertion and counter-assertion about whether psychology or theology should have normative priority. Constructing dialogue between the two in this area is hampered, however, by the limited scope of Balthasar's reading of Jung.

In terms of analogy, Balthasar's similarity-within-ever-greater-dissimilarity is not only different from Jung's appeal to direct correspondence, but Balthasar used this difference to argue for the rejection of the views of those who did not share his normative stance. It will become clear, in chapter seven, that Jung's attempt to link the divine drama directly to a pattern of human psychological development could not provide the basis for an agreed approach with Balthasar. The pressing of this aspect of Jung's way of working would be more suitable for a type 3 dialogue with a theologian likewise looking for direct links between theological and psychological ideas. However, since Jung himself recognized the importance of paradox as well as direct correspondence in correctly handling theological themes, in my view there is potential benefit for psychology for keeping this area of divergence actively in play. Nevertheless, Jung's search for direct correspondence between psychological and theological insights might also be useful in guarding against any tendency in Balthasar's type 2 approach to overemphasize the (normatively prior) dissimilarity of the theological perspective.

In substantive terms, for a critical comparison of Balthasar and Jung on the question of God's involvement with evil, the question of polarity has a central importance. It is a key normative feature of both Balthasar's type 2 contextualizing theology and Jung's type 4 reinterpretive psychology. It seems to me that it is important to not judge Jung over-hastily to be an advocate of dualism but to see that dualistic monism is normative for him. I shall also argue, particularly in chapter nine, that although it is important to give due weight to the difference between Balthasar's ('vertical') handling of a polarity between God and humanity, through his dialectic of contradiction, and Jung's ('horizontal') handling of the polarity of contrary opposites in human experience, through his dualistic monism, yet finding a way to hold these different approaches together in tension provides a key to a positive outcome to the attempt to construct a dialogue on the question of God's involvement with evil.

Notes

1 Note, however, that Jung immediately registers his disavowal of metaphysics lest it be thought that he has 'claimed the possibility of proving God' (*CW*12: 14; cf. ibid.: 29).
2 Kilby is not persuaded that Balthasar manages to maintain this position when he argues that the Cross and Christ's *descensus* are trinitarian events (Kilby, 2012: 121).
3 See also: 'God is light *and* darkness, the *auctor rerum* is love *and* wrath' (*L*2: 473).
4 Balthasar further refers to Jung on God shattering Basel cathedral (*MDR*: 52–8), the exclusion of evil from the Trinity (*PRTL*: 63), the possibility of God's involvement in original sin (*CW*12: 30), as well as the view that Job 'discerned the opposites in the divine nature' (Jung, 1952a) (*TD*1: 519 n. 30).
5 It has been argued that Balthasar's scriptural preferences here are influenced by German Idealism and Jung's psychology (Crammer, 2004: 106).
6 Schärf, 1948. My references are from the English translation, Kluger, 1967 [*SOT*]. See also Sanford 1981: 25–34.
7 Balthasar also notes that John 1:51 applies Jacob's dream of angels to Jesus, which is further developed by the Fathers (*TD*3: 475 n. 6).
8 Other examples cited include Exod. 3:2 cf. Exod. 3:4, Exod. 14:19 cf. Exod. 13:21, Judg. 13:17f. cf. Gen. 32:29 and Exod. 3:14 (*SOT*: 58f.).
9 Hillman in the introduction to Kluger, 1967.
10 The plural divine name, *elohim*, is a reminder for Schärf of 'the original plurality of the concept of God' (*SOT*: 101).
11 Jung may also be implicitly evoking dualistic monism when he credits Schärf with showing that 'the monotheism of the Old Testament' has to be understood in terms of what he calls the 'relativity' of God, containing 'opposite qualities' (*PADT*: 187).
12 For Irenaeus the purpose of this pedagogy is to overcome the original fall, understood as disobedience, and so to be 'never again tempted to taste disobedience to God' (*GL*2: 79).

Part III

God's involvement with evil

Chapter 6

Evil – its origins and reality

In the first two parts of this book, I constructed a framework and set out bases for a critical comparison of the question of God's involvement with evil in the works of Jung and Balthasar. In this third part, I explore the questions of the origin and reality of evil in the present chapter, Jung's exploration, in his Trinity essay, of God's involvement with evil in chapter seven, and Jung's and Balthasar's focus on the Cross as the expression of this involvement in chapter eight. This critical comparison shows that a dialogue between Jung and Balthasar would have had its limits. In conclusion, in part four (in chapter nine) I outline a cruciform model for God's involvement with evil which holds together in tension a Balthasarian approach to analogy and a Jungian approach to dualistic monism.

Divine and human involvement in the origin of evil

The terms for the discussion of the question of evil in recent centuries, particularly in the West, have been set primarily by Enlightenment thinkers. The British philosopher David Hume (1711–76) encapsulated the problem: the existence of evil is incompatible with the existence of a good God: 'Is [God] willing to prevent evil, but not able? then he is impotent. Is he able, but not willing? then he is malevolent. Is he both able and willing? whence then is evil?' (Hume, 1947: 198). 'Theodicy' is the term usually given (following Leibniz (1646–1716)) to attempts to give a justification for belief in a good God in the face of the evidence of moral and natural evil. Such attempts typically claim that 'there is some greater good that God could only achieve by creating a world in which moral and natural evil is possible or unavoidable' (Higton, 2007: 7).

D. Z. Phillips (1934–2006) is one of those who warned of the danger for theology of accepting the debate on these terms, since in it God is assumed to be a moral agent of exactly the same sort as a human moral agent (Phillips, 2005: 180). Balthasar, with his understanding of the analogy of being and his emphasis on the dissimilarity between God's infinite and humanity's finite freedom, would be sympathetic to this criticism; Jung, with his tendency to see analogy in terms of direct correspondence, might be less concerned. However, neither of them seeks to engage in constructing a theodicy based on the assumptions of the Enlightenment agenda. In a recent monograph, Jacob Friesenhahn relates Balthasar's trinitarian theology to the question of evil in terms of 'theodicy' in his title (Friesenhahn, 2011). But he advocates a Balthasarian approach because it shifts the focus of attention away from the classical, philosophical concerns of theodicy. Balthasar does not seek to justify God in relation to the existence of evil but rather, through the Cross as a trinitarian event. He argues for a transformation of the meaning of suffering based in God's inner nature (ibid.: 141; cf. ibid.: 1–2, 141–8).

However, within the broad category of 'greater good' defences, Jung and Balthasar exhibit some affinity with both the 'free will' argument (Plantinga, 1975) and the 'soul-making' argument (Hick, 1968). Balthasar stresses both that evil arises out of the finite but real freedom, given to humanity by God in the exercise of his infinite freedom, to choose evil rather than good, and that such finite freedom, in order to develop its full potential, must explore all its possibilities. Jung sees that the choice for moral evil provides the opportunity for a process of individuation towards greater wholeness to begin. However, for both men it is the contemporary importance of the question of evil in the practical experience of humanity that means that it will require significant attention. Balthasar could be taken to speak for both of them when he says that 'the problem of creaturely freedom, involving the possibility of evil … has acquired an urgency today quite different from the urgency it had in primitive Christian and medieval theology' (*TD*1: 48).

However, Balthasar will distance himself from the re-emergence of the view that evil is part of God, as he sees Jung suggesting with his Quaternity symbol of the Godhead which includes the Devil.

> *Jung* gives the potent expression of this new climate of thought and feeling when he calls for the Christian Trinity to be expanded into a Quaternity which would find a place for the opposition of good and evil, the good Son of the Father (Christ) and his counterimage, the wayward son (of [*sic*] the devil).
>
> (ibid.: 49)

The question of God and evil has shifted to a new ground: 'The emphasis changes when, in modern times, the darkness and fragmentation of creation is projected into the divine ground itself … Now it is *God* [according to some] who bears the contradiction (including hell) in himself' (ibid.: 48f.).[1]

On the question of the origin of evil, Balthasar and Jung hold largely similar views, emphasizing the role of human choice and the positive link between this choice and the process of salvation. Balthasar stresses more strongly sole human responsibility. Jung sees God involved, if somewhat surreptitiously.

Balthasar addresses the question of the origin of evil not from Enlightenment philosophy's articulation of questions, but in the light of biblical and patristic sources. Balthasar asks the Irenaean question: if evil is such a problem, why did God not create angels and human beings sinless? His response is that finite freedom needs the opportunity to explore all its options. The parable of the Prodigal Son articulates this 'primary experiential concept' (*TD*2: 216). For Balthasar, evil contains a paradox. Although humanity must bear responsibility for choosing evil, yet only through such choice can salvific 'soul-making' become possible: '[S]ince our redeeming God does not overpower our freedom, man retains freedom to decide for or against grace; he can refuse it …, in which case he himself "freely chooses separation from God, that is, death"' (ibid.: 144f. quoting Irenaeus). And further: 'finite freedom must experience its finitude and poverty, must, as it were, explore the whole area of its possibilities in order to learn by experience … that it can only fulfil itself by following the advice and counsel of God' (ibid.: 216).

The option to choose evil is God-given. Indeed, it is paradoxically the very gift of finite freedom which creates evil: it 'brings a danger with it: it has the power to create something that even God cannot create: evil' (ibid.: 220; cf. ibid. n. 29). The gift of finite freedom arises out of the decision made from within God's infinite freedom, and as an expression of the kenotic nature of God's love, to create humanity with the autonomy properly belonging to finite freedom, which includes the possibility of saying No to God.

Jung accepts the importance of recognizing human responsibility for choosing evil rather than good. However, for him it is an epistemological as well as an ethical issue. The ability to discern and choose between opposites is constitutive of consciousness. To an extent this relativizes the ethical aspect of the choice between good and evil. Human agents 'are the authors of moral value judgments' based on good and evil as 'a logically equivalent pair of opposites and, as such, the *sine qua non* of all acts of cognition' (*CW*9(ii): 47). He asserts, against the patristic view, for instance in Basil (330–79), that there is more to be said than that evil originates in human free will (ibid.: 46–8 *passim*). But since '[p]sychology does not know what good and evil are in themselves; it knows them only as judgments about relationships' (ibid.: 53), he hesitates to be specific about the author of the 'facts' of good and evil about which we exercise our moral judgement.

The question can be focused on the biblical account of the Fall, of which Jung and Balthasar both hold a non-catastrophic understanding. Balthasar, like Irenaeus, sees it as a mistake, such as might have been made by a child: 'the Fall came about through inattention, not through wickedness' (*TD*2: 145 referring to Irenaeus). Jung distances himself from the Protestant Reformers' enhancement of an Augustinian doctrine of the Fall which sees humanity as a 'mass of perdition', and asserts rather: 'The God-image in man was not destroyed by the Fall but was only damaged and corrupted ("deformed"), and can be restored through God's grace' (*CW*9(ii): 39). Jung goes as far as to suggest that the original sin of disobedience be seen as humanity's *felix culpa*, the happy fault, that enables the process of redemption to begin (*CW*12: 30; cf. Jung, 1958b: 358 and Jung, 1959: 460). Balthasar makes a similar point: 'Evil, in spite of the baffling freedom it has, has only enough power to manifest the far more baffling mercy of God, which causes the fountain of salvation to spring forth from the very wounds that evil has inflicted' (*TD*5: 503).

Despite these similarities, Jung seeks to argue for some involvement by God in the origin of evil in his creation. Initially Jung contents himself with a passing reference to the serpent in the Garden of Eden, who 'prods and persuades to knowledge' (*SM*: 240), acting on behalf of the God who 'introduc[ed] a distinction between good and evil and outlaw[ed] the evil' (ibid.: 196). And since 'without original sin the redemption of the world could never have come about', he conjectures whether 'in this very power of evil God might not have placed some special purpose which it is most important for us to know' (*CW*12: 30; cf. *PSF*: 230).

But also he develops an argument, which implicitly relies on analogy as direct correspondence, whereby everything that has real existence in creation must ultimately come from God. He argues that the choice of evil is a manifestation of resistance, and an aspect of the concreteness of creation, and if of creation, then ultimately of God:

> matter represents the *concreteness* [die Bestimmtheit] of God's thoughts and is, therefore, the very thing that makes individuation possible, with all its consequences. The adversary [the devil] is, quite logically, conceived to be the soul of matter, because they both constitute a point of resistance without which the relative autonomy of individual existence would be simply unthinkable. The will to be different and contrary is characteristic of the devil, just as disobedience was the hallmark of original sin. These, as we have said, are the necessary conditions for Creation and ought, therefore, to be included in the divine plan and – ultimately – in the divine realm.
>
> (*PADT*: 171f.)

Jung seeks to invoke what he takes to be early Christian sources in support of his view, [2] in order to show that it was a later development that separated evil from God in response to the threat of Manichaeism. Jung is aware of debate about the content and dating of the sources he cites – the Clementine Homilies and the *Ascension of Isaiah*. He acknowledges them as 'Gnostic-Christian', revising an earlier dating ('about 150 A.D.') to a more cautious one ('the beginning of the 3rd cent., if not earlier') (*CW*9(ii): 57 n. 54).

In the Clementine Homilies, Jung suggests, good and evil (who were, like brothers, begotten in the same way (ibid.)) do not 'have their substance outside of God, for there is no other primal source [αρχη]' (ibid.: 56 quoting the Clementine Homilies). They are not to be relegated for their origin to the created order, 'for they were of the same mind [ομοδοξοι] with him' (ibid. quoting the Clementine Homilies).

Jung notes, however, that the Clementine Homilies are not fully specific about the origin of evil. He attributes this to their 'distinctly "High Church"' or 'Petrine Christianity', which would find it difficult to 'attribute the cause of evil to the Creator in so many words' (ibid.). Creation begins with the bringing into being of a fourfold elemental substance, which is 'eternal … and God's child' (ibid). Creation continues by different forms of being made from difference mixtures of the original elements. But a mixing occurred 'from without', producing 'the preference which rejoices in evil' (ibid. quoting the Clementine Homilies), which Jung glosses thus: 'the tendency to evil was added from outside to the mixture willed by God' (ibid.).

Jung suggests that two views about the origin of evil are present: 'without intending it (and possibly without his [God's] knowing it) the mixture of the four elements took a wrong turning'; or is it a matter, as elsewhere in the homilies, of 'the opposite hands of God "doing violence to one another"' (ibid.)? Jung, at this stage, is only suggesting rather cautiously that Christianity might take on board some notion of evil originating from within God.

In the apocalyptic *Ascension of Isaiah* there is a great battle in the heavens against Sammaël and his angel hosts. Isaiah is transported to the highest heaven, closest to the throne of God, and even here the angels who stood '[c]n the right side of the throne … were more beautiful than the angels on the left' (ibid.: 57). Jung proposes that this text suggests that: 'The devil … dwells in the firmament … and his sphere interpenetrates with the divine sphere of the Trinity', from which he concludes: 'This paints a picture of complementary opposites balancing one another like right and left hands' (ibid.). For Jung this sort of 'yang–yin relationship … comes closer to the actual truth than the *privatio boni*' (ibid.: 58).

This points us to one of the key issues in relation to the reality of evil. Jung insisted that at all costs there be no downplaying of the experiential reality of evil, manifested in the shadow with its archetypal and (in the sense that is objective rather than subjective) absolute origins. He was very resistant to the theological position that evil is a privation of good, insofar as it seems to take the sting out of that reality.

How Jung and Balthasar understand the reality of evil

A major focus of Jung's correspondence with Victor White (a dialogue which Jung continues in his book *Aion*) is his concern that the Christian doctrine of evil as *privatio boni* threatens to undermine its reality. Jung's own view of evil is linked to his arguments for a doctrine of God as *complexio oppositorum*. For Balthasar the theodrama was paramount. In addition to some relatively brief remarks on the reality of evil under the heading of the mystery of iniquity, Balthasar seeks to establish (in dialogue with Barth) the reality of evil in dramatic terms, though he is not able ultimately to sustain the idea of evil spirits as *dramatis personae.*

Jung's understanding of evil

Though the question of evil was of continuing interest for Jung, it is hard to give a clear account of his understanding of it. Stein warns that 'it would be deceptive to try to make [Jung] look more systematic and consistent on this than he actually was' (Stein, 1995: 2). Jung wanted to assert the reality of evil and in his engagement with Christianity he was strongly averse to the theological tendency, as he saw it, to downplay that reality. Evil is an aspect of the archetypes – both those that Jung saw as naturally occurring, such as the alchemists' Mercurius (the spirit archetype) and those that occur in religion, such as the conflict between Christ and Antichrist (an expression of the archetypal theme of the hostile brothers) – but Jung's primary interest is in the resolution of the conflict.

Jung gives considerable emphasis to understanding good and evil as evaluative judgements of human consciousness. He sometimes goes as far as to say that without consciousness 'good and evil simply happen, or rather, there is no good and evil, but only a sequence of neutral events, … the uninterrupted causal concatenation leading to suffering, old age, sickness, and death' (*L2*: 311). It is important not to misread this in terms of debates, arising, for instance, from the materialist philosophy of logical positivism, based on a distinction between fact and value, in which private value judgements are assigned lesser status than public (scientifically provable) facts. For Jung, when something is psychologically real, no form of reductionism should be allowed to downgrade its importance. The judgement about good and evil is not a second, volitional step within the workings of consciousness (which might or might not be undertaken) but is integral within the working of the human psyche as a whole.

There are, for Jung, two aspects of the workings of the human psyche that call for sophisticated judgements of what is good and what is evil. The first of these relates to Jung's ideas about 'levels' of consciousness, which he discusses briefly in the Mercurius essay (*SM*: 199–201). Jung envisages a primitive level of consciousness (and borrows Levi-Bruhl's (1857–1939) anthropological concept *participation mystique*) where there is experience but no possibility of judgement because there is no conscious separation of the experiencing subject from the experienced object. The next level is that of the conscious discernment of difference between subject and object. Only after that does moral judgement enter the scene.

The second aspect of the psyche's functioning that relates to the question of good and evil is that part of the unconscious that Jung calls the shadow (*CW*9(ii): 8–10). The shadow's contents are of two sorts: first, those that (through conscious suppression and unconscious repression) a person hides and hopes to remain unconscious of, that is, those things of which he or she is ashamed; and, second, those that are potentially useful aspects of the total personality of which the person has yet to become conscious. However, an unconscious process of projection means that someone may react strongly when he or she perceives these shadow contents in others. This makes a judgement about evil possibly distorted unless, by recognizing and withdrawing one's shadow projections, a person can discriminate between what properly belongs to the other and what to himself or herself. Christians might call this the 'mote and beam' issue (Matt. 7: 1–5; Luke 6:41f.). Jung's view was that if people, individually and collectively, do not engage in this challenging work of discrimination, the unconscious shadow projections will come back with potentially catastrophic force. In the last thing Jung wrote for publication before his death, he continued to note the collective problems that arise when evil is unconsciously projected: as in the Cold War, '[i]t is the face of his own evil shadow that grins at Western man from the other side of the Iron Curtain' (Jung, 1978: 73).

When these processes of the archetypes of the collective unconscious are acted out collectively, the world can be drawn into frenzies of violent mutual destruction, overpowering the discriminatory powers of consciousness. In Jung's view similar processes can take place theologically. In the *Symbolik des Geistes* essays on Satan and on the Trinity, Jungian thinking envisaged an overwhelming archetypal power in 'God's need to incarnate His own dark destructiveness' (Stein, 1995: 15) and here, if anywhere, he locates the absolute reality of evil. In *Aion* Jung writes, 'it is quite within the bounds of possibility for a man to recognize the relative evil of his nature but it is a rare and shattering experience for him to gaze into the face of absolute evil' (*CW*9(ii): 10). If the need to address this had begun for Jung in the precincts of Basel Cathedral in his youth, it finally erupted in his 1952 *Answer to Job* when he 'was gripped by the urgency and difficulty of the problem [of the opposites in God] and was unable to throw it off' (Jung, 1952a: 358).

It may be the case that analytical psychology is unduly influenced by Jung's psychology,[3] particularly his fear of 'irrevocable splitting' (Stein, 1995: 15). But this is not an indication of a psychological (or theological) dualism in Jung. The process of individuation offers to bring healing to dividedness through greater wholeness. Even though he saw that the book of Job came within 'a hair's breadth' of Persian dualism, Jung preferred to follow his colleague Rivkah Schärf's thesis of an Old Testament monotheistic God-image 'relativized' (*PADT*: 187) insofar as being made up of good and evil elements. Jung set his face against the traditional Christian view of God as *summum bonum* and the idea of evil as *privatio boni*.

As Jung read Christian origins he saw that God as *summum bonum* soon became a foundational belief. This had initial value, in Jung's view, but it had unwelcome consequences, particularly an implicit tendency to downplay the reality of evil. This trend was increased as the threat of (Gnostic and then

Manichaean) dualism grew. Christian doctrine responded by developing the idea of evil as *privatio boni*. Jung's correspondence with Victor White highlighted the difficulty of reconciling a theological and a psychological reading of this doctrine. Jung's preference is for a doctrine of God as *complexio oppositorum*, which in his view maintains the importance of the reality of evil. In *Aion* he wrote: 'One could hardly call the things that have happened, and still happen, in the concentration camps of the dictator states [of Nazi Germany and Stalinist USSR] an "accidental lack of perfection" – it would sound like mockery' (*CW*9(ii): 53).

As he saw it, the foundational Christian starting point was 'omne bonum a Deo, omne malum ab homine' (ibid.: 41; cf. Jung, 1938/1954: 103) – all good comes from God, all evil from humanity. As we have seen, Balthasar stands within this tradition. It was Jung's long-held view that this sharp distinction between good and evil had served a useful function in challenging the unbridled instinctuality of the world of ancient Rome into which Christianity was born. Christianity offered a basis for moral discernment and action (*CWB*: 69ff. and ibid.: 70 n. 35). This was in part founded on the early Christian assertion of Christ's incarnation, as someone who, in modern terms, was a fully integrated, psychosomatic human being: 'There can be no doubt that the original Christian conception of the *imago Dei* embodied in Christ means an all-embracing totality ['the nearest analogy of the self' (*CW*9(ii): 44)] that even includes the animal side of man' (ibid.: 41). Nevertheless, Jung detected a docetic tendency within Christianity. He saw this beginning in John's Gospel and continuing in those Church Fathers, such as Origen and Augustine, who emphasized the spiritual perfection of Christ: 'The *imago Dei* [is] imprinted on the soul, not on the body' (ibid.: 37 referring to Origen (ibid. n. 7)); and 'that which is made after the image and similitude of God is our inner man, invisible, incorporeal, incorrupt, and immortal' (ibid.: 38 n. 10 quoting Origen).[4]

Jung saw continuing benefits in Christianity's ability to draw distinctions and make connections (for instance, between spirit and body). He saw this as a contribution to the development of human consciousness, even to laying the foundations for the emergence of modern science. But he believed that this facility would eventually contribute to the undoing of Western civilization and the Christianity embedded within it. For, although science and technology, based on a differentiation of matter/body from spirit/mind, has produced spectacular benefits for humanity, in his view, the basis of modern rationality has now been seen to be over-narrow. The belief that the exercise of conscious rationality alone can produce a world that is entirely good has been found to be a false hope. A doctrine of the entire goodness of God, in Jung's view, contributes to the problem.

Human experience makes it clear that evil persists. For Jung the seriousness of its persisting reality meant that it is important to take a view on the question of responsibility for evil. As he saw it, a further problem with the doctrine of the entire goodness of God is the corollary that humanity is entirely responsible for evil. If 'omne malum ab homine', humanity 'thereupon bec[omes] the real carrier of the *mysterium iniquitatis*' (Jung, 1938/1954: 103).

He found the earliest examples of this view in the Christian apologists Tatian (*c.*160) and Theophilus of Antioch (later second century) (*CW*9(ii): 46 and nn. 30, 31), and later in one of the Cappadocian Fathers, Basil the Great (ibid. nn. 32–4). Basil argues that a good God could not create evil, something contrary to himself. Consequently, as far as humanity is concerned: 'Each of us should acknowledge that he is the first author of the wickedness in him' (ibid.: 47 n. 34 quoting Basil). Jung thought both that this leads to a too pessimistic anthropology (ibid.: 61) and also that, given 'the colossal role that evil plays in the world' (ibid.: 62), this ascribed a too fateful power to humanity (ibid.). Jung's main thrust, however, was not so much to pursue the question of responsibility. He was not primarily concerned to develop a theodicy, but to stress that evil must not be undervalued. It must be engaged with in adequately serious ways. It is in relation to this that he found the *privatio boni* doctrine wanting.

Jung understood why Irenaeus wrote against the Gnostic dualistic opposition of light and darkness (ibid.: 45f.). He felt, however, that as Christian doctrine developed, in which he saw a conjoining of the idea of God as *summum bonum* with that of evil as *privatio boni*, it underestimated the force of evil and risked leaving 'a too optimistic conception of the evil in human nature' (ibid.: 61). Jung's assessment was that for Church Fathers, such as Origen, Basil the Great, (Pseudo-)Dionysius the Areopagite (late fifth–early sixth century) and Augustine, the view of God as *summum bonum* was taken as axiomatic, never seriously questioned. This doctrine was also, in his view, 'the effective source of the concept of the *privatio boni*, which nullifies the reality of evil' (ibid.: 46). In the case of Augustine, Jung concluded that '[t]his is how the christian doctrine gets out of its inherent dualism, i.e. Manicheism, by denying the existence of Evil' (Lammers and Cunningham, 2007: 200).

Jung cited Basil the Great, John Chrysostom (*c.*347–407), (Pseudo-) Dionysius the Areopagite, Augustine and Aquinas to illustrate how, in his view, the Church Fathers' denial of the reality of evil was linked to their opposition to dualism (*CW*9(ii): 49). He even suggested, though found it difficult to bring forward convincing evidence to prove, that 'Manichaean dualism first made the Fathers conscious of the fact that until then, without clearly realizing it, they had always believed firmly in the substantiality of evil' (ibid.: 58).

Jung credited Origen with originating the doctrine of the *privatio boni* in which 'evil was characterized as a mere diminution of good and thus deprived of substance' (ibid.: 41). Jung takes the view that Origen began with the idea of good and evil as contrary opposites but then went on to raise doubts about the reality of evil. He cited Origen as first asserting that Christ and Satan are 'diametrically opposed' (ibid.: 44 n. 28) to one another, for 'to turn aside from good is nothing other than to be perfected in evil' (ibid.). Given the starting 'premise "Deus = Summum Bonum"', it became unthinkable that 'the perfect good could ever have created evil' (ibid.: 52). Responsibility for evil was assigned to choice. Evil beings 'were not created evil but chose the condition of wickedness of their own free will' (ibid.: 44 n. 28 quoting Origen). Evil was then described in terms of the good. From one point of view it is 'a lesser good' in that it is 'an effect of the finiteness and limitedness of created things' (ibid.: 52); from another, evil is a lack of good, '[f]or it is certain that to be evil means to be deprived of good' (ibid.: 44 n. 28 quoting Origen). Jung concluded that the Church's teaching is that evil is an absence of good.

Jung was to discover, in his correspondence with Victor White, that Christian theology does not downplay the reality of evil in human experience. It does, however, seek to find different ways of speaking of evil in relation to God.

White's Thomism stressed that God is Absolute Being and that this Being is essentially Good (*summum bonum*); that the entire creation of this God is good, since God cannot create anything contrary to God's nature; evil as *privatio boni* is a privation, something which has lost its goodness, or fails to live up to the good. White's theology used the language of privation as a grammatical device to speak about the metaphysical status of evil in relation to the goodness of God.

Despite Jung's repeated assertions to the contrary, *privatio boni* is not a claim that evil is non-existent. In the context of human experience this would be manifestly wrong and potentially dangerous, as if, by ignoring it, it would cease to exist. Jung wanted the question of evil to be handled on a different basis, namely in terms of contrary opposites. In his view, in the realm of psychological experience, 'white and black, light and dark, good and bad, are equivalent opposites which always predicate one another' (ibid.: 54).

White made a number of attempts to recast the *privatio boni* in a way that would enable the dialogue to go forward with Jung, but to little avail (Weldon, 2007: 148–59, 161–5, 166–75, 181f.). White saw evil as privation, which Jung regarded as tantamount to treating evil as a negation, as non-existent rather than as a contrary opposite to good. White's repeated appeal was to the validity of a distinction between absence and non-existence. To say that (in relation to God) evil is an absence (μη ον), or privation, of good is not to assert that it is non-existent (ουκ ον).[5]

Jung's view was that good and evil are an example of 'logically equivalent contraries' and so 'if good is substantial' (reflecting the nature of the Creator) 'then so is evil' (ibid.: 150, 162). He seeks to relate this to God by means of direct analogy. Since in human experience good and evil are contraries where 'evil is ... just as substantial as good' (ibid.: 149), we need a doctrine of God as both *Summum Bonum* and also *Infinum Malum* [deepest evil] (cf. *RBLN*: 350). White's view is based on asymmetrical correspondence. In human experience we know good and evil as contrary realities; but metaphysically in relation to God, who is distinctively different from his creation, evil is opposite to goodness in a privative rather than a contrary way (ibid.: 170).

Eventually, in *Aion*, Jung conceded that he might have misunderstood Christian theologians in claiming that, through *privatio boni*, they were 'nullif[ying] the reality of evil' (*CW*9(ii): 46), asserting the non-existence of evil. He finally allows that the *privatio boni* may be 'a metaphysical truth' 'aiming to give expression to the tendency always to increase the good and diminish the bad' (ibid.: 54). Even here he wants psychology to have the last word. He pleads his preference to avoid the sort of arguments White had brought forward, since he has 'neither the inclination nor the competence to get mixed up in metaphysics' (ibid.). But he reserves the right to become 'polemical when metaphysics encroaches on experience and interprets it in a way that is not justified empirically' (ibid.).

If Jung were to have a doctrine of God to match his understanding of the psyche, it would need to be one that corresponded to his dualistic monism. In his view, God, like the archetypes of the collective unconscious, should be understood as a *complexio oppositorum*. He feared that, in maintaining the entire goodness of God, Christianity ends up with another form of dualism, a good God and an evil world. For, as Jung sees it, in Christian thinking, the archetype is hopelessly split 'into two irreconcilable halves, leading ultimately to a metaphysical dualism – the final separation of the kingdom of heaven from the fiery world of the damned' (ibid.: 42).

Try as it might, Jung insists, Christianity cannot rid itself of the reality of evil. In the New Testament, 'the shadow which lies over the world is, as we know from the Gospels, the *princeps huius mundi* [the prince of this world], the devil' (ibid.: 41 n. 23). Jung's point is that Christianity itself envisages the devil as 'complementing ... the bright but one-sided figure of the Redeemer', existing – and herein lies psychological (and so theological) danger – as 'the cut off counterpart': thus Antichrist is 'a true αντιμιμον πνευμα [opposing spirit], an imitating spirit of evil, who follows in Christ's footsteps like a shadow following the body' (ibid.: 42).

Although Balthasar accepted the crucial importance of the battle of the Logos, Christ opposed by Antichrist, he always sought to stand out against any sort of dualistic theology, such as that of second-century Gnosticism, where 'a life-and-death struggle with the question of evil' led to ascribing the origin of evil to 'a subordinate "God"' [demiurge] and then, in Manichaean dualism, to 'an "anti-God"' (*TD*1: 48). Despite this admitted danger Jung applauded the Gnostics of the early Church era for being willing to tackle evil 'on a broader basis than the Church Fathers' (*CW*9(ii): 41). Christian doctrine today, in Jung's view, would be better advised to follow the psychological insight which he had discovered, that '[i]n the empirical self, light and shadow form a paradoxical unity' (ibid.: 42).

Jung's case for a doctrine of God as *complexio oppositorum* is that psychological symbols and God-symbols can contain opposites held together within unity in a paradoxical dualistic monism. A key text in establishing Jung's case, drawn from psychological symbols, is his essay on Mercurius in *Symbolik des Geistes*.

Jung interprets the Mercurius figure, occurring in the works of philosophical alchemists of the late medieval/early modern period, as a natural symbol of the spirit archetype arising from within the collective unconscious. He argues that, since Mercurius has 'the contrary qualities of fire and water', among other things, he has an 'essentially antinomian [or, paradoxical] dual nature' (*SM*: 216) including 'both good and evil' (ibid.: 218; cf. ibid.: 223). It is fundamentally important for Jung that this is a 'united double nature', not a dualistic one (ibid.). Mercurius is thus 'a *complexio oppositorum*' (ibid.: 241). He 'consists of all conceivable opposites' and so is 'quite obviously a duality'; he 'is named a unity in spite of the fact that his innumerable inner contradictions can dramatically fly apart into an equal number of disparate and apparently independent figures' (ibid.: 237).

Jung discusses a number of links between the alchemical Mercurius symbol and Christ. Alchemy, for Jung, is a product of the collective unconscious arising in compensatory relation to the conscious dominants of society and religion. It is 'a dream-like statement about the Christian culture in which [alchemy] was practiced, representing the compensatory function of the unconscious in reaction to the dominant structures and images of collective consciousness' (Stein, 1995: 6). Consequently, Mercurius is not a replacement for Christ but rather a 'subtle compensatory counterpoint': 'If Christ is the archetypal dominant of collective consciousness, in the Christian West, Mercurius is the shadow brother of Christ, and as such he is compensatory and not an absolute opposite' (ibid.: 6; cf. *SM*: 245). In the context of the Christendom of Western European civilization, 'Christ and [Mercurius], the dark nature deity' appear respectively as 'the archetype of consciousness' and the 'archetype of the unconscious' (ibid.: 247).

Jung speculated on what underpins the connectedness of Christ and Mercurius in alchemy: is it the predominance of Christian theological ideas in Western medieval Christendom (leading some authors to relate Mercurius to the Holy Spirit, to Christ, to the Trinity); is it a manifestation of a more widespread cultural tendency to separate spirit and matter; is it an expression of the irresolvable conflict between good and evil, expressed in the conflict between Christ and the Devil – an example of 'the widespread [archetypal] motif of the two hostile brothers' (ibid.: 246 n. 9); or is it an example of Mercurius used as a (shadow) dumping ground for all that has been 'eliminated from the Christian model' (ibid.: 241)? Eventually Jung prefers the view of Mercurius as a symbol of totality. Mercurius has the potential to heal the splits that Jung himself has identified in Western European civilization and Christianity, because he is a symbol of dualistic monism, of wholeness comprising a *complexio oppositorum*.

Jung's strategy in the Mercurius essay was to allude to aspects of how this alchemical symbol functions healthily, in contradistinction from Christ. It is left to the reader to draw the implications of what this would mean for reasserting a doctrine of Christ that was similarly healthy (in Jungian terms). For some alchemical authors, Mercurius, like Christ, is 'made of "two natures" or "two substances"' (ibid.: 217), and in one text is referred to as 'divine and at the same time human' (ibid.: 222). However, this shared 'duplex' character manifests, in Jung's view, in a Mercurius who, unlike Christ, clearly has a shadow: 'his main characteristic is duplicity' (ibid.: 217). One of the consequences of the way that Western philosophical alchemy operates, in a symbiotic relation to the Christian dominant, is that Mercurius stands for Christ's opposing shadow. The Christian tendency would always be to identify such figures with the Devil (ibid.: 245). Jung believes that the alchemical figure just manages to retain its integrity as a further manifestation of an ancient pagan god, who is thus a 'natural' (rather than institutional) expression of the spirit archetype of the collective unconscious. Somewhat curiously, Jung imputed to Mercurius characteristics not dissimilar to the Christian theological assertion of Christ's sinlessness (of which Jung was so critical), that is, 'invulnerability and incorruptibility, the very qualities we so urgently need to heal the split in ourselves' (ibid.: 246).

However, the central point from Jung's discussion of Mercurius for his project in relation to Christianity is that, in line with the archetypal structure and dynamics of the human psyche, Mercurius represents a wholeness comprised of the reconciliation of opposites. Mercurius manifests dualistic monism, as a *complexio oppositorum*: 'The paradoxical nature of Mercurius reflects an important aspect of the self – the fact, namely, that it is essentially a *complexio oppositorum*, and indeed can be nothing else if it is to represent any kind of totality' (ibid.: 241).

In order to be convincing, in an engagement with Christianity, Jung must appeal not just to philosophical alchemy but also to the Christian tradition in support of a doctrine of God in which opposites are held together in unity, rather than descending into dualism. It is in sections of *Aion* that Jung makes this attempt.

Jung argued that it was the threat to Christianity from Manichaeism (perhaps from the late third century onwards) that made the Church Fathers sharpen their criticism of dualism. Jung hoped to show, however, that before Christian theology had to meet this challenge, it had been possible for theologians to hold the idea of good and evil together in God, when 'there was as yet no need for Christianity to fight against its Manichaean competitors' (*CW*9(ii): 57). In part, Jung drew again on the Gnostic Christian sources. He also wanted to find evidence in early Christian orthodoxy for God's involvement with evil.

It would have made a strong basis for his argument if his assertion (on a couple of occasions (*CW*18: 682 and Jung, 1952e: 313)) that the Apostolic Father Clement of Rome (*fl.* 96) saw God ruling the world with two hands, Christ and the Devil, had been well founded. Jung had, however, already acknowledged that this comes in the later, pseudonymous Clementine Homilies, which Jung acknowledges are 'Gnostic-Christian writings' (*CW*9(ii): 54).

Indeed, the sources to which Jung appeals all have Gnostic influence. In the Clementine Homilies creation is viewed as composed of 'syzygies, or pairs of opposites' with 'good and evil as the right and left hand of God' (ibid.).[6] Marinus, who was a follower of Bardesanes (*c.*154–222), a convert to Catholic Christianity who retained elements of Babylonian astrology in his theological system, 'sees good as "light" and pertaining to the right hand … and evil as "dark" and pertaining to the left' (ibid). And the pseudepigraphical *Ascension of Isaiah* is taken to illustrate that the sphere of the devil (Sammaël) 'interpenetrates the divine sphere of the Trinity', another instance of 'complementary opposites balancing one another like right and left hands' (ibid.: 57).[7] This appeal to Gnostic sources, however, undermines Jung's argument that, before the rise of the threat of Manichaeism, orthodox Christianity had been able to accept the idea of good and evil in God. He was not able to show that the first-century 'Clement finds this altogether compatible with the idea of God's unity' (ibid.: 55).

Despite this evidential problem, it remains clear that Jung was trying to establish, by appeal to the early Church, that an acknowledgement of 'the reality of evil [in God] does not necessarily lead to Manichaean dualism and so does not endanger the unity of the God-image' (ibid.). In Jung's view it is possible and proper for Christianity to hold a doctrine of God based on dualistic monism rather than one in which God is '*only* good'. Such a theology, he claims, 'does not damage monotheism in any way, since it unites the opposites' (ibid.: 58). Jung knows, from a psychological point of view, that such healing symbols of wholeness, expressing dualistic monism, are a gift of the collective unconscious rather than an achievement of consciousness. And just as we should not limit the unconscious to what consciousness can encompass, we should likewise not limit God. In a rare moment of appeal to an analogy based on dissimilarity Jung points to 'the dangerously anthropomorphic assumption that what man cannot unite … God cannot unite either' (ibid.).

If Jung's attempts failed to find evidence for a doctrine of God combining in unity both good and evil in early Christian sources, he hoped to appeal, in *Aion*, to the doctrine of God expounded by Nicholas of Cusa (1401–64). Previously, in his 1946 work on *The Psychology of the Transference*, Jung had cited Nicholas of Cusa as someone who supported the philosophical importance of contrary polarity. Just as for the alchemists 'anything unknowable could best be described in terms of opposites', so 'Nicholas of Cusa, in his *De docta ignorantia*, regarded antinomial thought as the highest form of reasoning' (Jung, 1946: 309; cf. ibid. n. 9). In Jung's view, 'The alchemists were as it were the empiricists of the great problem of the union of opposites, whereas Nicholas of Cusa is its philosopher' (ibid.: 320).[8]

Jung also sought to link the psychological process of wholeness through individuation to the doctrine of God by appeal to Nicholas. Jung is interested in 'a wholeness that resolves all opposition and puts an end to conflict, or at least draws its sting. The symbol of this is a *coincidentia oppositorum* which, as we know, Nicholas of Cusa identified with God' (ibid.: 319). If successful this would have enabled Jung to establish, by appeal to at least one theologian, a direct correspondence between dualistic monism in archetypes and in God. Balthasar, however, who registered Jung's interest (*TD*1: 520), sees that Nicholas' importance lies in the fact that he was the last medieval theologian to use the analogy of being to indicate similarity within an ever-greater dissimilarity where 'God is all *in* all, because he is inescapably all *over* all' (*GL*5: 209; cf. ibid.: 210).

In one sense, however, Balthasar also found a place for Nicholas of Cusa's *coincidentia oppositorum* within his own doctrine of God. He noted that with the right safeguards it is possible to envisage opposites in God, based on 'the cosmos as the *explicatio*, the folding out [*Auseinanderfaltung*], of what in God is perfect *complicatio*, in-foldedness [*Eingefaltetsein*]' (*TL*2: 210). This involves the paradoxical relationship in Nicholas of Cusa of macrocosm and microcosm. Balthasar notes that, for Nicholas, God is the one 'in whom the greatest coincides with the smallest' (ibid.: 212). Jung, too, notes the paradox in Nicholas' view that the Maximum has no opposite even though it is also its opposite, the Minimum (Jung, 1946: 320). Balthasar relates it to the incarnation. Since God takes on human form in Jesus 'he can be *omnia contracte* [all things in contraction], so that "all fullness can dwell" in him' (*TL*2: 213 referring to Nicholas of Cusa). Jung saw the main application of this to God as Creator, who, for Nicholas, 'is also above the opposites' (Jung, 1946: 320 quoting Nicholas of Cusa). Jung understood that, for Nicholas of Cusa, as White pointed out to him (White, 1960: 283 n. 55), God is beyond the process of the tension and union of opposites, but he attributed this to the constraints of the context within which Nicholas was working. If Nicholas had included evil in God, Jung suggested, 'he would have been roasted long ago' (*CW*18: 725). Even so, Jung tended to write as if Nicholas of Cusa could be cited as an example of a theologian who accepted that God is a *coincidentia oppositorum* (Henderson, 2010).

Despite the admitted limitation of his appeal to Nicholas of Cusa, Jung's main point, again, is that Nicholas' use in his context of the principle of *coincidentia oppositorum* at least provides a resonance within the Christian tradition of the psychological insight about symbols of wholeness which stands at the centre of Jung's analytical psychology. Although archetypal symbols contain opposites, the psyche is not fundamentally dualistic. It is rather a dualistic monism. It is the same dualistic monism that Jung, on the basis of direct analogy, wants to see reflected in the doctrine of God. For archetypal '[p]sychological opposites ... are never incommensurables; if they were they could never unite. All contrariety notwithstanding they do show a constant propensity to union, and Nicholas of Cusa defined God himself as a *complexio oppositorum*' (Jung, 1947/1954: 206f.).

The most important feature to draw from an exploration of Jung's understanding of evil is that he asserts both that it be seen as the real contrary opposite of good and that this be taken as implying not a psychological or theological dualism but a wholeness based on the resolution of contrary opposites, a *complexio oppositorum*. We shall see in chapter eight that this is central to Jung's reading of God's involvement with evil in his view of the Cross-*descensus*. Again the background to the theological implications of Jung's psychological proposals is the difference between himself and Balthasar in the theory of analogy. The remaining task of this chapter is to explore some of the key components of Balthasar's understanding of evil.

Balthasar's understanding of evil

It would have pleased Jung to know that Balthasar asserted the (psychological) reality of evil: 'since the world contains so much horror, it would be pure aestheticism to lock ourselves in a realm of beautiful forms. The hideous form [Ungestalt] is part of the world's form [Gestalt]' (*TD*2: 27). Balthasar rejects Barth's concept of evil, *das Nichtige*, as 'speculative' and he further seeks to include Satan, on biblical grounds, among the *dramatis personae* of the action of the theodrama. But Balthasar will not countenance the idea of opposites in God, and he challenges all ideas suggesting that God holds responsibility for evil. Balthasar hopes to find those for whom 'the constant reality of confrontation with the demonic' is understood as about a 'more-than-human, more-than-psychological power' (*TD*3: 467).

Jung would be surprised to learn that Balthasar sees him diminishing the reality of evil, by what Balthasar sees as an appeal to the 'all-revealing' insights of depth psychology (ibid.: 469). Balthasar acknowledges that Jung is among those who approach the phenomenon of evil with 'a serious and sober openness to facts and observation' and not just out of 'curiosity or fascination' (ibid.: 466). But he sees a dangerous reductionism in the idea that angelic and demonic powers are understood as 'aspects of human (individual and collective) … and of cosmic existence' rather than as 'dimensions of biblical revelation' (ibid.).

Balthasar specifically commends Jung when he 'correctly recognizes that the full notion of the devil only emerges with Christianity, as a counterreality to Christ' (*TD*1: 519 n. 30 referring to *MDR*: 118). Late in life Jung recalls that, in his student days, 'I was … not aware … that the devil, properly speaking, had been born with Christianity' (*MDR*: 118; cf. *CW9*(ii): 42, 61). Later, in *Aion*, referring to the advent of the Antichrist, Jung writes: '[it] is not just a prophetic prediction – it is an inexorable psychological law … [for] every intensified differentiation of the Christ-image brings about a corresponding accentuation of its unconscious complement, thereby increasing the tension between above and below' (*CW*9(ii): 43).

If Balthasar is to find a satisfactory theological account of evil, it will have to meet the criteria for the inclusion of angels and demons in 'the list of *dramatis personae*, ... characters acting in this play that deals with God and the world' (*TD*3: 465; cf. ibid.: 463–501). It will also have to be soundly based on Scripture and tradition (ibid.: 471; cf. ibid.: 470 and n. 12, ibid.: 471 and n. 21, ibid.: 475 nn. 8, 10–12 referring to Haag, and ibid.: 479 referring to Barth). Balthasar admits that the biblical sources are 'strange', perhaps 'deliberately fragmentary', even contradictory, the product of a variety of historical and cultural contexts, expressed in 'nonlogical' terms. Nevertheless they represent something real. But since there is no clear biblical picture of the good and evil powers' 'origin, nature, and destiny', we should not overexert ourselves in what would prove a fruitless attempt to 'adequately systematize them' (ibid.: 466; cf. ibid.: 479 referring to Barth).[9]

If modern rationality makes us disinclined to accept the reality of spiritual beings, of angels and demons, Balthasar recommends that we listen to the promptings of poets, sociologists and novelists. Rainer Maria Rilke's (1875–1926) 'angels' 'are at least ciphers for something very real ["beings"] that the poet has experienced' (ibid.: 467). Among twentieth-century sociologists, Peter Berger is 'trying to prepare us for something like an "encounter with angels"' (ibid.; cf. ibid. n. 4). Fyodor Dostoevsky's (1821–81) Ivan Karamazov (in his dialogue with the Devil), Mikhail Bulgakov (1891–1940) in *The Master and Margarita*, and particularly Herman Melville (1819–91) in *Billy Budd*, all address the 'mystery of iniquity' (ibid.; cf. ibid. nn. 6, 7).

Melville's posthumously published *Billy Budd, Sailor* is the story of the unwarranted antagonism of Claggart, master-at-arms,[10] towards the young foretopman, Billy Budd, epitome of the 'Handsome Sailor' (Melville, 1986: 299). Melville portrays Claggart's nature as inexplicably evil and associates it with the biblical notion (in 2 Thess. 2:7) of the mystery of iniquity. For Claggart was someone

> in whom was the mania of an evil nature, not engendered by vicious training or corrupting books or licentious living, but born with him and innate, in short 'a depravity according to nature.' Dark sayings are these, some will say. But why? Is it because they somewhat savor of Holy Writ in its phrase 'mystery of iniquity'[11]?
>
> (ibid.: 326; cf. *TD*3: 467 n. 7)

This is an example, for Balthasar, not of '"proof" of the existence of the devil' but of what in Jung's terms is the psychological reality of evil, that is, 'an existential demonstration of the fact that people are aware of it' (*TD*3: 468). More generally, it is, for Balthasar, 'evidence of a real encounter between the more-than-human "powers" and their prevailing influence' (ibid.: 469).

Balthasar has further reflections on 'Mysterium Iniquitatis' (*TD*4: 442–52) in which the focus is on 'the intensification of the dramatic confrontation' in the time after Christ, expressed in 'the No to the claim of Jesus, who concentrates everything "religious" on himself' (ibid.: 444). In modern times, since the Enlightenment, this manifests itself as the '(anti-Christian) idea of freedom as total autonomy' (ibid.) and produces the bitterest of struggles, 'the complete Antichrist endowed with total power, as the No to Christ's total powerlessness' (ibid.: 447). The mystery of iniquity is the 'perverse mirror-image' (ibid.: 448) of the christological mystery, resisting the reconciliation of the tension of human polarities, which was itself put to death, through the Cross (as in Ephesians 2 and 3 *passim*). Christ 'disarms [the mystery of iniquity] from within by enduring suffering. "When I am weak, then I am strong" (2 Cor. 12:10)' (ibid.: 449). And although we are now, since Christ, in the 'final phase', the Church's mission until the End is the witness of 'sharing in the Passion of Christ' (ibid.). This redeeming mystery, which takes on the mystery of iniquity, is simultaneously christological and trinitarian ('the *mysterium Trinitatis*' (ibid.: 450)) – which eventually confronts, as in Revelation, hell's counter-trinity.

The self-giving mission of Christ on the Cross is a revelation of the inner-trinitarian processions, the mutual, kenotic, letting-be and being let-be. On the Cross Jesus

> manifests the glory of divine power in … self-surrender … [and] unveils a totally unexpected picture of God's internal, trinitarian defenselessness. … Only thus can the Son really reveal the Father; only thus can the Spirit who proceeds from both be the revelation of their loving fellowship. Truth, at its origin, is unreserved self-surrender and hence the opening-up of the depths of the Father. Truth is the Son's humility, which makes room for, and expresses, the whole sublimity of the Father's love. Truth is the Spirit who both attests and seals this divine relationship and communicates it to the world.
>
> (ibid.)

Jung sees this divine threefold pattern mirrored inversely in triadic demonic images (*PSF*: 235), but Balthasar rejects any such idea: in Revelation 'hell's attempt to produce a countertrinity' (ibid.) (the Dragon, Antichrist and the lying 'spirit' – 'the final shape of evil' (*TD*4: 452)) must not be engaged with as if it somehow related to revelation but must be seen as an aspect of the contradicting blasphemy of Antichrist (ibid.: 450). For in this polarity, between Christ and Antichrist, 'the opposition is so total that there is no similarity whatsoever' (ibid.: 451). The Church must bear witness against evil until the End. In this sense, Balthasar seems to confirm Jung's view of the inability of christocentric Christianity to resolve the Christ–Antichrist conflict: 'This eschatological opposition between the apparent omnipotence of evil and the apparent mortal powerlessness of believers [truly witnessing to Christ] cannot be dismissed as a mere vision. It is genuine prophecy' (ibid.: 452).

The significance of this confrontation with evil illustrates why for Balthasar the reality of evil has to be taken seriously. When he considers the dramatic status of angels and demons, therefore, he dismisses any programme of demythologization, such as that advocated by Bultmann, for whom 'belief in spirits and demons has been superseded as a result of our knowledge of the powers and laws of nature' (*TD*3: 469 quoting Bultmann). Balthasar challenges Bultmann's a priori assumption 'that such beings are incompatible with the "modern world view"' (ibid.). The persisting 'sense of much deeper layers of being' (ibid.: 468) than the modern world view would allow also leads Balthasar to set aside a non-committal stance about the personality or existence of the devil, as advocated, for instance, by Karl Rahner (ibid.: 470).

Balthasar gives serious attention to Barth's view of evil, particularly his concept of *das Nichtige*. Although he focuses on two short passages in Barth's *Church Dogmatics* ('God and Nothingness' (Barth, 2009: 1–78) and 'The Kingdom of Heaven, The Ambassadors of God and Their Opponents' (ibid.: 79–243), Balthasar recognizes that 'the doctrine developed here has been long in the making and later is developed further' (ibid.: 471 n. 19; cf. Rodin, 1977; *TD*5: 205–9, 236–9).

Although *das Nichtige* is usually translated as 'nothingness', there needs to be an appropriate caution, holding back from saying Barth's is a doctrine of the unreality of evil (Quash, 2005: 120), since the 'nothingness' in question is an apparently positive reference to God's response to everything that refuses or resists his grace (Hardy, 2005: 34). For Barth, *das Nichtige* functions to deepen understanding of 'the role of evil within the creation especially as it relates to his insistence on a shadowy side [*Schattenseite*] of the created world' (Rodin, 1977: 181). Although Balthasar is suspicious of Barth's use of a (Protestant) Hegelian dualism (*TD*3: 478), he recognizes that through *das Nichtige* God is involved with evil in that it is 'what God has rejected and consigned to oblivion' (ibid.: 471), what 'in connection with God's creative plan … [God] denies, rejects and condemns' (ibid.: 478). *Das Nichtige* represents 'a negative attitude on God's part' (ibid.: 479; cf. ibid.: 478–85). On the one hand, this sort of active involvement by God in evil comes dangerously close, when ignoring the analogy of being, to attributing humanity's innate polarity structure to the Being of God. And yet, on the other hand, it is hard for Barth to maintain a positive account of what the reality of *das Nichtige* consists in. God in Christ on the Cross 'allows himself, for his creature's sake, to be attacked by "nothingness" – and he is the only one who can deal with it' (ibid.: 484). But Balthasar is concerned that it is not sufficient to say that what is dealt with is 'a fleeting shadow', 'simply what God *did not* wish, *does not* wish, and *will not* wish' (ibid. quoting Barth). For Balthasar it would be less speculative and more biblical to say that Christ bore and overcame evil on the Cross (ibid.) and died there for our sins, rather than saying that Christ was there dealing with 'nothingness' (ibid.: 486). In terms critical of Barth (and perhaps implicitly of Jungian thinking), Balthasar holds that on the Cross 'Jesus is eye to eye with the "adversary", whose concreteness does not come merely from God's No or from the shadow cast by Jesus' (ibid.: 485).

Further, since *das Nichtige* has been 'overcome by Christ', demons, for Barth, cannot be regarded as *dramatis personae* (ibid.: 471). Balthasar is critical of this position. It does not sufficiently reflect the biblical account of angels and demons. Balthasar also finds no basis in Scripture for the proposal that *das Nichtige* has 'a mode of being distinct from the being of God and the being of the creature' (ibid.: 478). Balthasar will rather attempt to give a biblically based theodramatic account of angels and demons, holding that they can be understood as *dramatis personae.* In these terms Balthasar's exploration initially looks fruitful: both angels and demons, it seems, fulfil the criteria of *dramatis personae.* However, in the end, in relation to demons, this position is not sustained.

The three criteria for *dramatis personae* are: being persons in the sense of exercising freedom of choice, being 'persons in Christ', and being persons in Christ whose mission is oriented to his (ibid.: 489).

Within the analogy of being, those who are candidates to be considered *dramatis personae* must have 'a freedom vis-à-vis God' (ibid.: 482f.). Barth 'clearly denies that the angels possess this freedom' (ibid.: 483). For Balthasar, however, 'the angel must be able to opt freely for God … [and] the freedom of this choice provides the possibility and (according to the New Testament) the reality of a negative choice' (ibid.: 487). Further, within this same criterion, demons (who 'cannot have been created evil in the first place') 'must have become evil as a result of a decision (to turn away from God)' (ibid). Freedom of choice is illustrated insofar as some angels 'left their proper dwelling [Jude 6],' and some 'sinned [2 Pet. 2:4],' with the devil doing so 'from the beginning [1 John 3:8]' (ibid.). In relation to the first criterion, then, Balthasar concludes that 'we must regard these [evil] spirits as *dramatis personae*' (ibid.: 488).

In relation to angels, the second and third criteria, which establish full theological personhood, are met. Angels are 'persons in Christ' on the basis of Colossians 1:16 ('in [Christ] all things were created, in heaven and on earth, … all things were created through him and for him'); further, their mission, on the basis of Hebrews 1:3–14, serves Christ's ('Are they not all ministering spirits sent forth to serve, for the sake of those who are to obtain salvation?') (ibid.: 489). As well as continually beholding and adoring God, they participate in mission: 'From their home in heaven, their mission is to "provoke" and trigger history in the world' (ibid.: 492) in a preparatory and subsidiary role. There are examples both in the Old Testament (ibid. and n. 7) and in the New, in the Gospels, Acts and Revelation (ibid. n. 5 and ibid.: 494).

In relation to demons, the case initially looks promising in relation to the second and third criteria. Whereas in the Old Testament their role was primarily to highlight 'the uniqueness and oneness of the living God', and in the inter-testamental period their greater independence began to emerge, matters are qualitatively different in the New Testament. Here it is a matter of the 'eschatological conflict between good and evil', and in this context

> [t]he demonic undeniably plays a 'role' (*persona*) in the Gospels: it is provoked to rear its head at the coming of Jesus, it features in the great scene of the Temptation, in Jesus' exorcisms and when he gives his disciples power over the same demonic element (to say nothing of its role in the Church's history).
>
> (ibid.: 495f.)

But this as far as it goes, for the second criterion of their being 'persons in Christ' is not fully met by simply by taking up a role: 'It is questionable, however, whether the demonic can be regarded as a theological person on this basis' (ibid.: 496).

Eventually, demons fail the test of the third criterion, being persons in Christ whose mission is oriented to his. Human beings become theological persons 'by striving toward and reaching [a positive relationship to Christ's destiny and mission] (which is made possible by grace)' (ibid.). The case is somewhat different, however, for spiritual beings who relate to this criterion in a special way: 'Unlike man, however, the pure spirit is in a position to attain its ultimate goal in an indivisible act by which it grasps itself completely' (ibid.). The consequence for the demon is disastrous. The demon is the angel who has chosen to say No to God. In refusing to align its mission with Christ it also destroys itself as a 'person' and thus cannot be among the *dramatis personae* in the theodrama:

> Accordingly, if [the demon] totally renounces this goal, it loses its personality; it cannot even hold on to itself as a quasi-intact conscious subject since … this conscious subject does not have a 'purely natural' goal. … This means that the subject that has fallen from its personal truth can only continue to exist in a fragmentary form, full of internal contradictions: perversion, the lie, the lack of communication, but also the urge to destroy everything that lives by truth and communication.
>
> (ibid.: 496f.)

In the end it emerges that evil, as exemplified by demons, does not have for Balthasar full theodramatic reality. Jung might be tempted to complain that this is *privatio boni* in another guise, since evil is on this account comparatively privative, deficient in relation to good and not its opposite contrary. Evil, for Balthasar, is, it seems, an ultimately secondary reality, not a primary transcendental partner of good. Viewed from the perspective of the triumph of the good, 'even the most deliberate of evil' has a comparative quality of 'nothingness': in the end 'nothing remains of it except what it has achieved in terms of fruitful suffering' (*TD*5: 503). At best its fascinating profundity turns out to be boringly pseudo (ibid.).

Jung's commitment to asserting the reality of evil never waned. If Balthasar shied away from according the devil the fully functioning status of one of the *dramatis personae*, Jung's enthusiasm led him to assert too boldly that Satan is a Son of God.

Jung seems to have over-read the significance of the Old Testament notion of the *bene ha'elohim*. In the English Authorised Version, this phrase (for instance, in Job 1:6) is translated 'the sons of God'. In the *NRSV* a footnote acknowledges this as a literal translation, but in the text uses the phrase 'the heavenly beings' (Metzger and Murphy, 1991: (OT)626). Drawing on Schärf's argument, Jung, in his essay on the Trinity and in *Aion*, acknowledges the process whereby one of those sons 'took [up] the role of Satan' (*CW*9(ii): 245), emphasizing that Satan remained 'one of God's sons and on familiar terms with Yahweh' (ibid.: 42; cf. *PADT*: 173 n. 19). He acknowledges, however, that it is in a limited sense that the Old Testament Satan 'is in fact one of God's sons' (*PADT*: 170 n. 8 referring to Schärf).

However, on his own account Jung goes further and eventually argues that Satan is a Son of God, since if Christ and Satan are a manifestation of the archetype of the hostile brothers then they will be fundamentally equal as well as each other's contrary opposite.

In the essay on the Trinity in *Symbolik des Geistes*, Jung initially restricts himself to an extension into the New Testament of the Old Testament idea that Satan is a son of God: 'Since Satan, like Christ, is a son of God, it is evident that we have here the archetype of hostile brothers' (ibid.: 173 n. 19); and '[a]s the adversary of Christ, [the Devil] would have to take up an equivalent counterposition and be, like him, a "son of God"' (ibid.: 169f.). Balthasar notes that such ideas can be read as reducing theology to entirely psychological categories. However, he grants that for Jung 'through God's becoming man, Christ has become a historical archetype' (*TD*1: 519 based on Zacharias, 1954: 22ff.).

But, in relation to Christ and Satan, Jung's primary interest was in their archetypal equivalence. Schärf had noted those who thought that 'it was not Christ but Satan who was the firstborn son of God' (*SOT*: 99 n. 51). Jung sets out some of the Gnostic and alchemical sources propounding the same view (*SM*: 222f., 223 n. 21, and *CW*9(ii): 42f.). Associating these ideas with numerological thinking, Jung argues that:

> Once the indefinable One unfolds into two, it becomes something definite: the man Jesus, the Son and Logos. This statement is possible only by virtue of something else that is not Jesus, not Son or Logos. The act of love embodied in the [begetting of the] Son is counterbalanced by Lucifer's denial.
>
> (*PADT*: 173)

And, despite his usual agnosticism about 'the metaphysical position of the devil' (ibid.), Jung eventually makes the fully theological assertion that: 'Inasmuch as the devil was an angel created by God and "fell like lightning from heaven", he too is a divine "procession" that became Lord of this world' (ibid.).

For Jung, then, the psychological reality of evil must not be undervalued and it must be understood as functioning within a framework of contrary opposites and their resolution into a greater wholeness. This approach to the reality of evil is not dualistic. It expresses, rather, a dualistic monism.

One of the issues central to Jung's correspondence with Victor White is that the doctrine of an all-good God came to require a doctrine of evil as *privatio boni* and that this improperly downplays the reality of evil. Jung eventually saw that, in theological terms, the *privatio boni* doctrine does not necessarily amount to a denial of the reality of the human experience of evil. But his disavowal of metaphysics indicates that there were probably few further prospects for continuing dialogue with White.

On his own account, Jung seeks to involve God with evil through a doctrine which gives expression to his dualistic monism. In *Symbolik des Geistes*, in the Mercurius essay, he invokes this alchemical figure as evidence that such a symbol of wholeness comprising a *complexio oppositorum* was a product that emerged from the collective unconscious. However, Jung's further attempts, in *Aion*, to provide historical evidence from early orthodox Christian sources for the one God encompassing both good and evil are not successful. Even his appeal to Nicholas of Cusa's principle of *coincidentia oppositorum* is hardly fit for purpose.

For Balthasar, the question of the reality of evil is equally important. He appealed to poets, sociologists and novelists for evidence of the persisting sense of evil as a more-than-psychological reality. However, the primary reason, for Balthasar, for needing to take evil seriously is the Christ/Antichrist conflict. Balthasar sets aside theological views that downplay evil, even eventually Barth's *das Nichtige*, in favour of a biblically based account of demons as *dramatis personae* in the theodrama. In the end, however, demons fail to meet the criteria to be classed as fully theological persons. If this would have disappointed Jung, Balthasar in turn would not have countenanced Jung's move in the opposite direction, seeking to understand Satan as a (second) Son of God.

Jung's most notable proposal for addressing a one-sided Christian emphasis on the entire goodness of God, with an accompanying reduced understanding of evil, is that the Christian Trinity should become a Quaternity, with the inclusion of the Devil. This is how Balthasar read Jung's essay on the Trinity (*TD*1: 49). In the next chapter I look again at this reading of Jung, and argue that the Quaternity proposal is better seen as an attempt to highlight the problem of a christocentric theology for which the solution, for Jung, is a 'Joachimite' view of the work of the Holy Spirit, in collaboration with humanity.

Notes

1 Karen Kilby also argues that the questions to which theodicies seek to give an answer are not fruitful for theology, since the real mystery of evil is its 'inexplicability' (Kilby, 2003: 26).

2 This is a complicated argument to maintain. It involves taking a view about texts which seem to have had currency in Christian circles whilst containing Gnostic ideas. Since the discovery of the Nag Hammadi library in 1945 much more is known about Gnostic writings in their own terms. Further, recent research into the non-canonical Gospels shows that the sharp distinction that Irenaeus drew in the second century between orthodox Christianity and heretical Gnosticism is not easily maintained. What became two separate streams were much more complexly intertwined than he suggests. Some would argue that the complexity is such that the term 'Gnostic' has very little use since it covers such a wide variety of meaning. Others maintain that on key points, such as that of good and evil in the divine, the term still has important usefulness (Foster, 2009; Foster, 2008).

3 For instance, 'Jung's interest in the healing of the psyche was unmistakably rooted in the conflicts with a troubled father and a mentally ill mother in his own childhood' (Smith, 1996: 1). More neutrally, 'the analytical psychology devised by Jung in all important respects grew out of his own psychology' (Stevens, 1990: 5).

4 Jung further invokes Augustine insofar as he confines the *imago Dei* in the creature to a non-bodily aspect of our humanity, to the '*anima rationalis* ... the understanding' (*CW*9(ii): 38). However, Jung's further attempt to use Augustine in support of this same point misfires, since in the quotation that he cites the concluding phrase 'a complete human soul' clearly refers to a psychosomatic unity: 'The Word took on complete manhood, as it were in its fullness: the soul and body of a man. ... [W]hen I say a human soul and human flesh, I mean he took upon him a complete human soul' (ibid.: 39).

5 Lammers (2005: 18f.) thinks that μη and ου had become interchangeable by New Testament times; Weldon (2007: 279 n. 54) contests this.

6 For Balthasar, the Father's 'two hands' are the Son and the Spirit (*TL*3: 165–218).

7 Marinus' work was refuted in the 'Dialogue of Adamantius', at one time attributed to Origen.

8 Jung notes, however, that 'the opposites which Nicholas had in mind were very different from the psychological ones' (*PADT*: 187 n. 11).

9 Balthasar's argument is rather paternalistic. We are shown only enough to enable us to 'act in faith' for we need to be protected from what would harm us if we knew more (*TD*3: 469).

10 This role is 'a sort of chief of police charged ... with the duty of preserving order on the populous lower gun decks' (Melville, 1986: 313).

11 Note το μυστηριον της ανομιας is more literally translated the 'mystery of lawlessness' (Metzger and Murphy, 1991: (NT)297).

Chapter 7

Jung on God's involvement with evil

In Jung's *Symbolik des Geistes* collection, the essay on the Trinity was the most heavily revised. The first version was a lecture given at the 1940 Eranos conference, containing a short foreword and two parts, on 'The Trinity' and on 'The Problem of the Fourth'. As the table shows, almost the whole of the 1940 lecture was included in the 1948 version,[1] although some of the paragraphs in 'The Trinity' section were edited in the light of further material Jung had gathered. The section on 'The Problem of the Fourth' is reprinted in its entirety in the 1948 version.

Table 1 A comparative synopsis of *PCT* and *PADT*

Eranos lecture on the Trinity, 1940 (*PCT*)	*Symbolik des Geistes* essay on the Trinity, 1948 (*PADT*)
Title: On the Psychology of the Concept of the Trinity [p. 7]	Title: A Psychological Approach to the Dogma of the Trinity [p. 107] Epigraph [p. 107]
Foreword [paras 1–2, p. 8]	Introduction [paras 169–71, pp. 109–11]
	1. Pre-Christian Parallels
I. The Trinity [para. 3, p. 9]	I. Babylonia [paras 172–76, pp. 112–5]
	II. Egypt [paras 177–8, pp. 115–17]
I. The Trinity [paras 4 –6, pp. 9–10]	III. Greece [paras 179–93, pp. 117–28]
I. The Trinity [paras. 7–22a, pp. 10–15]	2. Father, Son, and Spirit [paras 194–206, pp. 129–37]
	3. The Symbola [paras 207–21, pp. 138–47]
	4. The Three Persons in the Light of Psychology
	I. The Hypothesis of the Archetype [paras 222–5, pp. 148–52]
	II. Christ as Archetype [paras 226–33, pp.152–7]
I. The Trinity [paras 22b–9, pp. 1–19]	III. The Holy Ghost [paras 234–2, pp.157–63]
	5. The Problem of the Fourth
II. The Problem of the Fourth [paras 30–54, pp. 19–27]	I. The Concept of Quaternity [paras 243–67, pp. 164–80]
	II. The Psychology of the Quaternity [paras 268–79, pp. 180–7]
	III. General Remarks on Symbolism [paras 280–5, pp. 187–92]
	6. Conclusion [paras 286–95, pp. 193–200]

Balthasar identified a single purpose behind Jung's 1948 Trinity essay, namely to include the Devil within the Godhead. The twofold structure of the 1940 Trinity lecture highlights, however, that Jung wanted both to address the doctrine of the Trinity from a psychological perspective and also to resolve the question of Quaternity. The 1948 essay, as well as expanding on these themes, can further be read performatively as a psychotherapeutic treatment of Christianity (Stein, 1985; cf. Rowland, 2005: 2). Jung's wider range of aims in 1948 include: discussion of the problem of the fourth, and of the patristic elaboration of the doctrine of the Trinity, the application of his therapeutic method, including anamnesis and reconstruction, drawing on two types of psychological interpretation and the therapeutic relationship, and discussion of his specifically theological interpretations, including an attempt to offer a psychologically based theological reflection on the Trinity, his assessment of the Christ/Antichrist conflict, and his 'Joachimite' theology of the Spirit in relation to the Trinity.

The problem of the fourth

The problem of the fourth in Jung's project on Christianity was there from the start, in the 1937 Terry lectures. It reflects a difficulty for his psychology that was posed for him by accepting Christian theological themes as archetypal. The puzzle for Jung centred on what account he was to give of three- and fourfold dream images of wholeness and had arisen earlier in the 1930s when he gained access to a series of over four hundred dreams.[2] Jung's reflections on these dreams were the subject of an Eranos lecture (Jung, 1940: 96–204), and a main source for his Terry lectures (*PRTL*: 24 and n. 13) and for part two of *Psychology and Alchemy* (*CW*12: 39–223).

Jung's preference for fourfold images of wholeness has been the subject of criticism. There are twofold images of wholeness, recognized by Jung, such as yin–yang. White argues that threefold images tend to be 'dynamic' whereas fourfold ones 'static' (White, 1960: 107). James Olney goes as far as to suggest that Jung is engaged in 'deifying the quaternity, discovering the holy four almost everywhere and projecting it where [he] fail[s] to find it' (Olney, 1980: 164).

However, Jung is clear in his Terry lectures that it was not simple numerical fourfoldness that was important as an indicator of wholeness. What he found in the Pauli dream series (as he had found since his own discovering of the mandala image in 1916, and was increasingly finding in alchemical symbolism) was the image provided by the internal structure of such symbols, a circle divided into four, indicating wholeness resulting from the union of opposites. In summary, Jung says that he 'showed … with the help of dreams, how the unconscious produces a natural symbol, technically termed a mandala, which has the functional significance of a union of opposites' (*PRTL*: 90). The key point is that wholeness arises as that integration which results from the resolution of the tension of contrary opposites.

Pauli 'was a Catholic by education', but he was 'no longer a practising one, nor was he interested in religious problems' (ibid.: 24). Nevertheless, some of his dreams contained explicitly Catholic religious material (ibid.: 24–6). Jung recognized that, in its own terms, the Trinity is a symbol of wholeness since 'the three persons of the Trinity are one and the same God' (ibid.: 62). Archetypal quaternity symbols arise from within the collective unconscious and 'quaternity is entirely absent from the dogma' (ibid.: 73) of the Trinity. This poses no particular problem for Jung as long as he sees dogma as a function of an institutionalization of individual religious experience. He can simply note, in the first Terry lecture on 'The Autonomy of the Unconscious', that there would be considerable consequences should Christianity accept the promptings of the unconscious and 'transform [the Trinity] into a quaternity, which is at the same time a unity' (ibid.: 62) by including, for instance, either the feminine or evil. This becomes more problematic for Jung, however, once he accepts, in the second Terry lecture on 'Dogma and Natural Symbols', that certain central Christian dogmas, including the Trinity, are themselves archetypal. How then are threefold dogmatic archetypal images of wholeness to be related to fourfold natural archetypal images?

This is clearly exercising Jung in his 1940 Eranos lecture on the Trinity, which was very much a work in progress. Another contributor at the same conference had linked the Trinity to Platonic ideas (Speiser, 1942) and the next day Jung gave his impromptu response (Jaffé, 1986: 7f. and *PCT*: 9). The second of its two sections addressed 'The Problem of the Fourth' (*PCT*: 19–27).

Jung's primary argument is based on his fourfold theory of functional types (arranged in two paired opposites, thinking–feeling and sensing–intuiting), and in particular the difficulty of integrating into consciousness the fourth, inferior function. In *Psychological Types* he sets out the idea that 'it is practically impossible … for anyone to develop all his psychological functions simultaneously' (*CW*6: 450). One is likely to become predominant, one or both of the other pairing (the auxiliary functions) may be able to be integrated into conscious life, but the fourth (inferior) function, the opposite of the dominant, is less available. This inferior function can be part of consciousness, but little used. However, with increasing one-sidedness of conscious functioning (favouring the dominant and auxiliary functions) it may lose its energic (libidinal) strength and sink into the unconscious. It now becomes 'incompatible with the conscious, favoured function' (ibid.). In therapeutic analysis the psychic products of the inferior function can be brought into consciousness and integrated into a more whole way of living in the world. Without this treatment, the inferior function will be inaccessible and is likely to be troublesome.

Jung finds hints in literature of the reluctance of the fourth to come into consciousness – in the opening of Plato's *Timaeus* and the Cabiri scene in Goethe's *Faust* (*PCT*: 19). In the fairy-tale essay in *Symbolik des Geistes* Jung argues that the inaccessible and reluctant unconscious fourth is likely to be troublesome since the inferior function is 'inaccessible to our will', appearing as spirit, as 'a teasing and distracting imp' or 'as a *deus ex machina*' of 'its own volition' (*PSF*: 238). This is the spirit that 'bloweth where it listeth' [John 3:8, Authorized Version]. The independent character of the collective unconscious also finds expression in the figures representing the spirit archetype. The inferior function acts as 'a painfully disturbing factor', apparently the 'worst enemy' (shadow) of the dominant function. The more the dominant function represses the inferior function, the more strongly will its troublesome features appear, for instance as 'the devil who delights in disguising himself as an angel of light' (ibid.). The missing fourth is 'the Achilles heel of even the most heroic consciousness' (ibid.: 237).

For Jung, the 'quaternity is an archetype that occurs universally' (*PCT*: 19) in Pythagorean numerology, as well as four compass points, elements (earth, air, fire, water), primary colours, (Indian) castes and Buddhist paths, among others (ibid.: 19f. *passim*). These examples are intended to support his view that the fourfold aspect represents the minimum for a determination of completeness: 'Ideal completion, naturally, is round, is the circle. But its minimum, natural division is the four' (ibid.: 20).

This view of wholeness is then applied to the threefold Christian Trinity, with the additional proposition that if such a threefold form represents 'the good and beautiful' and has 'all positive qualities' attributed to it, it would be concomitantly 'deprived of evil and imperfection' (ibid.). Jung complains that the doctrine of *privatio boni* robs Christianity of a sufficiently robust view of the reality of evil. He affirms the psychological and theological reality of the Devil and proposes a Quaternity. This, however, as we shall see below, is not a mere matter of adding the Devil to the Trinity, but involves a new way of giving an account of the processions and missions of the divine Persons, in which Jung gives an important role to the Cross and an even more important one to the collaboration between humanity and the Holy Spirit (ibid.: 20–7).

The patristic elaboration of the doctrine of the Trinity

In the first section of the 1940 Eranos lecture on the Trinity, Jung gives a positive account of the development of the doctrine of the Trinity by the Church Fathers. He laments the fact that, by the twentieth century, the Trinity has become in effect a forgotten idea, for people in general as well as in academic disciplines – theology included. With the exception of historians, '[p]eople have … largely stopped thinking about … a conception like the Trinity … [and its] meaning and [no longer] consider [it] a possible object of reflection' (ibid.: 9).

It is to the work of the Church Fathers that we should look when seeking to understand the Trinity, rather than, for instance, to the mathematical basis of a Platonic relationship of threeness to oneness (ibid.: 9f. referring to Speiser). Whilst acknowledging that the image of an equilateral triangle 'makes it possible for us to think at least somewhat logically ... about the mysterious essence of the Trinity [yet] [t]he true contours of the dogma ... have very little to do with the logical formula [of $a=b=c$]' (ibid.: 10). Jung insists that in order to understand the Trinity 'we have to depend on psychological factors, on irrational [that is, unconscious] data that cannot be logically predetermined' (ibid.). In particular, as Christian doctrine was developed, although Son, being begotten, is related, by biological analogy with Father, yet the Holy Spirit's procession uses the idea of 'a "being breathed"' (ibid.).[3]

Jung then offers his reading of the patristic doctrine of the third Person of the Trinity as the life-soul of the Godhead. Breathing is a bodily function but 'when conceived as autonomous it is a substance apart from the body' for, although the body lives, '"life"' is imagined as an additional, autonomous quality, namely as 'a soul independent of the body' (ibid.). Although not made explicit in the Eranos lecture, there are clear associations here with Jung's vitalist notion of libido as life energy, which he links directly with 'the divine pneuma' (*L*1: 384). He goes on to make a further association with his own concept of the spirit archetype of the collective unconscious:

> Applied to the formula of the Trinity, one would therefore have to say, 'Father, Son' and 'Life' where the latter emanates from both or is lived by both. The Holy Ghost as 'Life' is a concept that simply cannot be derived from the identity of Father and Son. It is much more a psychological notion, that is, a factor based on an irrational, primordial [i.e. archetypal] idea.
>
> (*PCT*: 11)

If the identification with life seems to undermine the Personhood of the Holy Spirit, Jung is clear that: 'We are ... dealing with ... personalities: the unbegotten Father ..., the Son ... begotten by the Father, and the *Spiritus Sanctus* ..., the life of both that they have in common' (ibid.).

Jung is insistent that the Trinity is something more than another example of a significant triad of divinities. It 'is not a matter of a tri-theistic coexistence' (ibid.: 12). In his view, the Church Fathers achieved an impressive outcome. They maintained the archetypal foundations not despite but through a conscious human process of reflection. The Trinity is a matter of 'a unity effected through reflection from internal and external relationships' (ibid.). If the Church Fathers had followed natural analogies the outcome might have been very different. Unlike some Gnostics they do not speak of Father, Mother and Son (*PCT*: 16). The Christian Trinity comes in Jung's view from reflection (that is, 'a mental act in a direction other than the natural course', an 'act of becoming conscious' (ibid.: 27 n. 12)), which joins the Spirit 'to the natural succession of Father/Son. From Nature, this reflection abstracts life and its particular soul and recognizes the latter as an extraordinary existence: Father and Son are united in the same soul' (ibid.: 16). He sees in what was achieved in the doctrine of the Trinity not only a theological but also a psychological advance: 'Undoubtedly the Trinity is a higher form of the notion of God than a simple Unity inasmuch as it corresponds to a condition of greater reflection, of consciousness, in human beings' (ibid.: 14). Given that human thinking, by the use of images, can only attempt to speak about God imperfectly since God is unknowable 'other than by something of a similar nature' (ibid.: 15),[4] we 'would have no dogma of the Trinity had the Church Fathers not expended an unbelievable intellectual effort toward its creation. In actuality, they developed Trinitarian thinking' (ibid.).

This contributed towards humanity developing higher levels of consciousness. Trinitarian thinking was an example of 'the human mind [being] able to think not only beyond nature but in opposition to it' (*PADT*: 176). However, the question of the fourth (particularly of evil) remained. In compensatory fashion, because fourfold thinking was suppressed by the cultural dominance of Christian trinitarian orthodoxy, such patterns of thought reappeared in late medieval philosophical alchemy (ibid.: 176f.) (comparable to others that were to be found in ancient Chinese philosophy (Jung, 1929a)).

The application of Jung's therapeutic method

In the much-expanded 1948 essay on the Trinity, a further factor needs to be taken into account. This piece of writing now acts performatively, as a therapeutic intervention directed as treatment by Doctor Jung towards his patient, Christianity: 'I write as a physician, with a physician's sense of responsibility' (*CW*9(ii): x). Jung sets out this intention towards the end of his 1948 essay:

> In order to interpret the Trinity-symbol psychologically, we have to start with the individual and regard the symbol as an expression of his psyche, rather as if it were a dream-image. ... We can treat the Trinity the more easily as a dream in that its life is a drama, as is also the case with every dream that is moderately well developed.
>
> (*PADT*: 180f.)

This is not merely taking methodological advantage of the fact that 'trinity symbols ... occur fairly frequently in dreams', as well as in other sources of unconscious material used in therapy, such as 'folklore and myths' (ibid.: 189). These sources are primarily useful to Jung therapeutically since this 'empirical material ... shows ... how the archetype works' and where the 'individuation process' towards wholeness 'culminates' (ibid.: 190). Trinity symbols are included by Jung among those 'aiming at wholeness' and he will try to show how they can 'be correctly understood by the doctor' (ibid.: 191).

Stein finds three aspects of Jung's therapeutic method operating in Jung's late works on Christianity: anamnesis and reconstruction, two types of psychological interpretation (association and amplification), and the therapeutic relationship (Stein, 1985: 21–68). He uses these to inform his reading of Jung's 1948 essay on the Trinity (ibid.: 111–35).

Anamnesis and reconstruction

A first aspect of Jung's method in therapy is anamnesis and reconstruction of the patient's history, not used to clarify the story of past experience for its own sake, but, first, to get as much of the story as possible into conscious recollection and, then, to seek historical causal interpretations of 'the present structures of personality and consciousness … by considering earlier events and developmental outcomes' (ibid.: 22). The past is important for the light it might shed on present experience and future wholeness.

Jung briefly reminds Christianity, his 'patient', of the story of the development of the Trinity idea over several centuries with a historical account of New Testament triadic formulae and the creeds ('The Symbola') (*PADT*: 138–47), affirming the level of sophistication achieved by the Church Fathers, in discerning the archetypal nature of the interrelations within the one God, of Father, Son and Holy Spirit (ibid.: 129–37).

Two types of psychological interpretation

One indication that the 1948 essay would focus on therapeutic treatment rather than on intellectual argumentation is the change of title. The 1940 lecture is 'On the Psychology of the Concept of the Trinity'; the 1948 essay is (in German) 'Versuch zu einer psychologischen Deutung des Trinitätsdogmas' (Jung, 1948a: 321). The key word is 'Deutung', which in this context means psychotherapeutic interpretation. 'A Psychological Interpretation of the Dogma of the Trinity' might have been preferable to the 'Approach' of the title in the English *Collected Works* (*PADT*: 107).

Jung's principal psychotherapeutic method was dream analysis by association ('a careful and conscious illumination of the inter-connecting associations objectively grouped round particular images' (Jung, 1934b: 148)) and amplification (offering 'striking and unmistakable analogies with other systems' (Jung, 1914a: 187 and n. 12)) and the use of active imagination (by which an emotional 'mood' 'and its contents are brought nearer to consciousness' (Jung, [1916]/1957: 82; cf. Casement, 2001: 94–7)).

One form of interpretation, arising directly out of the anamnesis, is reductive, looking for historical causes of present experience, by finding remembered associations between dream images and the patient's life story. The other form is prospective, seeking the integration of psychic contents emerging from the unconscious to help form a more nuanced, integrated and whole conscious attitude. The key method in this second form of interpretation is amplification, drawing on the symbolism of folklore, myth and religion, particularly as it illustrates the structure and dynamics of the archetypes of the collective unconscious. The hope is that this second form of interpretation will enable the emergence and integration of a symbol that encapsulates for the patient a greater sense of wholeness. He was also interested in whether and how dream symbols might enable his patient to take responsibility for the future direction of his or her life, insofar as a dream image is compensating for a contextually rooted one-sided conscious attitude in the dreamer. Some dreams are archetypal and come from the realm of the collective unconscious and can be a significant contribution to a person's process of individuation. In such so-called 'big dreams' it was important for Jung to use amplification, to explore potentially meaningful links to 'universal imagery … using mythical, historical and cultural analogies' (Casement, 2001: 80; cf. Stein, 1985: 45–8).

The section on 'Pre-Christian Parallels' to the Trinity (*PADT*: 112–28) is an example of the first form of interpretation. It indicates a historical context of ideas associated with what became the Christian Trinity, with illustrations of triads of gods from Babylonia and Egypt and numerological ideas in Greek philosophy. These associations are brought forward, not to identify historical causes of the Christian understanding of the Trinity, but rather to establish the Trinity as an archetypal idea that will need to be interpreted prospectively. Not only threefold but also triune thinking is archaically archetypal. Its re-emergence can take place *de novo*, independent of historical causes (ibid.: 129). What eventually became the Christian doctrine of the Trinity was dependent upon an initiating archetypal experience: 'The trinitarian drama of redemption (as distinct from the intellectual conception of it) burst upon the world scene at the beginning of a new era, amid complete unconsciousness of its resuscitation from the past' (ibid.: 138).

The section on 'The Hypothesis of the Archetype' (ibid.: 148–52) makes the same point. An expression of the archetype of trinity, comparable to the Christian one, is found in the 'homoousia of Father, Son and Ka-mutef' in Egyptian theology but this should not be thought of as the cause of the Christian idea (ibid.: 148). For whenever an archetype 'starts functioning at a given moment', arranging 'the material of consciousness into definite patterns', this is not primarily a matter of historical causes or deliberate intentionality, for there 'is never any conscious invention' (ibid.: 148f.). That granted, Jung's overall approach is anthropological: 'the history of the Trinity presents itself as the gradual crystallization' (ibid.: 151) of archetypal psychological products. This contrasts with a primarily theological understanding, of a history initiated, in Balthasar's terms, by God deciding out of his infinite freedom to step onto the world stage to make real there the trinitarian theodrama. For Jung it is the 'archetype *an sich*' by which 'man's conceptions of God are organised into triads and trinities' (ibid.: 148f.) and which 'moulds the anthropomorphic conceptions of father and son, of life, and of different persons into an archetypal and numinous figure, the "Most Holy Three-in-One"' (ibid.: 151).

Partway through the section on 'Christ as Archetype' (ibid.: 152–7), Jung brings a prospective interpretation more strongly into play (ibid.: 153ff.).[5] He wants to offer a therapeutic interpretation of the meaning of Christ in terms of the archetype constellating around him: 'we must ask ourselves what it was in man that was stirred by the Christian message, and what was the answer he gave' (ibid.: 154). Jung's amplificatory method of interpretation compares the

Christ-symbol in the New Testament, in patristic sources and in medieval iconography with the archetypal content of the unconscious psyche in order to find out what archetypes have been constellated. They are those of the hero and the God-man 'born without sin, more complete and more perfect than the natural man' (ibid.: 155). The Christ-symbol also represents the wholeness of the Self, and 'it was this archetype of the self in the soul of every man that responded to the Christian message' (ibid.: 156).

An important aspect of Jung's method is the indistinguishability of psychological and theological symbols (ibid.: 160, 194; cf. ibid.: 180, 199). Jung says that

> Christ realized the idea of the self. But as one can never distinguish empirically between a symbol of the self and a God-image, the two ideas, however much we try to differentiate them, always appear blended together, so that the self appears synonymous with the inner Christ … and Christ with God ('of one substance with the Father').
>
> (ibid.)

A by-product of this is that Jung can make theological assertions, while at the same time claiming that they are psychological interpretations. It also allows Jung, in the section on 'The Psychology of the Quaternity' (ibid.: 180–7) (following a Christian theological tradition at least as old as Augustine), to link an account of the Trinity directly to a psychological account of human development.

The final interpretation, in the section on 'Christ as Archetype', is that, though a Self-symbol represents an archetype of totality, it only needs to have relatively greater totality than the individual has currently consciously achieved to be therapeutically sufficient. Not every symbol of the Self, therefore, expresses entire totality (ibid.: 156). This is Jung's psychotherapeutic solution to the puzzle, raised in his Terry lectures, of the unconscious producing three- and fourfold images of wholeness. Jung cashes this out theologically in terms of Christ's lack of a dark side. He links this not only to the inclusion of the Devil in a Quaternity, but also to the 'Joachimite' orientation of his theology (ibid.: 156, 158).

The sections on 'The Holy Ghost' and 'The Concept of the Quaternity' (ibid.: 157–63 and 164–80), which are reproduced largely unedited from the 1940 Eranos lecture, are likewise well characterized as prospective interpretations of archetypal material. They contain significantly more amplificatory connections to non-Christian sources. Also embedded in them are Jung's own theological proposals about the Quaternity and his 'Joachimite' account of the divine drama.

The therapeutic relationship

A third aspect of Jung's method focuses on the nature of the relationship between therapist and patient, in terms of transference (Jung, 1946). In order to be effectively therapeutic the relationship must be two-way, with both therapist and patient 'functioning as emotionally engaged partners, both prepared to undergo change, and both experiencing transformation during the course of therapeutic treatment' (Stein, 1985: 24).

Jung's emotional engagement with Christianity spanned decades. He recalled, when writing *MDR*, that he had been 'profoundly disappointed' that his father had nothing to say about the Trinity during his teenage confirmation classes (*MDR*: 70). In the introduction to the 1948 essay Jung overrides the resistance he anticipates to treating central Christian symbols psychologically (by those who calmly accept his psychological treatment of the symbols of other religions) by asserting forcefully that 'what is sauce for the goose is sauce for the gander ['*was dem einen recht ist, soll dem andern billig sein*' (Jung, 1948a: 323)] (*PADT*: 109; cf. Stein, 1985: 114).

Within the therapeutic relationship, the patient's emotional reaction to the therapist (transference) needs a similarly emotionally engaged response from the therapist (countertransference). In the usual circumstance, therapeutic treatment does not begin unless the patient takes the initiative to present themselves to the therapist in the search for a means to address a present sense of dysfunction. Perhaps Jung was wise to be cautious in circumstances in which he had initiated the offer of therapeutic treatment for Christianity. In relation to treating the doctrine of the Trinity in the 1948 essay, Jung's starting point (given the problem of the missing fourth, as explored in the 1940 Eranos lecture) was that the Christian dogma was a one-sided and only partially adequate symbol in relation to his understanding of a healthy structuring of consciousness.

In the section on 'Christ as Archetype', Jung suggests that the Church Fathers, despite their achievement in their own day, have 'failed to bequeath to posterity an intellectual understanding of the dogma that would lend the slightest support to belief in it' (ibid.: 153). The situation has been made worse by those liberal, nineteenth-century theologians (such as D. F. Strauss (1808–74)) who attempted to rely on the intellectual tools of modernity with its 'rationalistic and intellectualistic assumptions', narrowly confined to the workings of consciousness, when what has to be dealt with are 'irrational [unconscious] psychic phenomena' (ibid.).

Although this is presented as a historical, causal interpretation, Jung's countertransference, his own emotional involvement with Christianity, may also be a factor, even though it is in the background, 'present but quite unconscious' (Stein, 1985: 134). When Jung and his father failed to be able to discuss the Trinity, Jung felt that the only option Swiss Reformed Christianity offered him was to insist on faith. On the one hand Jung speaks about this in objective terms as a comment on the collective historical process. As the patristic world view, within which the doctrine of the Trinity made sense, began to disintegrate, in Jung's view '[t]here remained only submission to faith and renunciation of one's desire to understand' (*PADT*: 153). If this personal issue for Jung had begun for the teenager in his father's study, it was still a live issue more than half a century later, when he wrote the 'Introduction' to the 1948 Trinity essay:

> Faith is a charisma not granted to all; instead, man has the gift of thought, which can strive after the highest things ... People who can believe should be a little more tolerant with those of their fellows who are only capable of thinking.
>
> (ibid.: 110)

Jung's specifically theological interpretations

It is clear from the text of the 1940 Eranos lecture and the much-expanded 1948 essay on the Trinity that Jung is not only engaging in an attempt to treat Christianity psychotherapeutically, but that he also has specific theological suggestions for the development of Christian doctrine. Four of these can be identified: to link the divine drama to a pattern of human psychological development, to use a Quaternity to highlight the Christ/Antichrist conflict, to promote a 'Joachimite' understanding of the Holy Spirit in relation to the Trinity, and to refer briefly to his interpretation of the Cross. The first three of these make up the remainder of the present chapter; the fourth is discussed in chapter eight.

The divine drama linked to human development

Jung's attempt to link the divine drama to an account of the process of human psychological development is in the section 'The Psychology of the Quaternity', newly written for the 1948 essay (ibid.: 180–7).[6] Had he known of it, Jung might have been encouraged in his attempt to link an account of human development to an account of the life of the Trinity from Balthasar's comment that 'while the life of the Trinity must not ... be described as a "becoming" (since ... [the Persons] are coeternal, the creaturely process of becoming can present an "image" of this primal life' (*TD*2: 261). Jung himself wants this section to be seen in the context of the 'development of the Trinity into a quaternity', understood by analogy with human psychological development as 'a collective process, representing a differentiation of consciousness that has been going on for several thousand years' (*PADT*: 180).

Jung's suggestion is that religion in the age of the Father is related to the psychological position of the small child in relation to its parent (and implicitly to the age of the Old Testament): 'the father denotes the earlier state of consciousness when one was still a child, still dependent on a definite, ready-made pattern of existence which is habitual and has the character of law' (ibid.: 181).

The human developmental process for the son is initiated by imitation ('the son starts to put himself in his father's place') but it goes on to involve a separation towards autonomy, with 'conscious differentiation from the father and from the habitus represented by him' (ibid.). Jung emphasizes that aspect of (New Testament) Christianity that promotes the role of discernment and knowing: 'The Christianity symbolized by the "Son" therefore forces the individual to discriminate and to reflect, as was noticeably the case with those Church Fathers who laid such emphasis on ... knowledge' (ibid. and n. 3 referring to Justin Martyr and Clement of Alexandria).

In this account of human development Jung argues that '[t]he "Son" represents a transition stage, and intermediate state, part child, part adult. He is a transitory phenomenon' (ibid.: 182). This period, in which autonomy is being established with '[i]ncreased discrimination' through the exercise of 'reason and reflection', is beset by two endemic problems, 'opposition' and 'dissociation' (ibid.: 182, 183): 'This state is not only in opposition to the still-existing earlier state, but, by virtue of its conscious and rational nature, it contains many latent possibilities of dissociation' (ibid.: 182). It can be typified, by association with Christ, as a crucifixion (ibid.). But this stage in human development needs to be superseded, whilst retaining the gains in consciousness represented by reason and reflection.

The third stage of human development, adulthood, is characterized by the ability to recognize that the insights of knowledge are not truly the achievement of autonomous consciousness but rather 'come from an unconscious function' (ibid.: 183). In this stage of understanding (associated with the age of the Spirit), the true meaning of 'inspiration' brings with it a realization that '"gnosis" ... is inspired by a higher authority which, in projected form, is known as the "Holy Ghost"' (ibid.).

The process has come full circle but has also developed. The mature adult now voluntarily submits to a paternal authority (as when the Christian 'recognizes the authority of the Church's teachings' (ibid.)) though with continuing discrimination. The higher authority is (psychologically) the Self, (theologically) the Holy Spirit. This involves 'articulating one's ego-consciousness with a supraordinate totality ... which is best visualised as a more comprehensive being ... and is known in Christian parlance as the "Holy Ghost", the breath that heals and makes whole' (ibid.: 185). Further, the transitions – from the dependency of the child on the father to the striving for autonomy of the son and then the further transition to accepting the authority of the unconscious – involve 'sacrifice': 'Just as the transition from the first stage to the second demands the sacrifice of childish dependence, so, at the transition to the third stage, an exclusive independence has to be relinquished' (ibid.: 183).

Yet again in the background of this theological interpretation there is the question of the psychotherapeutic countertransference. For this is an account of human development that has resonance with Jung's own issues with his father, which were interwoven with his attitude to his father's embodiment of Christian faith.

Nevertheless, a psychological approach to understanding the Trinity has a venerable pedigree. For Augustine there are vestiges even in fallen humanity of creation in the image of the triune God as evidenced in the triad of memory, intellect and will. Jung himself invokes this pedigree in a quote from Augustine as his epigraph for the 1948 Trinity essay: 'Go not outside, return into thyself. Truth dwells in the inward man' (ibid.: 107). Balthasar points to the inadequacy of such an approach, since the human analogy based on similarity is not capable of giving a fully truthful account of the greater dissimilarity of God. Jung might argue that his approach offers a partial way of understanding the divine life insofar as his psychology relies on a dissimilarity (as well as a similarity) between the conscious and the unconscious aspects of the psyche.

Jung's assessment of the Christ/Antichrist conflict

A key feature of Jung's understanding of the Christian Trinity and the question of God's involvement with evil is his idea that the stage of the Son is not only endemically conflictual but that this conflict can be suffered but not resolved by the Son. Resolution can only be granted in due course by human spiritual collaboration with the Holy Spirit. To address this issue Jung develops his Quaternity suggestion in terms of the battle between Christ and the Devil, which he represents diagrammatically.

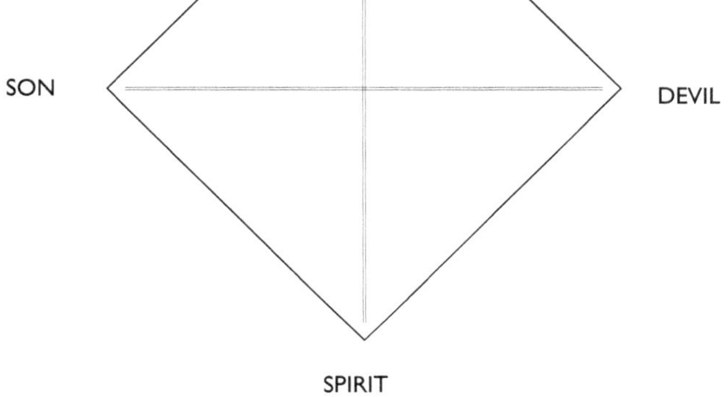

Figure 2 Jung's Quaternity Diagram

Jung writes:

> In our diagram, Christ and the devil appear as equal and opposite, thus conforming to the idea of the 'adversary'. This opposition means conflict to the last, and it is the task of humanity to endure this conflict until the time or turning-point is reached where good and evil begin to relativize themselves. … In the age of Christianity and the domain of trinitarian thinking such an idea is simply out of the question, because the conflict is too violent for evil to be assigned any other logical relation to the Trinity than that of an absolute opposite. … The unspeakable conflict posited by duality [between Christ and the Devil] resolves itself in a fourth principle [Spirit], which restores the unity of the first [Father] in its full development.
>
> (ibid.: 174f.; cf. *PCT*: 22)

Jung bases this aspect of his Quaternity proposal on a judgement about Christ as an expression of the archetype of totality. In the section on 'Christ as Archetype' he says that this version of the Christ-figure 'is not a totality, for it lacks the nocturnal side of the psyche's nature, the darkness of the spirit, and is also without sin' (*PADT*: 156). The Christ-figure 'corresponds to only one half of the archetype' of wholeness; the 'other half [the dark aspect] appears in the Antichrist' (*CW*9(ii): 44). Jung's assertion is that '[w]ithout the integration of evil there is no totality' (ibid.). In *Aion*, he argues:

> Psychologically the case is clear, since the dogmatic figure of Christ is so sublime and spotless … everything else turns dark beside it. It is, in fact, so one-sidedly perfect that it demands a psychic complement to restore the balance.
>
> (*CW*9(ii): 42)

A Quaternity image states what Jung sees to be the problem of an entirely good God-image. It does not resolve the problem. For Jung's own theology is anti-christocentric. In his letter to Père Lachat, Jung points out that conflict between Christ and the Devil is quite rightly seen to culminate on Calvary, but what the Cross symbolizes 'is a state of suspension between the opposites, that is to say, an unresolved conflict' (Jung, 1954a: 689).

Jung's 'Joachimite' theology of the Spirit in relation to the Trinity

On this reading a key purpose of Jung's Quaternity proposal is to highlight what he perceives as a central problem with christocentric theology as an adequate account of God's involvement with evil, namely that it cannot bring saving resolution to the problem of the conflict of good and evil. For Jung (in his 'Joachimite' theology) it is the Holy Spirit who resolves the irresolvable conflict of the Son.

For Jung the Holy Spirit is the 'figure that replaces Christ as his equivalent' (*PCT*: 14; cf. *PADT*: 135 'deputizes for Christ'; cf. *CW*9(ii): 88) but, unlike Christ, effects the desired resolution:

> As he is the third term common to Father and Son, he puts an end to the duality, to the 'doubt' in the Son. ... The point is that the unfolding of the One reaches its climax in the Holy Ghost after polarizing itself as Father and Son.
>
> (*PADT*: 135; cf. *PCT*: 14)

For 'the Holy Ghost is a reconciliation of opposites [Christ and the Devil] and hence the answer to the suffering in the Godhead which Christ personifies' (ibid.: 176). For Jung, 'the Paraclete is the crowning figure of the work of redemption on one hand and God's self-revelation on the other ... and represents the completion of the Godhead and the divine drama' (*PCT*: 14; cf. *PADT*: 136).

Not only that but humanity now has a potentially exalted role to play in the divine drama, for 'the Holy Ghost continues the work of redemption' in collaboration with those 'who perform works that are even "greater" than those of the Son' (ibid; cf. *PADT*: 136). What is important is what can be achieved by humanity in the age of the Spirit:

> The life of Christ is on the one hand only a short, historical interlude for proclaiming the message, but on the other hand it is an exemplary demonstration of the psychic experiences connected with God's manifestation of himself (or the realization of the self). The important thing for man is not ... what is 'shown' and 'done' [in Christ], but what happens afterwards: the seizure of the individual by the Holy Ghost.
>
> (ibid.: 158)

It amounts to a theology of deification:

> Just as the Holy Ghost is a legacy left to man, so, conversely, the concept of the Holy Ghost is something begotten by man and bears the stamp of its human progenitor. And just as Christ took on man's bodily nature, so through the Holy Ghost man as a spiritual force is surreptitiously included in the mystery of the Trinity.
>
> (*PADT*: 161)

Although Jung realizes it is an idea resisted by the Church and associated with 'explosive schisms', he nevertheless insists (in yet another example of his direct understanding of analogy) that in the Holy Spirit we are made Sons of God:

> The dogmatic assertion ... speaks of the Holy Ghost making us 'children of God,' and this filial relationship is indistinguishable in meaning from the

> υιοτης (sonship) or *filiatio* of Christ. We can see from this how important it was that the homoousia should triumph over the homoiousia (*similarity* of substance): for, through the descent of the Holy Ghost, the self of man enters into a relationship of unity with the substance of God.
>
> (ibid.: 194f.)

It would not be unreasonable to conclude that on this point there are very few options available for continuing to engage in a dialogue between Jung and Balthasar other than spelling out their theological incompatibility.

Jung's attempt to link the Trinity to an account of human psychological development relies on direct correspondence. It seems to me that one of the important contributions that Balthasar makes to a theology–psychology dialogue is his insistence upon an analogy of similarity-within-ever-greater-dissimilarity. This understanding of analogy holds together, in a way that Jung himself was unable to, his view about the importance of both similarity (direct correspondence) and dissimilarity (paradox) in religious discourse, and thus could help him with the issue of psychologism, collapsing religion into psychology, which he strongly asserted he wanted to avoid.

Jung also offers a model of the drama of salvation along a pneumatological trajectory which is anti-christocentric. Jung was right if he feared that this proposal would be regarded as heretical, as were Joachim's similar views in the Middle Ages. Even before the rediscovery in the twentieth century by Balthasar, among others, of a christocentric theology, it would be surprising if anyone in the mainstream of Christianity would take on Jung's ideas of Satan as Christ's brother and as a Son of God or accept that, since the conflict of these hostile brothers is unresolved, Christianity should set aside the claim that Christ's death is salvific once for all. Although Jung's view on the role of the Spirit might be taken up by those in the burgeoning charismatic churches (and not just by those interested in New Age spirituality), the idea that there are three ages (of the Father, the (two) Son(s), and the Spirit), with the second and third both being needed to overcome the limitations of its precursor, would find it hard to win a hearing in a period of revival of interest in the doctrine of the Trinity. Three such ages seem to imply a tri-theistic rather than a triune God. And even if Jung restores a fuller sense of oneness to God in the age of the Spirit than in the age of the Father, this has needed (according to Jung) an unsuccessful involvement by God in the historical process of the Christ-event and co-partnership by human beings with the Spirit in the present age. Such a God, dependent on historical and psychological processes for his evolution, is not Balthasar's infinitely free God who in his inner-trinitarian divine life creates the space for creation and the stage for the theodrama which he freely enters in the incarnation.

Despite all these very real difficulties, I want to suggest in the next chapter that there is one final area for undertaking a critical comparison of God's involvement with evil in Jung and Balthasar, namely their respective ways of understanding the Cross. Jung's performative, therapeutic method involved putting forward numerous suggestions, leaving the patient to choose which, if any, he will work with for himself. Jung's prime concern is to initiate dialogue. At the close of the 1948 Trinity essay he reiterates his interest in the psychology–theology connection, between 'archetypal statements' and their 'ultimate ramifications [which] penetrat[e] to the very ground of the universe'; and, notwithstanding his continued disavowal of his own theological positions, he ends by inviting dialogue: 'If I have merely succeeded in stimulating discussion, then my purpose is more than fulfilled' (ibid.: 200).

Notes

1 The paragraph numbers I have assigned in the table for the English translation of *PCT* do not form part of the printed text.
2 These were the dreams of the physicist Wolfgang Pauli, who was being treated by another Jungian analyst and with whom Jung later collaborated on synchronicity.
3 Jung does not always distinguish carefully between terms such as 'procreated' and 'begotten'. In the Nicene creed the Son is 'begotten', that is 'incarnate' rather than 'created'. In the Athanasian Creed, the Son was 'not made, nor created'. Jung writes that the Son is the result of 'a "procreation" (being "begotten")' (*PCT*: 11).
4 A rare acknowledgement by Jung of God's analogical 'greater dissimilarity'.
5 The transition is done somewhat clumsily by using terms from the (first) quest for the historical Jesus to suggest that in the New Testament, from Paul onwards 'the real Jesus of Nazareth … is completely … smothered, by metaphysical conceptions' turning him into Christ, 'a dogmatic figure who has no more need of historicity' (*PADT*: 152f.). This is not, however, Jung's main point.
6 There is an earlier version of this (*PADT*: 133–6) which is taken from *PCT*: 12–4.

Chapter 8

The Cross in Jung and Balthasar

In this chapter I explore Jung's understanding of the Cross and link it to his theory of symbol formation, which involves a descent into the unconscious, as a basis for a psychological understanding of God's involvement with evil. I then explore Balthasar's understanding of Christ's Cross and descent to the dead as the basis of his theological account of God's involvement with evil. Balthasar's dramatic soteriology emphasizes what the Cross, as an economic trinitarian event, reveals about the fundamental nature of God (in the eternal processions within the immanent Trinity), namely God's kenotic love. The focus of Jung's interpretation is opposition of good and evil and the challenge of its resolution. It will be a key aim of chapter nine to seek to bring these two approaches together.

Jung and the Cross

A focus on the Cross is a minor feature of the 1948 essay on the Trinity, but it was important from the start of Jung's project in relation to Christianity. Linking Jung's interpretation of the Cross to his theory of symbol formation provides an important key for reading his fairy-tale essay, revised for inclusion in the *Symbolik des Geistes* collection and some further reflections about the Cross in *Aion*.

Jung's project in relation to Christianity became theoretically possible during his 1937 Terry lectures. His inspiration to address this in the context of Western European civilization seems to have been prompted by a dream during his 1938 visit to India, where he saw an approach to the question of suffering that contrasted with the Western perspective. Jung felt 'that a feasible thing would be to try and find at least a way to enable people to endure the inevitable misery which is the lot of every human life' (*L*1: 236). One of his initial hunches was that this would need to relate to the centrality of the Cross.

Shortly after his return home Jung was visited by a Protestant pastor, Walter Uhsadel (1900–85),[1] who gives an account of their meeting:

> When I visited Jung for the first time in the year 1938, our conversation revolved around the question, which pastoral means of assistance the old but neglected Protestant forms of spirituality and practice [*geistlichen*

> *Lebensordnungen*] could be offered to present-day man if he were correctly guided in how to make use of them. I was able to give Jung an account of many practical experiences in this respect, which I had collected during a period of pastoral care and which, even if to a modest degree, still sustained their use. As I took my leave, he led me into a small room in which he treated his patients. He had in this room a copy of a very lovely Gothic stained-glass window of the Crucifixion. Through this, the room had acquired the character of a spiritual place. [*Der Raum hatte dadurch das Gepräge einer Sakristei*[2] *bekommen*.] While Jung was pointing to this window he said to me: 'Just look, this is the crucial thing for us.' When I asked him why he said that, he replied in his calm, collected way: 'I have just returned from India, where this problem has arisen for me anew. Mankind has to be able to cope with the problem of suffering. Eastern man wishes to free himself from the problem of suffering by stripping off life. Western man, on the other hand, attempts to suppress suffering with drugs. However, suffering must be overcome, and it will only be overcome insofar as one endures it. This we learn solely from him.' And with this he pointed to the Crucified One.
>
> (Uhsadel, 1966: 120f. – my translation[3]; cf. *L*1: 236 n. 1)

The conflict of opposites is fundamental to Jung's psychology and, in *Psychology and Alchemy*, he associates that tension, itself seen as a crucifixion, with the only appropriate way to relate to religious symbols:

> Without the experience of opposites there is no experience of wholeness and hence no inner approach to the sacred figures; … [and] the reality of evil and its incompatibility with good cleave the opposites asunder and lead inexorably to the crucifixion and suspension of everything that lives.
>
> (*CW*12: 20f.)

Likewise, a Quaternity symbol in which opposites are contained is the epitome of wholeness. In the Terry lectures Jung sees Christianity's Trinity symbol in these terms. Even though later dogma excludes Quaternity, such a symbol is to be found in early iconography, that is, 'the cross with equal arms enclosed in the circle' (*PRTL*: 73). Jung notes this again in the 1940 Eranos lecture on the Trinity, and goes on to make a theological point:

> The Church fathers most vehemently opposed the notion of a quaternity of divine principles while making the attempt to assign three persons to the nature of God. This resistance against the quaternity is extraordinary given that the central Christian symbol, the cross, is unmistakably a quaternity. It represents, however, God's suffering in the direct collision with the world.
>
> (*PCT*: 20f.; cf. *PADT*: 170)

Further, in the 1940 lecture, Jung presses the point that the Cross is the event through which redemption is effected, referring to his quaternity diagram, which combines, in cruciform manner, 'the oppositional identity of Christ and his adversary' with 'the unfolding of the Father's unity into the multiplicity of the Holy Ghost. The cross produced in this manner is the symbol of the Godhead's suffering that redeems humanity' (ibid.: 25; cf. *PADT*: 174f.).

Eventually, Jung's theology comes to prioritize the notion of a conflict between the good and evil in God and the consequent role of the Holy Spirit, whilst retaining an assertion of God's real engagement with suffering in human existence:

> If however, God wants to be born as a human being and to unite humanity in the community of the Holy Ghost, he will suffer the terrible torment of having to bear the world in its reality. It is a cross; yes, he himself is the cross. The world is God's suffering and each individual human being who also wishes even to approximate his own totality knows very well that that means carrying a cross. But the eternal promise of bearing a cross is the Paraclete.
>
> (ibid.: 26; cf. *PADT*: 179)

And God as Paraclete 'drew closer to real human beings and their darkness even more than he had as the Son. The light God stepped onto the bridge of Man from the day side; God's shadow, however, from the night side' (ibid; cf. *PADT*: 179).

Once God had become involved in the world in the age of the Son, the originating conditions could not remain for ever unchallenged.:

> By definition, the Father is the creator, the maker, the *auctor rerum*, the author of things, who, at a cultural level where there is not yet reflection, can simply be the One. The Other results from the One through separation. This separation need not take place as long as no one takes any kind of critical position toward the *auctor rerum*, that is, as long as a culture does not reflect on this unity and begin to criticize the work through which the creator makes himself known.
>
> (ibid.: 12; cf. *PADT*: 133)

Jung himself seeks tentatively for a way forward to relate the interpretation of the Christ-event with the inner life of God. On the one hand, in relation to the economic Trinity:

> The descent into human form signifies a becoming 'Other,' a setting-itself-in-opposition to itself. From this moment, there are two, the 'One' and the 'Other,' which means a certain tension. This tension expresses itself in the suffering of the Son and finally in his acknowledgement of God's forsaking him (Matt. 27:46).
>
> (ibid.: 14; cf. *PADT*: 135f.)

On the other hand, in relation to the immanent Trinity:

> the 'One' [Father] and the 'Other' [Son] are still bound in the original One and are, in a manner of speaking, eternally on the point of becoming two. For this reason, the Son is 'eternally' begotten by the Father and his sacrificial death an 'eternally' present act.
>
> (ibid.: 27 n. 8; cf. *PADT*: 136 n. 9)

Allowing for Jung's 'Joachimite' take on the shift from the age of the Father to that of the Son ('The world of the Father is thereby fundamentally changed and superseded by the world of the Son' (ibid.: 13; cf. *PADT*: 134)), the Cross as a symbol of the tension of opposites is clearly important for Jung theologically. He also thinks that understanding it (from a psychotherapeutic perspective) as a symbol of healing is important, particularly in the context of Western European civilization.

> The stage of the 'Son' is therefore a conflict situation *par excellence*: the choice of possible ways is menaced by just as many possibilities of error. 'Freedom from the law' brings a sharpening of opposites, in particular the moral opposites. Christ crucified between two thieves is an eloquent symbol of this fact. The exemplary life of Christ is in itself a 'transitus' and amounts therefore to a bridge leading over to the third stage.
>
> (*PADT*: 182)

But the last word about this opposition, even if it constellates an archetype of the hostile brothers, need not be that of irresolvability, for 'Christian symbolism is particularly concerned with healing, or attempting to heal, this very wound'; rather '[i]t would be more correct to take the open conflict' (between good and evil, Christ and the Devil) 'as a symptom of the psychic situation of Western man, and to deplore his inability to assimilate the whole range of the Christian symbol' (*CW*12: 27).

Jung's reading of the Cross and his theory of symbol formation

In order to be able to relate Jung's reading of the Cross to Balthasar's of the Cross-*descensus* it is important to show how Jung's thinking relates to his theory of symbol formation, which can be illustrated from Jung's fairy-tale essay in *Symbolik des Geistes.*

Jung writes briefly about the process of symbol formation in *Psychological Types.* (*CW*6: 478ff.) The opportunity for a new 'living symbol' will arise out of a person's need for a more encompassing world view, when 'already existing symbols offered by established tradition … [are] no longer the unified expression of consciousness and the archetypes of the collective unconscious' (ibid.:

478). The new symbol has to be the product of humanity's 'highest spiritual aspirations' and 'at the same time spring from the deepest roots of [our] being ... the lowest and most primitive levels of the psyche'(ibid.).

New symbols are forged in the conflict of opposites, fundamentally between the spiritual aspirations of rational consciousness and the instinct-like forces of the collective unconscious. This opposition must be brought out into the open: 'For this collaboration of opposing states to be possible at all, they must face one another in the fullest conscious opposition' (ibid.). The risk involved, in psychological terms, is dissociation and psychic splitting, because the conscious ego, bearing the opposition, acknowledges its full involvement in both states: 'This necessarily entails a violent disunion with oneself, to the point where thesis and antithesis negate one another, while the ego is forced to acknowledge its absolute participation in both' (ibid.). This means not only that healthy, living symbols are not the products either of consciousness or of the unconscious alone, but also that, for the process to take place, there needs to be an important moment of relinquishing conscious control. For, 'when there is full parity of the opposites, attested by the ego's absolute participation in both, this necessarily leads to a suspension of the *will*' (ibid.: 479). This does not mean that the psyche goes into a state of mere passivity in the face of the unresolved tension of opposites. Rather, since Jung's energic view of the psyche requires libido to be constantly flowing, 'a damming up of vital energy results', which in turn produces a 'regression of *libido*' in the collective unconscious (ibid.). Jung, in the *Red Book*, associated this regressive descent into the unconscious (as a necessary part of the process of individuation) to motifs in literary classics and also to Christ's descent into Hell (Shamdasani, 2012b:100ff.):

> This is really Good Friday, upon which the Lord died and descended into Hell and completed the mysteries. This is the Good Friday when we complete the Christ in us and we descend to Hell ourselves. This the Good Friday on which we moan and cry to will the completion of Christ, for after his completion we go to Hell.
>
> (*RBLN*: 304)

So, Jung argues, the tension of opposites, after the descent of libido into the unconscious, 'produce[s] [from within the unconscious] a new uniting function that transcends [the opposites]' (*CW6*: 479). What it is that happens in the unconscious (seen as a pool of 'archaic' archetypal contents, existing 'in a state of promiscuity' (ibid.)), that allows a new symbol of greater wholeness to emerge, remains a mystery. Jung liked to refer to it (challenging the classic law of the excluded middle in conscious logical thinking) as a *tertium non datur* (ibid.: 45, 46, 105, 460) – something which could not be logically predicted from the opposites. However, what emerges unites the opposites and provides

> a new content that governs the whole attitude [psychic orientation], putting an end to the division [of opposites] and forcing the energy of the opposites into a common channel. The standstill is overcome and life can flow on with renewed power towards new goals.
>
> (ibid.: 480)

Jung's name for this process of symbol formation as a whole is the transcendent function (ibid.). The process represents the internal dynamic of Jung's process of individuation, through which the threat of dissociation (arising from the tension of opposites) is resolved into an integrated wholeness.[4] He stresses that this involves a descent of psychic energy into the unconscious (which contains the archetype of the Self, wholeness comprised of a *complexio oppositorum*), whence arises the new, living symbol. It is this emphasis on the descent into the (different but not external) unconscious which is useful in a critical comparison of Jung and Balthasar, not least because, as in the quote above from Jung's essay on 'The Transcendent Function', he sees this as a 'movement out of the suspension of opposites' (which suspension itself cannot produce the new symbol), which elsewhere he links in theological terms with the Cross.

Jung's reading of the fairy tale 'The Princess in the Tree'

An example of the process of individuating symbol formation, based on an interpretation of 'The Princess in the Tree' (*PSF*: 231–3 summarizing Zaunert, 1912: 1–14), is offered by Jung in the fairy-tale essay in *Symbolik des Geistes*. While Jung suggests that his analysis will be of primary interest to psychotherapists, he nevertheless makes comparisons at several points with his reading of the Christian theology of salvation.

In this fairy tale, a young swineherd comes across a tree in the woods that reaches to the heavens. He climbs to the top, where he finds a princess (A) held captive in a magic castle by a wicked magician, in the form of a raven. The young man disobeys a prohibition against entering one of the rooms. In it the raven is being crucified. The young man frees the raven, who at once recaptures the princess (A) and takes her back down to earth. The young man is assisted in his quest to find the princess (A) by three animals. She is now imprisoned in a hunting lodge. The young man and the princess (A) make an unsuccessful attempt to escape on the hunter's magic three-legged horse. The princess (A) remains captive but the young man is spared because the hunter was the magician (in the form of a raven) whom the young man had earlier released from his crucifixion. The young man continues his quest and discovers that a witch breeds these magic horses. He manages to secure the witch's own four-legged magic horse by realizing that this requires the sacrifice of lambs to feed (and distract) her guarding wolves.

The young man now rescues the princess (A), destroys the hunter/magician/raven and captures his three-legged horse. The swineherd hero and princess (A) ride away (he on a three-legged; she on a four-legged horse) and are married in her father's kingdom. The young man accedes to the two magic horses' plea to be killed, but their beheading transforms them back into a prince and princess (B), who are thereby released to return to their own kingdom.

In Jung's reading of the fairy tale the (masculine) individuating process of the young swineherd gets under way when he seeks a larger perspective on life by climbing the tree. He responds to his own question to himself: 'How would it be ... if you were to look at the world from the top of that great tree?' (*PSF*: 231). This can be seen in terms of the fulfilment of higher spiritual aspirations. However, he does not yet realize that this will involve engagement with the depths of the collective unconscious, bearing the tension of opposites. This engagement is only enabled to begin because of his response to a prohibition, not to enter one of the rooms of the treetop castle. His disobedience (like that of Adam and Eve in Paradise) turns out to be a *felix culpa* (ibid.: 236).

The opposites that the young man encounters in the higher spiritual realm of the treetop are aspects of himself. There is his (positive) anima, princess (A) (ibid.: 239) (who 'belongs to the upper region of light near the sun' (ibid.: 235f.).) She is 'a kind of *anima mundi* ['soul of the world'] who has got herself into the power of darkness' (ibid.: 236) represented by his (negative) shadow, the raven. The tension of opposites is already in play, for the raven has imprisoned the princess (A). There is an early hint that the resolution of the tension of opposites will involve suffering, in that the raven is being crucified. The young man releases the raven, who recaptures the princess (A) and takes her back down to earth.

The quest for greater wholeness continues, following this descent into the realm of consciousness, where the young man has to strive for an integrated relationship with his anima and his shadow, involving the integration of a fourth, inferior function (ibid.: 238). Here the challenge may be more manageable, since in the earthly realm (of consciousness) anima and shadow 'dwindle to human proportions and thus become approachable' (ibid.: 240). It is now a matter of the four typological functions of consciousness in the young man, where the hunter 'personifies his inferior function' (his dominant function's shadow) and 'the three-legged, all-knowing horse' represents his shadow's spiritual power (ibid.).

In the fairy tale a paired symbol of wholeness (the prince and princess (B)) eventually emerges and is taken by Jung to represent the goal of the quest. As in Christian redemption so also in psychological individuation, this cannot be achieved without sacrifice, requiring 'a work of patience, self-sacrifice and devotion' (ibid.: 241). The young man has to learn from his shadow, the hunter. There can be a failure to gain access to wholeness if the issue of evil is not attended to. A further descent is required into the realm of the unconscious.

The hunter sought to bring a four-legged horse from the unconscious domain by robbery. But the horse lost a leg in an attack by the witch's (evil) wolves. This could have been averted by the sacrifice to the wolves of twelve lambs (which Jung associates with Christ's redemptive 'lamb-sacrifice' (ibid.: n. 53), but 'he forgot to pay tribute to the chthonic powers' (ibid.: 241). As a consequence, the hunter's three-legged horse represents the evil aspect of the Spirit archetype, 'the dark, nocturnal, lower, chthonic element' (ibid.: 234). However, all such symbolic representations of archetypes are ambivalent (since archetypes are by Jung's definition a *complexio oppositorum*): the three-legged horse 'represents a principle which ... betrays affinities with evil, though it is by no means certain that it expresses nothing but evil' (ibid.).

Although in the fairy tale the young man eventually kills the hunter, this is so that he can have access to the three-legged horse as an aid in carrying the process forward. This is interpreted in line with Jung's insistence that the negative opposite must be engaged with, rather than destroyed, for a greater symbol of individuating wholeness to be formed and integrated into living. Thus 'it is possible for a man to attain totality, to become whole, only with the co-operation of the spirit of darkness, indeed ... the latter is actually a *causa instrumentalis* of redemption and individuation' (ibid.: 251f.).

The magician's three-legged horse is not sufficient to enable the young man to journey onward toward wholeness with the princess (A). This happens only when he has secured the witch's four-legged horse, with the necessary lamb-sacrifice. It is the quaternity symbol of the four-legged horse that enables the hero to 'gain possession of his soul' and an integration is effected of 'that which was still needed in order to become whole' (ibid.: 241). Thus, the swineherd and princess (A) return to her father's kingdom and are married.

But we finally discover that what has carried them to this new state of integrated wholeness is an underlying archetype, hidden in the three- and four-legged magic horses. These horses plead to be slain and a semi-divine brother–sister pair, a prince and princess (B), emerge, representing an archetype of the collective unconscious, beyond the consciousness and the personal unconscious of the young man and the princess (A). They are a 'royal brother-sister pair of whose existence the hero and his anima have no notion, and who appear very much out of the blue in the story itself' (ibid.: 246). The princess (B) comes from within the slain three-legged horse. She had been imprisoned within the masculine shadow of the hunter/magician represented by his three-legged horse (ibid.: 245f.). Upon their release the semi-divine pair return to their realm, signifying the *hieros gamos*, the heavenly marriage (ibid.: 229), the *coniunctio oppositorum*. Jung sees such pairings throughout the fairy tale – the young man and the princess (A), the hunter and the witch, the prince and the princess (B) whom he links in theological terms with 'the central Christian idea of *sponsus et sponsa*, Christ and his bride, the Church' (ibid.: 250).

For Jung the individuating symbol-making process involves bearing the tension of opposites. This is a dynamic matter and 'The Princess in the Tree' is a good example for Jung's purposes because it 'reveals with unusual clarity ... the bewildering play of antinomies' involving the alternating movement of life energy oscillating between the extremities of polar opposites, the higher, spiritual, divine and the lower, material, evil, 'all aiming at the great goal of higher consciousness' (ibid.: 239). This is not because Jung held an ontologically dualistic world view; rather, it is an expression of his belief that the spirit archetype is a dualistically monistic entity. The theological intention implicit within this psychological interpretation is for the Christ-symbol to be interpreted in the same way.

Jung argues for the idea of the 'two hands' (ibid.: 240) of the unconscious, and thus 'the essentially antithetical nature of the spirit archetype' (ibid.: 239) with 'a positive, favourable, bright side that points upwards' and a side 'that points downwards, partly negative and unfavourable, partly chthonic' (ibid.: 226). In the fairy tale this manifests as figures that are helpful or obstructive to an individuating consciousness. It appears in a helpful, theriomorphic triple guise of a wolf, a lion and a bear who, by the gift of talismanic strands of hair, help the young man pass the witch's test and gain the magic four-legged horse essential to his quest to rescue the princess (A). It appears in obstructive guise as raven/hunter/magician. The raven in particular represents the struggle with evil. But Jung in making a link with the Cross seems to be looking to interpret that symbol in terms of bearing the tension of opposites. Jung refers to the raven being crucified in the treetop magic castle as 'a state of agonising bondage and suspension' (ibid.: 236). He made an obvious association from this to 'the Saviour who freed the soul of humanity from the domination of the prince of this world' and further linked the (psychological) fairy tale with the (theological) Christ-event with the suggestion that the 'triad of nails' crucifying the raven points to something done 'in the triune name' (ibid.; cf. ibid.: 235).

Jung's final reflection on 'The Princess in the Tree', in a section added when he revised the essay for inclusion in *Symbolik des Geistes* (ibid.: 243–54), notes that this is a German fairy tale and should be read in terms of a thousand-year-old theological conflict between the Christian God and Wotan. Jung thinks that 'in the figure of the hunter we meet an *imago dei*, a God-image' of Wotan (ibid.: 246). The triad of three nails (an inverse symbol of the crucifixion of Christ) with which Wotan imprisons the evil aspect of the spirit archetype shows his involvement in the battle between the nature god who has become more and more evil in conflict with the entire goodness of the Christian God. That is to say,

> in so far as the hunter is a pagan God-image and thus exalted above the world of heroes [swineherd] and paramours of gods [Princess A], the parallelism goes beyond the merely magical into a divine and spiritual sphere, where the evil spirit, the Devil himself – or at least *a* devil – is bound by the spell of an equally mighty or even mightier counter-principle [the

> Christian God] indicated by the three nails. This supreme tension of opposites, the mainspring of the whole drama, is obviously the conflict … in theological terms, between the Christian God and the devil who has assumed the features of Wotan.
>
> (ibid.: 248)

Jung's persistent theme is that this conflict cannot be addressed by the perpetuation of the battle with evil but rather humanity can 'attain totality, … become whole, only with the cooperation of the spirit of darkness' (ibid.: 251).

For Jung the 'worst sin is unconsciousness' (ibid.: 253). He is clear that 'the archetype of the spirit is capable of working for good as well as for evil, but it depends upon man's free – i.e. conscious – decision whether the good also will be perverted into something satanic' (ibid.). This is a cultural and a religious opportunity: 'the most vital task of civilization' (ibid.: 254) and a great challenge for Christianity. For although it 'has shown us the way [in the pattern of redemption] … it has not penetrated deeply enough below the surface' (ibid.: 254). Failure to do so means we will continue to be delivered up to evil. In Jung's view the final reading of 'The Princess in the Tree' arises from the contemporary cultural context of the Christ/Antichrist conflict being fought out, as he wrote, in the war with Nazism (Jung, 1936a; Jung, 1945a) and which provides the urgency for the need to address the conflict of opposites in Christianity. Some of the things that Jung has to say about the Cross from a Christian point of view offer an opportunity to use his pattern of the process of symbol formation as a means of expressing God's saving involvement with evil.

When Jung discusses symbol formation in *Psychological Types* his final comment is that he sees major examples of this process in 'the conflicts experienced by the founders of religion during their initiation period, e.g., the struggle between Jesus and Satan' (*CW*6: 481). This is no doubt a reference to Christ's Temptation. It can also be applied to the Cross.

Jung's further reflections on the Cross in *Aion*

Jung has further reflections in *Aion* on the Cross in relation to this process of symbol formation. Christ finds that his presence in the world provokes the opposition of his adversary. They find themselves increasingly locked into an irresolvable opposition. Humanity in its handling of this primordial conflict needs divine assistance: 'Indeed, it took the intervention of God himself to deliver humanity from the curse of evil, for without his intervention man would have been lost' (*CW*9(ii): 62). The focus of that necessary intervention is the Cross: the 'passion of Christ signifies God's suffering on account of the injustice of the world and the darkness of man' (*PADT*: 157; cf. Dunne, 1987: 25). Christ takes the opposition into himself and bears the suffering of the tension between good and evil by dying on the Cross: 'the crucified Christ hanging between two thieves' ('one of whom goes to paradise, the other down to hell' (Jung, 1952a:

455)) represents 'a real suspension between opposites' (*CW* 9(ii): 69; cf. Jung, 1942/1954: 225, 269; Becker, 2001: 82, 341–4 *passim*). Jung specifically makes the Cross the site of the Christ/Antichrist struggle, for when Christ and Antichrist are held together as a paired symbol this is, for Jung, the meaning of the crucified Christ. The bearing of this conflict of the opposites of good and evil is the sacrifice necessary for salvation:

> the image of the Saviour crucified between two thieves [is the] great symbol [that] tells us that the progressive development and differentiation of consciousness leads to an ever more menacing awareness of the conflict and involves nothing less than a crucifixion of the ego, its agonizing suspension between irreconcilable opposites.
>
> (ibid.: 44)

This illustrates the individuation process, as Jung sees it, 'with an exactness and impressiveness far surpassing our feeble attempts' (ibid.: 45).

This crucifying tension was endured to the death. The loss of psychic energy is signified in the abandonment at the point of death. The life energy sinks with the buried Christ in his descent into hell. It is important for Jung that the scope of redemption goes beyond the limit of human death, 'suggested by the *descensus ad inferos*, the descent of Christ's soul to hell, its work of redemption embracing even the dead' (ibid.: 39), for this allows the depths of the psyche to be activated: 'The psychological equivalent of [the *descensus*] is the integration of the collective unconscious which forms an essential part of the individuation process' (ibid.). Jung also recognizes the importance of the *descensus* in a Christian theology of salvation, for instance, as exemplified in the symbolism of the Roman Catholic Mass. The fraction, the breaking of the Host, is symbolic of Christ's death. Further it symbolizes that the descent into hell was the necessary precursor to the exaltation to glory. Jung speaks of the descent in terms of 'the breaking of the infernal power' (Jung, 1942/1954: 218f.), 'conquering death' (*CW* 12: 339). In the Terry lectures he links this image explicitly to the pattern of the process of symbol formation:

> The three days' descent into hell during death describes the sinking of the vanished value [God] into the unconscious, where, by conquering the power of darkness, it establishes a new order, and then rises up to heaven again, that is, attains supreme clarity of consciousness … [N]o small difficulties stand in the way of finding and recognizing the transformed value.
>
> (*PRTL*: 90)

On one occasion the association of the descent with victory is replaced by a more passive image, where 'Christ lay as one asleep or in the fetters of death during the three days of his descent into hell' (*CW* 12: 354).

From these mysterious depths of the descent there arises the 'transfigured' symbolic figure of greater wholeness, the Risen Christ (Jung, 1946: 305; cf.

*CW*12: 422), who contains and transcends the tension of opposites, a symbol of the *coniunctio oppositorum*. Jung understands that, for Christianity, rather than the resolution of the human conflict of contrary opposites what is at play is the reconciliation of God and creation. He sees this as enacted in the *commixtio* of bread and wine in the Catholic Mass, a reuniting 'mingling of the heavenly and earthly nature of Christ' (Jung, 1942/1954: 220).

In a larger perspective this process of symbol formation illustrates for Jung that the pattern of the process of individuation and the pattern of salvation revealed in Christ correspond. Individuation is 'an heroic and often tragic task' which 'involves suffering, a passion of the ego', suffering 'from the violence done to him by the self'; a similar pattern befalls the incarnate one: 'The divine hero born of man is already threatened with murder; he has nowhere to lay his head, and his death is a gruesome tragedy' (*PADT*: 157). God's action in Christ offers the human being the opportunity to 'get to know the real meaning of his suffering' (ibid.). In individuation there is a process of 'integration of conscious and unconscious', ego and Self, where the 'ordinary, empirical' person, who thought that he or she was fully free and autonomous, 'is burdened with the fate of losing himself in a greater dimension and being robbed of his fancied freedom of will'; as it were, 'his ego enters the "divine" realm, where it participates in "God's suffering"' (ibid.).

Balthasar and the Cross

Jung's reading of the Cross includes the necessity of a psychological *descensus* and the rationally non-predictable emergence of new life possibilities in a symbol of greater wholeness. Balthasar's theodramatic account of the Cross likewise gives a fundamental place to Christ's Holy Saturday *descensus* and to the fundamentally unpredictable nature of the resurrection. Balthasar's dramatic soteriology is set within his entire theological conspectus of events – creation, incarnation, salvation, eschatology – which are first and foremost for him trinitarian events revealing the intra-divine trinitarian life, to which the key is the divine love. These are the themes at large in 'The Action' and 'The Last Act' (volumes four and five of Balthasar's *Theo-Drama*), in his essay *Mysterium Paschale* and in parts of 'The Truth of God' (volume two of his *Theo-Logic*), particularly for this chapter, the section on 'Hell and the Trinity' (Nichols, 2000: 137–248, Wigley, 2010: 103–21). We shall discover, however, that whereas Jung's interpretation begins with the 'horizontal' experience of the tension between good and evil as contrary opposites and only arrives at a resolved symbol of greater wholeness by a 'vertical' descent to the unconscious, Balthasar's interpretation focuses primarily on the 'vertical' action of the theodrama, addressing the dialectic of contradiction arising from humanity's No to God. I discuss his understanding of God's involvement with evil in terms of kenosis, *descensus*, resurrection and the End.

Kenosis

For Balthasar it is 'the pathos of the world stage', the drama of human existence, which provides the locus for the theodrama (*TD*4: 69–201). Christ enters the world's drama 'as God's representative' (ibid.: 427) for the sake of the human inability to resolve the issues of finite human existence, in particular the consequences of humanity's No to God. The theodramatic God who is revealed is trinitarian – the Son shows us the Father and gives us the Spirit. Balthasar's handling of God's involvement with evil through Christ is likewise thoroughly trinitarian, in that he links theological insights in the economy, on the world stage, with the inner-trinitarian life of the God of love.

Balthasar understands creation in terms of God's trinitarian life (*TD*5: 61–109). He distances himself from views that make God dependent upon his creation: 'God does not need the world to confirm him as God or to provide him with a series of stages to go through and so perfect himself' (*TD*2: 261). He also rejects ideas in which creation flows out of the being of God: 'The living God does not pour himself forth by nature' (ibid.).

There is a 'decision to create' (ibid.) a world of finite freedom and this is an entirely non-contingent decision, God exercising his infinite freedom. God freely determines that the world shall exist out of the generosity of kenotic love. This world-creating action is itself an expression of the inner nature of God in Godself: '[a]ll earthly becoming is a reflection of the eternal "happening" in God' (*TD*5: 67), namely the procession within the Trinity, expressing God's kenotic love. This is the essential precondition for a world of space and time: the world's 'primal origin in the Trinity lies in the way in which the Persons of the Trinity "make room" ("space") for one another, granting each other freedom of being and action' (ibid.: 93). Because the being of God, the decision to create and the Christ-event are all expressions of God's love, Balthasar's dramatic soteriology begins at creation rather than incarnation: 'The creation of finite freedom by infinite freedom is the starting point of all theo-drama' (*TD*2: 271). The action that takes place in the world (revealing the economic Trinity) has its source in the life of God (in the immanent Trinity). '[W]ith the unveiling of God's radical activity on the world's behalf in the Christ-event', it is revealed that 'the absolute source of all the dramatic interplay between God and the world is the mystery of that life in God which is shared by the divine life-centres ("Persons")' (*TD*1: 129).

Central to the dilemma of human existence for Balthasar is the dissimilarity between God and his creation. Finite freedom is similar to infinite freedom because the former is real rather than delusional, but dissimilar because finite freedom is inherently limited. Finite humanity cannot fully comprehend infinite being. Consequently,

> man's historical situation in this world is in a state of permanent tension: he is constantly on the lookout for a solution, a redemption [*Erlösung*], but

> can never anticipate or construct it from his own resources; nor does he even have an intimation of it.
>
> (*TD*4: 75)

It is important for Balthasar that his soteriological account of God's involvement with evil in the Christ-event is seen as a trinitarian dramatic action (ibid.: 319–32; cf. *MP*: 136–40). God's ('vertical') response to the contradicting No to God is a manifestation of God's being as love. The nature of that love (revealed in the economic Christ-event) is an (immanent) eternal relationship of mutual self-giving between the Father and the Son through the Spirit. The key, then, to understanding the divine love is kenosis, for

> it is the drama of the 'emptying' of the Father's heart, in the generation of the Son [in the immanent Trinity], that contains and surpasses all possible [economic] drama between God and a world. For any world only has its place within that distinction between Father and Son that is maintained and bridged by the Holy Spirit.
>
> (ibid.: 327)

For Balthasar the key to gaining what insight we can into the divine mystery of salvation as an economic manifestation of the life-love of God is kenosis. The dereliction and *descensus* reveal God's essential kenotic love, which is of a piece with that love within the processions in the eternal Trinity. The abandonment on the Cross

> must lie within the Trinity, in the absolute distance/distinction [*Abstand*][5] between the Hypostasis [the Father] who surrenders the Godhead and the Hypostasis [the Son] who receives it. And while the distance/distinction between these two is eternally confirmed and maintained ('kept open') by the Hypostasis [the Spirit] who proceeds from them, it is transcended in the Godhead that is the absolute gift they have in common.
>
> (ibid.: 333)

The Father's surrendering is a letting-be of self-emptying love. The Son's receiving is a being-let-be of self-emptying love. The Spirit's holding of the resulting distance/distinction is a self-emptying of not demanding any greater separate place or function, content to be the bond of love, maintaining and bridging the distinction.

Descensus

Balthasar gives significant attention in his soteriology not only to the Cross and resurrection but also to Christ's descent into hell, which, like the Cross, is to be understood primarily in terms of the kenotic trinitarian life and love.

Balthasar's vision is of a God who in Christ triumphs over evil by depotentiating it. This is hinted at when Balthasar refers to the Father's missional incarnation of the Son as showing the 'abyss of divine love' (*TD*5: 203). One of the purposes of reflecting on the *descensus* is to allay any hint of triumphalism in the meaning of the Cross, particularly in the light of the continuing reality of evil. In his discussion of the reality of evil Balthasar draws back from sustaining the idea of the Devil as one of the *dramatis personae* and ends with a view of evil as meaninglessness. Evil, nevertheless, remains present and active in the world and, as such, represents a failure of part of God's plan of salvation, 'an eschatological "tragedy" in the very midst of "God's victory"' (ibid.: 212). For Balthasar, even this must somehow be included in what is revealed by Christ of the life and love of God. The *descensus* is important to Balthasar because it enables him to explore further the trinitarian meaning of the cry of dereliction on the Cross through the silence of Holy Saturday: 'It is for the sake of this day that the Son became man' (*MP*: 49; cf. Williams, 2004: 37). As Nichols summarizes: 'Because the Descent is the final point reached by the Kenosis [of the Son], and the Kenosis is the supreme expression of the inner-Trinitarian love, the Christ of Holy Saturday is the consummate icon of what God is like' (ibid.: 7).

It is important for Balthasar that Christ not only suffered separation from God on the point of dying on the Cross whilst still living, but entered into death itself in the *descensus*. Here Christ learns more of the Father, in that:

> During the Son's earthly life the Father had not shown the Son his own 'darkness' – the darkness of sin in the form of his anger – but had 'kept it in his own power'. But when 'the Son passes through hell on Holy Saturday, he does so as one to whom the Father shows his secret because he no longer keeps it for himself.'
>
> (*TD*5: 267 quoting Speyr)

The Son's obedience takes him into hell, 'into the pure essence of sin that has been separated from the world, into what has been condemned by God, in which God cannot be found' (ibid.). It is only in the *descensus* that the mission of the Son is completed.

In insisting that the descent into Hell is part of, indeed the completion of, the Son's mission in the theodrama on the world stage, Balthasar faces inevitable difficulties in seeking to give an account of a place or state or action that is unseeable from the finite, worldly point of view. The language will necessarily be metaphorical. Balthasar prefers Adrienne von Speyr's everyday images of what takes place as a trinitarian event on Holy Saturday to biblical or traditional images of Christ preaching to the imprisoned spirits (1 Pet. 3:18–20), or the harrowing of Hell, the triumphal release of Hell's captives, Adam and Eve and the righteous of the Old Covenant era (*MP*: 7, 151–60).[6] He speaks of the Father offering the Son the mystery of the kenotic separation in Hell in a sense indirectly: 'The dead Son "therefore accepts the mystery of darkness just as the Father offers it to him: in the turning away of the Father himself"' (ibid.: 268 quoting Speyr).

After the ideas opened up in *The Last Act* (*TD*5), Balthasar extended his exploration in *Mysterium Paschale*. He is still searching for the most satisfactory way of describing the state of Christ in Hell. On the one hand, he asserts quite straightforwardly that 'Jesus was really dead', yet he does not think that this amounts to the 'obliterating [of] the human subject altogether' (*MP*: 148). He seems to give approval to a line of thought that 'opens the way to a psychic solidarity between the dead Christ and those who dwell in the Hades of the spirit' (ibid.: 163; cf. *MDR*: 339).

But, rather than pursue this line of thought, Balthasar settles on the ideas of passivity and solidarity with the dead (ibid.: 7). Hell, then, is a state in which activity is no longer possible, where 'the vital activity [is] brought to its end' (ibid.: 148). The emphasis on the passivity of the realm of the dead implies for Balthasar a caution even in using the word 'descend' insofar as it contains 'the unintended and unexamined meaning of an action' (ibid.: 149). Balthasar prefers 'being with the dead' (ibid.: 150; cf. ibid.: 152–60); that is, 'the solidarity of the Crucified with all the human dead' (ibid.: 160). It is in this light that he interprets the small number of New Testament texts referring to Christ among the dead between his death and resurrection.

Solidarity with the dead involves sharing the inability to take action. Christ is one with those who are deprived of strength. Thus he cannot continue to 'conduct an active struggle' (ibid.: 173). Balthasar draws on the distinction between action and contemplation, Good Friday and Holy Saturday: 'This contemplative and objective (passive) moment is what distinguishes Holy Saturday from the subjective and active experience of suffering in the Passion' (ibid.: 172). What Christ experiences as Hell is the 'vision of death' (ibid.: 170f. quoting Nicholas of Cusa) together with the life-consuming reality of 'sin in itself' (ibid.: 173). The tradition has used many images to represent the foulness of this reality, its self-consuming nature, destroying all possibility of life (ibid.: 173f.). It is this in which Christ, in fulfilling his redemptive mission, participates to the full, experiencing 'the absolute emptying of life, which he knew as the Dead One' (ibid. referring to Speyr; cf. ibid.: 185 n. 7).

But it is only by understanding Christ's *descensus* as a trinitarian event that we get the fullest insight into it. The New Testament Hell goes beyond the Old Testament Sheol for Balthasar because, following the letter to the Hebrews, before Christ the theological consequences of humanity's life choices are neither 'in this world nor in the world to come … absolutely definitive'; but because of 'the uniqueness of Christ', humanity 'comes to the unique and definitive decision' (ibid.: 171). Rather than focusing on the rejection of God's grace offered in Christ barring the way to salvation, Balthasar sees this as the Hell of ultimate separation from God which Christ uniquely embraced with saving intent. For Balthasar,

> Hell in the New Testament sense is a function of the Christ event. Now, if Christ has suffered, not only for the elect but for all human beings, he has by this very fact assumed their eschatological 'No' in regard to the event of salvation which came about in him.
>
> (ibid.: 172)

Because all humanity is structurally involved in the No to God arising from the misuse of finite freedom, righteous and sinners alike suffer the consequences of sin, which can be seen as imprisonment within the realm of death. Balthasar affirms this aspect of the Christian theological tradition:

> As yet unexpiated, it followed that all human beings who lived before the coming of Christ, even the holy ancestors, descended into the *infernum*. And so, in order to assume the entire penalty imposed upon sinners, Christ willed not only to die, but to go down, in his soul, *ad infernum*.
>
> (ibid.: 164)

This is on the Irenaean ground that 'only what has been endured is healed and saved' (ibid.: 165 referring to Irenaeus; cf. ibid.: 184 n. 60). Balthasar turns away from seeking to unravel the complexities of why the righteous and sinners alike have to wait in the Sheol of death for redemption, to the assertion of the all-encompassing nature of the divine initiative, understood within the asymmetrical analogy of being: '[In Christ[7]] does not God … englobe, by his own ever greater depth, all the deep places of the underworld? [*Dans le Christ, Dieu n'englobe-t-il pas, … par sa propre et indépassable profondeur, toutes les profondeurs du monde infernal?* (Balthasar, 1981: 160)[8]]' (*MP*: 167).

This shows that the scope of kenotic love in the Godhead can encompass both the experience of finite creation's No to that love (in sin, moral evil) and also its consequences in the inability to escape death as the ultimate horizon of finite life. The place of the 'restorative action is necessarily the place of the original rupture: death, Hades, lostness from God' (ibid.: 12). Christ is the one who

> has undergone [humanity's] fate, including every possible remoteness and alienation from God. Such distance is possible, however, only within the economic Trinity, which transposes the absolute distinction of the Persons in the Godhead from one another into the dimensions of salvation history involving man's sinful distance from God and its atonement.
>
> (*TD*5: 257)

This is accomplished not through a battle with evil but by meeting evil with the good of depotentiating love. The powers of sin and death originate in the misuse of finite freedom in saying No to God. Finite humanity is unable to overcome in its own strength the horizon of finitude, including death. Because

Christ has descended to the realm of the dead, these powers, 'among which is certainly included "the last enemy ... death" (1 Cor. 15:26)', are deprived of their potency. They 'no longer have power to hold men prisoner' (*MP*: 154; cf. ibid.: 154ff. *passim*). By going into death it is God who puts in place the 'boundary stone marking the place where the lowest pitch is reached and the reverse movement set into operation' (ibid.: 167).

The specifically trinitarian aspects that Balthasar explores in *Mysterium Paschale* are aptly summarized by Nichols:

> the God revealed by the Redeemer is a Trinity. Only if the Spirit, as *vinculum amoris* [bond of love] between the Father and the Son, can re-relate Father and Son in their estrangement in the Descent, can the unity of the Revealed and Revealer be maintained ... [even in] its lowest pitch of self-giving love.
>
> (ibid.: 7)

Christ's experience of Holy Saturday is for Balthasar supremely a trinitarian event. In the eternal procession there is through kenotic love an infinite distance/distinction between Father and Son simultaneously held within the greatest intimacy of unbroken union.

Paradoxically, separation is a mode of union:

> the God-forsakenness of the Son during his Passion was just as much a mode of his profound bond with the Father in the Holy Spirit as his death was a mode of his life and his suffering a mode of his bliss.
>
> (*TD5*: 257)

In this sense Balthasar accepts Nicholas of Cusa's play of the opposites of maximum and minimum: in Christ 'the *coincidentia oppositorum* [coincidence of opposites] is also realized, since on the Cross he descends into the uttermost humiliation, without losing his divine majesty' (*TL2*: 213 referring to Nicholas of Cusa; cf. ibid.: 213 n. 99). The Cross-*descensus* event brings together the opposites of exaltation and humiliation: 'for the maximum coincides with the minimum, maximum humiliation, for example, with exaltation' (ibid. n. 99 quoting Nicholas of Cusa). He even goes beyond Nicholas of Cusa, for whom God was *non aliud* [Not-Other], to insist on a place for otherness within God: theology must embrace the realization that 'Jesus Christ's revelation of the Trinity, in which the coessential equality of Father and Son (*aequalitatis*) does not exclude their difference (*alteritas*)' (ibid.: 215f.).

But it is in the world, where finite freedom rejects this kenotic–reconciling love in its No to God, that kenotic love suffers unreconciled separation. God enfolds (englobes, reaches under) this separation to the uttermost in Christ not only by the abandonment of the Cross (which combines the human separation from God and God's separation from God) but also in Hell where sin-separation in itself is experienced by the Father and the Son in the lifelessness of death. Even here the kenotic–reconciling bond of love is not broken in God. The reconciling love revealed through the Spirit in the resurrection is the true ground of hope for humanity. What is eternally and finally new has been eternally true in the triune life of love (*MP*: 174-6):

> That the Redeemer is solidary with the [really] dead, or, better, with [ultimate, 'second'] death ... is the final consequence of the redemptive mission he has received from the Father ... [as] the ... obedient ... dead Christ ... By [this obedience] Christ takes the existential measure of everything that is sheerly contrary to God ... But [the *descensus* also] ... gives the measure of the Father's mission in all its amplitude: the 'exploration' of Hell is an event of the (economic) Trinity.
>
> (ibid.: 174f.)

Because the Father, in his infinite freedom, created human finite freedom 'with all its foreseeable consequences', Hell is within the scope of the initial divine creative initiative. Salvation thus requires the experience by Christ of Holy Saturday. Hell is the ultimate limitation of finite freedom from which created humanity, once locked into the consequences of its No to God, cannot of its own resources break free. However, the Redeemer's 'exploration of the ultimate depths has transformed what was a prison into a way' (ibid.: 175). These depths are formlessly chaotic and are cut off from the vision of the kenotic–reconciling life-love of God. The Redeemer has to see and experience this for himself in order to open up the way of salvation. Again following Irenaeus, Balthasar asserts that '[t]his vision of chaos by the God-man has become for us the condition of our vision of the Divinity' (ibid.; cf. ibid.: 186 n. 95 and ibid.: 185 n. 94).

But it is Adrienne von Speyr whom Balthasar thinks eventually elucidates the trinitarian understanding of the *descensus* better than anyone else 'not only in theory, but also in the most rending depth of experience' (*TL2*: 346; cf. ibid.: 345–61). In drawing particularly on her work *Kreuz und Hölle* (Speyr, 1966; cf. *TL2*: 345 n. 75), Balthasar now sees his idea, in *Mysterium Paschale*, of the *descensus* as 'solidarity with the dead', as a 'compromise' (*TL2*: 345 n. 75). What he now stresses, more radically, is God's own godforsakenness. In the *descensus* Christ is 'dead, no longer speaking as God's Word, [but] "having become the Father's silent Word"', which silence is for humanity an impenetrable mystery, a 'Hell [that] cannot even be "negatively described"' (ibid.: 347 quoting Speyr), nor understood from within. During the *descensus*, the Son 'no longer understands' either his abandonment on the Cross 'or the Father' (ibid.). All is 'absolute meaninglessness', 'sheer futility' – in a word it is 'incomprehensible' (ibid.: 348 referring to Speyr).

In another sense Hell is ultimate contradiction: simultaneously finite and infinite – 'at once atemporal-eternal and self-destroying, perishing', having all being and none, sinless and sin; 'he is at once who he is (the sinless Son of the Father) and who he is not, insofar as he is the bearer of all the sins of the world', travelling in opposite directions at once – '(with the thief on his right) toward paradise and (with the one on his left, in order to fetch him) into deep hell' (ibid.: 351 referring to Speyr). Significantly, whereas Jung relates the image of the two thieves to Christ bearing the contrary opposites of good and evil, Balthasar relates it to him bearing the dialectic of contradiction between heaven and hell: 'The contradiction is, then, that he is at once the farthest from hell, and, as sin-bearer, the closest to it' (ibid. referring to Speyr).

Nevertheless, Balthasar does not link paradoxical difference within God to the worldly experience of contrary opposites, especially not those of good and evil. He sees it as a 'Platonic' mistake (even by 'great Christian thinkers') to see the 'interplay of contrasts', such as light and darkness, 'as indispensable for the beauty of the cosmos and of history' (*TD*5: 503). He rejects what he calls 'purely horizontal' (*TL*2: 353) theologies, like Luther's, with its dialectic of *simul justus et peccator*. His view (*pace* Aquinas) is that the divine plenitude of goodness will be a fulfilment of inexhaustible variety, in which, by the grace of God, creatures, who have known some of that richness, will participate. God's plenitude, a 'kaleidoscopic fullness' of contrasts, must not have imported into it 'the opposition between good and evil' (*TD*5: 503). Such an aesthetic theodicy would be in Balthasar's view a false step. This is the challenge – how to relate Balthasar's 'vertical' and Jung's 'horizontal' views of God's involvement with evil – that will be the focus of chapter nine.

It is indeed the vertical dimension that continues to be explored by seeing that 'hell is a trinitarian event' (*TL*2: 352). For Hell is not a place of horizontal dualistic contrariety but rather the place of the ultimate vertical contradiction of God, and it is this that provides a locus of the saving theodrama. For Balthasar, the eternal intra-divine processions are of a love that reveals simultaneously a distinction and unity of Persons. In *Mysterium Paschale* Balthasar envisaged Hell as the farthest point of distinction between Father and Son, where, in the Spirit as the bond of love, the turning-back occurs. In *TL*2 he adopts Speyr's heightening of the paradox: Hell (as an 'event' in the economy) reveals the distinction and unity simultaneously. Again the key role is played by the Holy Spirit 'in the mystery that the greatest proximity lies hidden in what seems to be the greatest distance' (ibid.: 353). That is to say, there is (in Jungian terms) an *enantiodromia*: Hell thus serves the intra-divine mysteries and their revelation:

> it vividly exhibits and demonstrates the supreme distinction of the Persons and their unimaginable unity. At the point where the Son believes he is most abandoned by the Father, abandonment becomes the means to break open the prison of abandonment, hell, and to admit the Son, along with the redeemed world, into the heaven of the Father.
>
> (ibid. quoting Speyr)

The particular contribution of the Son in this mystery is his obedience. In the eternal procession, there is the kenotic obedience of being-let-be by the Father.

This is played out in the fulfilment of obedience in his mission on the Cross and in Hell: 'proximity and distance are "bound together through obedience"' (ibid.: 355), both 'the hypostatic obedience of the eternal Son' (ibid.: 354) and the obedience of 'the carrying through of his mission' (ibid.: 355). It is in this paradoxical contradiction that the Son's identity consists and by means of which 'from below' he 'vanquishes' (ibid.: 354) the No to God that flows from disobedient misuse of the analogical paradox of similarity-within-ever-greater-dissimilarity between Creator and creation.

It is worth noting in passing that Balthasar does not draw universalist conclusions from his understanding of the *descensus* as a trinitarian event, though there are those who think his denial of universalism belies his underlying attitude (Pitstick, 2007: 270). Balthasar's own view is less certain that all will in the end be saved. In relation 'to the judgment that awaits every single human being, the appropriate attitude will be a hope that is not without a certain fear' (*TD*5: 321). Balthasar prefers to rely on 'God's longsuffering patience' as one who 'does not wish that "any should perish, but that all should reach repentance [2 Pet. 3:9]"' (*MP*: 158). Nevertheless, the final judgement is reserved to God. Balthasar makes a distinction between that part of humanity, once cut off from God as a result of the No of finite freedom, entirely redeemed, and that part finally lost to God. To illustrate from the parable of the Prodigal Son, the younger son is reincorporated into the father's home, but the issue of the eventual loss of the elder son remains open and dependent upon his response to the father's continuing invitation. It is here, according to Balthasar, that

> the distinction between Hades and Hell acquires its theological significance. In rising from the dead, Christ leaves behind him Hades, that is, the state in which humanity is cut off from access to God. But, by virtue of his deepest Trinitarian experience, he takes 'Hell' with him, as the expression of his power to dispose, as judge, the everlasting salvation or the everlasting loss of man.
>
> (ibid.: 177)

This, for Balthasar, must not lead to 'the restrictions of a doctrine of double predestination' but must rather hold fast to a 'universal purpose of salvation' (ibid.: 179) without, however, proceeding to assert a dogmatic universalism, 'the construction of a doctrine of apokatastasis' (ibid.: 181; cf. *TL*2: 359).

The *descensus* shows that God has to go into and beyond the worst of what needs to be addressed by the theodramatic action, not only sin and dying but also the realm of death itself:

> The central issue in theo-drama is that God has made his own the tragic situation of human existence, right down to its ultimate abysses; thus, without drawing its teeth or imposing an extrinsic solution on it, he overcomes it.
>
> (*TD*2: 54)

It seems that insofar as Balthasar discerns a nuanced difference between procession and mission, he relates the kenotic life and love of God to the procession and the reconciling life and love of God to the mission. The 'Son's trinitarian mission' (to reveal and live in obedience to the paradox of the kenotic love that enables the entire distance/distinction of Persons to be held within the eternal (comm)union of the Godhead) 'is at the same time a mission of reconciling the world to God' (*TD*5: 250). The asymmetrical analogy of being can be used to prevent the realities with which the kenotic and reconciling love have to engage in a world that is structurally disordered in its No to God being imputed to the life of Godself.[9] Nevertheless, the similarity finds expression in that in both the processions and the missions there is the same bond of love which maintains unity unbroken. This is true even in the economic realm, where the No to God turns distance/distinction into irreparable separation and calls to the fore the reconciling aspect of the bond of the Spirit.

Resurrection: kenosis–reconciliation

Before we look in more detail at Balthasar's views on resurrection it is important to note that comparison with Jung cannot be extended beyond his views on Cross and *descensus*, since Jung has so little to say on resurrection.

Jung on resurrection

There are only a handful of references to the resurrection of Christ in Jung's *Collected Works* (Forryan and Glover, 1979: 155). In response to a query about this omission, in 1954 Jung wrote a short note, 'On Resurrection' (Jung, 1954b). He does not wrestle as Balthasar does with the issue of the resurrection as a unique ('meta-historical') event set within a historical context (*MP*: 189; cf. ibid.: 189–266 *passim*), even though he acknowledges that the resurrection is 'one of the most – if not the most – important item in the myth or the biography of Christ and in the history of the primitive church' (Jung, 1954b: 692). Indeed, for Balthasar, 'Had Christ not arisen, there would have been neither Church nor faith' (*MP*: 191) Jung notes the tension in Christianity between aspects of the resurrection accounts which, on the one hand, point to 'an individual as well as collective vision' and, on the other, 'insist upon the material concreteness of Christ's [Risen] body' (Jung, 1954b: 693). In the end he counsels setting aside the latter in favour of the former.

Historicity is undermined for Jung because the 'chronology of the eyewitnesses' is 'unreliable' (ibid.). And the concreteness of Christ's bodily resurrection, for him, leads to the unfortunate suggestion of a 'new and incorruptible body' both for redeemed believers and for unredeemed sinners. This has the 'grotesque' consequence for the latter 'that they could be plagued in hell or purgatory for any length of time' (ibid.). On the other hand, Jung takes the accounts of the empty tomb as more historically reliable and concludes that 'the resurrection as a historical and concrete fact cannot be maintained, whereas the vanishing of the corpse could be a real fact' (ibid.).

Jung is, however, clearer about the importance of the resurrection as a psychological (spiritual) event (ibid.: 693–6), which he associates with accounts of the archetypal hero of mythology (who, 'though mortal, death does not annihilate … [and who] continues living in a somewhat modified form'), and of 'the type of the dying and resurrected god' 'who becomes the greater personality in every individual' (ibid.: 694).[10] Jung sees this archetypal process as taking place in Johannine christology, where Christ is 'the complete … man, the self' (ibid.: 693). Thus for Jung 'the Resurrection represents the projection of [a] … realization of the self [as Christ] that had appeared in the figure of a certain man, Jesus of Nazareth' (ibid.: 694).

Jung cannot bridge the gap (Lessing's ugly ditch) between the historical Jesus and the Christ of faith. While we know what Paul and the Gospel writers made of Jesus, 'we don't know to what extent this picture has anything to do with the truly historical man, smothered under an avalanche of projections. Whether he was the eternally living Christ and Logos, we don't know' (ibid.: 695). From a psychological point of view, this is of little importance (though Jung seems to think he probably was not the Logos), since the value of Jesus is that he became the manifest focus of an archetype of the Self, which is already within all humanity, and which, once revealed and appropriated (in the West and its Christianity), enables people to realize their humanity by participating (in the same way as Christ does) in the divine life:

> the [archetypal] image of the God-man lives in everybody and has been incarnated (i.e., projected) in the man Jesus, to make itself visible, so that people could realize him as their own interior *homo*, the self. Thus they had regained their human dignity: everybody had divine nature … and as such they were his brethren, of his nature, and had overcome annihilation … through physical death. They were 'resurrected with Christ.'
>
> (ibid.)

However, what Jung is referring to is resurrection understood not as a transformation through an action of redeeming divine initiative (as in Balthasar), but as the expansion of human consciousness into a realization that the true horizon of life is not space, time and death but timelessness. The integration of archetypal images provides consciousness with 'the feeling of continuing before and after our existence' bringing with it the realization that 'our psychic totality reaches beyond the barrier of space and time' (ibid.), making them (in terms of Jung's concept of synchronicity) 'relative' in relation to the 'eternity or timelessness' (ibid.: 696) of the unconscious.

Jung excuses his lack of greater attention to the resurrection on the grounds that he is 'not a theologian' (ibid.: 692). However, there is ample evidence that Jung has specific theological commitments, with the ongoing mission of the

Holy Spirit as the focus of his interest. Thus he ends his short piece on resurrection by advising Christianity to set aside as primitive the need to express spiritual events and realities in concrete and materialistic ways. In his view the adherents of Christianity cannot move forward while they 'maintain this shocking anachronism' of belief in the resurrection as a solely 'concrete, materialistic event' (ibid.: 696).

Balthasar on resurrection

For Balthasar the resurrection is unexpected. It illustrates various aspects of a trinitarian event. It needs to be understood in relation to eschatology. In relation to the question of God's involvement with evil, it provides another opportunity to state a position about the connection between 'vertical' and 'horizontal' perspectives.

The resurrection itself, despite the emerging belief at the time of Christ in a general resurrection at the end of history, was experienced by the disciples as an unexpected surprise. The resurrection is the starting point for the exploration of the saving meaning of the Cross, binding Cross and resurrection together as a single event (*MP*: 200f.). It is important for Balthasar that the Father makes his risen Son visible in the resurrection, as in the incarnation. What has to be opposed is a spiritualized understanding of the resurrection (such as is found in Jung), as it were, reversing the incarnation:

> We are not to believe that Jesus had to disappear in his bodiliness and become spirit, so that faith in him might be liberated from the obstacle which his personality set up and in that way achieve for the first time its own perfect purity as faith in the invisible.
>
> (ibid.: 206)

Balthasar's primary focus is to understand the resurrection as a trinitarian event. In the New Testament '[t]he Resurrection of the dead Son is consistently ascribed to the action of the Father, and in the closest possible connexion with the Resurrection there is presented to us the outpouring of the divine Spirit' (ibid.: 203). Although Cross and resurrection are separate scenes which follow one another as the theodrama unfolds, they are also to be read as a single event. Balthasar says: 'The whole New Testament is unanimous on this point: the Cross and burial of Christ reveal their significance only in the light of the event of Easter, without which there is no Christian faith' (ibid.: 189). He would resist a distinction between the Cross as a solely human, historical event and the resurrection as a solely divine, suprahistorical event. For him, both reveal aspects of the drama that results from God in Christ entering upon the world stage. This is important in order to avoid any sense that the separation between Father and Son in the dereliction of the Cross is seen as something which then requires a further divine action to rectify. In the eternal Godhead, rather, Father and Son are both distinct and one and this mystery must not be torn apart by an improper reading of the process of change between Cross and resurrection looked at from the perspective of time, since Father and Son within the inner-trinitarian divine life are eternally at an 'extreme distance' from one another and 'always one' (*TD*4: 361f.; cf. *TD*5: 260).

Thus it is together that Cross and resurrection reveal the nature of intra-trinitarian life and love, kenotic and reuniting. Christ's mission was salvific when, on the Cross and even in Hell, divine distance/distinction ('Godforsakenness') is also the 'profound bond' of divine unity (*TD*5: 257). It is through this 'distinction-in-relation' that the 'God-man' on the Cross can redeem that contradicting alienation of finite freedom's No to God (ibid.: 260). It is through the Spirit that Father and Son do not become subject to this alienation, 'since, [he] is not separated like the Son from the Father, [... and] can establish union in the separation of the Son without abolishing the separation' (ibid.: 262 quoting Speyr).

The only 'action' available to Christ in the *descensus* is to endure the end point of kenotic love, that is, utter lonely separation. The Spirit, who has divine infinite freedom to blow where he wills, for Balthasar, 'is the one who brings things into effect' (*TL*3: 238). Only as the resurrection takes place does it become clear that the bond of love has not been broken and that the divine generative, re-creative life continues:

> The mystery of Good Friday and Holy Saturday is thus a mystery of the loneliness of love between Father and Son in the Spirit, so much so that the outcome of these events (in their reunion, in the Resurrection), which is a 'mystery of eternal life', can take place only in 'full loneliness'.
>
> (*TD*5: 269 quoting Speyr)

The separation on the Cross and in the *descensus* is not one of a conflict, needing reconciliation within Godself. Nevertheless, Balthasar speaks of the resurrection in terms of reunion at the completion of the Son's mission, which had involved the utter separation of God from God on Holy Saturday: 'what transpires is the reunion with the Father of the Son who was sent into the world, and to the Cross, a reunion which takes place after the complete fulfilment of his mission' (*MP*: 210). This is realized in and through the work of the Spirit in a way that is continuous with the trinitarian life revealed throughout the mission of the Son:

> The Spirit accompanies the entire work of incarnating the Son in such a way that the Son, in his humanity, can be the Father's word of love both *in* the Spirit and *through* the Spirit who brings the Father's will to him.
>
> (*TL*3: 238)

The Son's accomplishment of his mission is as the one who is 'obedient to the Father in the Spirit', the Spirit who 'creates a seamless unity between the

Father's will and [the Son's] divine–human readiness to accept everything, including the agony on the Mount of Olives' (ibid.: 239) and the abandonment on the Cross and the separation of God from God in Hell in the *descensus*.

The End

The resurrection, together with the other aspects of the event that make up Christ's theodramatic incarnate mission, is to be seen in terms of eschatology. For Balthasar the incarnation is the eschatological starting point, decisively affirmed in the resurrection (*MP*: 196f.), for '[w]ith the Resurrection, the End is, fundamentally, already inaugurated, and what is still to be awaited is merely its definitive entry into vigour' (ibid.: 198). The resurrection is simultaneous (in John 20) with the 'sending forth of the Spirit to the Church and to the redeemed world' (ibid.: 210) until the End.

Balthasar and Jung shared an acceptance of the continuing post-Easter reality of the conflict of good and evil seen in theological as well as moral terms. However, their understandings were significantly different.

Jung was enthralled by the massive conflicts of the twentieth century. His reading of these events included the idea that, as in New Testament times, they were a highly significant outburst, in Western European civilization, of the Christ/Antichrist conflict. As we saw earlier, as Jung persisted with his project in relation to Christianity, this became for him a symptom indicating that the Son-phase of the divine drama could not release itself from the irresolvable conflict of the hostile brothers, Christ and Satan. This could take place, within his 'Joachimite' theological orientation, only in a new work of salvation by the Holy Spirit with human (and analytical psychological) cooperation.

Balthasar, with his *corpus triforme* theological orientation, resists any such 'Joachimite' idea of progressive periodization (cf. *TD*4: 428f. referring to Hegel and ibid.: 457f. referring to Joachim de Fiore). Balthasar says rather: 'Only after Christ does there arise that concentration of satanic and anti-Christian powers in world history' (*TD*2: 145 referring to Irenaeus). Balthasar relates this intensification to a direct opposition to the mission of Christ: Satan 'must come forward when what is at stake is Jesus' mission as such' (*TD*3: 476). He notes in relation to Christ's temptations in the wilderness that the 'very point the Tempter ("Satan", Matt. 4:10) wishes to attack … is Jesus' mission as the "Son of God" (Luke 4:3, 9)' (ibid.: 477; cf. ibid.: 475, 476).

Balthasar's trinitarian pattern is one of mutual coinherence at every stage: on the Cross

> the sinful world, alienated from God, is taken into the infinite Father/Son relationship (which is now 'economic'); when the Son accomplishes his mission… and gives [the Spirit] back to the Father, the Spirit is breathed into a mankind that has been redeemed by the Passion, namely the Church of Christ. For the Spirit accompanies the Son's entire mission, shares

> in the experience of it and, as it were, enfolds this mission in himself. He is simultaneously the Spirit of the Father who surrenders his Son and that of the sacrificed and glorified Son; his is the trinitarian Spirit, yet he informs the entire 'economy', and so he contains within himself, in unity, both the movement toward the Cross and the movement from Cross to Resurrection.
>
> (*TD*4: 384)

Balthasar accepts that 'the battle of the Logos' continues, for although

> Jesus Christ stands in world history as God's representative … [and] emerges from this battle victorious, through his death on the Cross, his *descensus* and his Resurrection, … this does not mean that all his work is done … [for he cannot yet] hand the perfected kingdom over to the Father.
>
> (ibid.: 427)

The period of history after the Christ-event has to be viewed eschatologically and as an application of his law of proportionate polarization ('the more God intervenes, the more he elicits opposition' (ibid.: 51)). That is to say, after Christ the conflict with evil intensifies until the end, until the completion of the last act. This is because of the 'provocation' offered by Jesus in claiming 'to have reconciled the world in God' (ibid.: 442).

Balthasar, thus, holds a version of realized eschatology. One view would maintain a linear (horizontal) view of history which would at the eventual end of chronological time be rounded off by a surprising, finally transformative completion. On this view Christ's life and work would be seen primarily in linear historical terms, starting to make this qualitatively different sort of ending real by (proleptically) embodying it and thereby making it a factor to be taken into account. Balthasar's (Johannine) version is more radical:

> For John, the Christ-event … is the vertical irruption of the fulfilment into horizontal time; such irruption does not leave this time – with its present, past and future – unchanged, but it draws it into itself and thereby gives it a new character.
>
> (*TD*5: 25)

For Balthasar this is not first and foremost a historical statement as if to suggest that the primary theological datum was the birth of Christ. It is rather that the Trinity is revealed on the world stage by the advent of the Logos, so that 'the real "last thing" is the triune life of God disclosed in Jesus Christ' (ibid.: 57).

There are in Balthasar's discussion of the Cross-*descensus*-resurrection indications of how he sees the 'vertical' understanding of the Christ-event in tension with any 'horizontal' understandings, such as that of Jung. In chapter nine, I construct a model in which Balthasar's and Jung's views of the Cross-*descensus* are brought together, drawing on psychological and theological insights, in an account of God's involvement with evil.

Notes

1 Uhsadel was pastor at St Gertrude, Hamburg in the 1930s and Professor of Practical Theology at Tübingen after the Second World War. He promoted the use of psychology in practical theology (Uhsadel, 1966: 99).
2 'Sacristy' in English refers to a room (or storage area) in which sacred objects can be kept when they are not in use in worship. But Uhsadel seems to be suggesting that the stained-glass window made Jung's consulting room a place of religious or spiritual activity.
3 I acknowledge the help of Jack Herbert with this translation.
4 Huskinson, in comparing Jung with Nietzsche, notes that Jung has a greater emphasis on a 'third thing' to provide resolution (Huskinson, 2004: 70 quoting Jung, 1916/1957: 90), whereas Nietzsche, reading Heraclitus differently from Jung, envisages that the energy of opposites in themselves can produce greater wholeness (ibid.: 81–5): 'Jung relies on a third thing external to the opposites to initiate their union, while Nietzsche does not' (ibid.: 161). Jung's third thing, however, does not come from a source entirely external to the opposites themselves (as Jung's use of the word 'transcendent' might be taken to indicate), for it is the same psychic energy, charged by the opposites themselves, that produces the new, living symbol of greater wholeness.
5 '*Abstand* can mean either' (Williams, 2004: 41).
6 Pitstick argues that this improperly shifts the emphasis on the Descent from 'the beginning of the glory of Easter Day' to 'a continuation of the suffering of Good Friday' (Pitstick, 2007: 84). By contrast Oakes argues that Balthasar's ideas are an 'authentic development' of Roman Catholic doctrine (Oakes, 2007a: 184).
7 Omitted from *MP*: 167.
8 The English translation for *MP* is using the French second edition. At this point the German new edition has: 'Untergreift Gott in Christus nicht, ... durch seiner eigene je größere Tiefe alle Tiefen der Unterwelt?' (Balthasar, 1990c: 160), which speaks of God 'reaching under' all the deep places.
9 Kilby is not persuaded that Balthasar has avoided this (Kilby, 2012: 115–22).
10 Balthasar sees this as an idea from the history of religions that is 'barely pertinent at all' as the background to the biblical texts (*MP*: 199).

Part IV

Conclusion

Chapter 9

A cruciform model for God's involvement with evil

Jung's project in relation to Christianity sought to address the wound of the irresolvable conflict between good and evil, epitomized for him in the Christ/Antichrist conflict. Balthasar likewise speaks of theodramatic salvation in terms of healing 'the wounds that existence bears', namely death, freedom, power and evil; these are the wounds that 'sharpen the problem of existence to the point of rendering it unbearable', and as a consequence (which Jung could claim his psychology affirms) 'all human life becomes an uninterrupted, chaotic searching and feeling after a totality of meaning' (*TD*4: 77). In this chapter I make use of aspects of both Jung's and Balthasar's approaches to Christ's Cross-*descensus* in order to construct a model of God's involvement with evil. For both men the Cross-*descensus* functions as a means of exploring the healing of aspects of the polarity of good and evil. The central theme to be explored is that of the relation and interplay of God's 'vertical' theodramatic action in relation to the divine/human contradiction, in Balthasar, held in creative, cruciform tension with the 'horizontal' human struggle with good and evil as contrary opposites, in Jung.

Jung makes a few remarks about the Cross in relation to good and evil. I have related these to his theory of symbol formation. Likewise I have drawn out from his predominant, though largely implicit, 'Joachimite' theological agenda further thinking about the Cross. This constructive approach is at least consonant with Jung's psychotherapeutic method, leaving it to his 'patient' to work with what seems important from among his proffered interpretations. Also, although Balthasar has a considerable amount to say about the Cross-*descensus*-resurrection and the question of God's involvement with evil, he does not conduct this discussion explicitly in relation to Jung. The focus of this exercise in construction is to explore whether and how Balthasar's and Jung's ideas can be brought together fruitfully even if the discussion goes in directions they themselves might have resisted.

There are three aspects to the model that I suggest: first, holding together at right angles Balthasar's 'vertical' and Jung's 'horizontal' understanding of the Cross; second, taking account of the fact that Jung's reading of the Cross-*descensus* (as an illustration of his theory of symbol formation) involves a descent into the unconscious, which can be related analogically to Balthasar's understanding of Christ's descent to the dead; and, third, allowing the Balthasarian suggestion that God's 'vertical' involvement with evil in the Cross-*descensus*-resurrection encompasses a Jungian 'horizontal' understanding of the Cross-*descensus.*

Balthasar's approach can be characterized as 'vertical' in that he was concerned with a polarity of contradiction between God and humanity. Evil arises by humanity's misuse of finite freedom, defining itself in terms of its own (limited) autonomy, rather than as in receipt of finite freedom as a gift from the triune Creator. This fundamental No to God sets up an opposition which is a contra-diction, a polarity of contradictory refusal. This disobedience produces the structural fault in humanity as a consequence of which it has to endure sin and death. With the advent of Christ, in Balthasar's theology, the contradictory No to God is intensified in the struggle between Christ and the counter-speaking Antichrist. God responds not with force but with an intensification of the kenosis of love in Christ's Cross-*descensus.*

For Jung's 'horizontal' approach a key starting point is the human experience of the tension of good and evil as contrary opposites, whose meaning finds expression in the Christ/Antichrist conflict, in the archetypal theme of hostile brothers. In his Quaternity suggestion Jung proposes that this conflict is not able to be resolved except through the further work of the Holy Spirit and the (psychologically aware) human being. But in his passing remarks about the Cross as a numinous archetypal symbol, Jung envisages that (God in) Christ bears in himself the tension of the contrary opposites of good and evil. Balthasar is wary of founding his theology on the psychological struggle by Christ with evil as the contrary opposite of good, in part to avoid the danger of a dualistic theology. His emphasis is, rather, that Christ responds to the challenge of Antichrist in keeping with the nature of the infinitely free life and love of the triune God.

The Cross is not, however, the end of the matter. For neither Jung nor Balthasar does it represent an entire resolution of either contradiction or contrariety. For both there needs to be a *descensus*. Balthasar struggles to find an account with which he is fully satisfied but, as well as exploring from an experiential point of view what being among the dead might mean, he also sees this as a trinitarian event in which God undergoes godforsakenness. For Jung, Christ's dying and *descensus* are analogous to the sinking of libidinal psychic energy into the unconscious (which calls for an act of sacrifice by the ego), when consciousness has failed to resolve the conflict of contrary opposites. There, at the archetypal level, inaccessible to consciousness, the tension of opposites mysteriously produces (by what in his theory of symbol formation Jung calls the transcendent function) a numinous, energy-rich symbol of greater wholeness, which sustains psychologically integrated living. For both Jung and Balthasar the outcome is humanly speaking an unpredictable surprise. For Balthasar the appearance of the Risen Lord is unexpected from any human perspective. But in the *descensus* as a trinitarian event, even at the ultimate point of distance/distinction between Father and Son, the bond of love in the Holy Spirit remains unbroken. This mystery is the unpredictable source of resurrection as the healing of the divine–human contradiction. For Jung the emergence into consciousness of a symbol of greater wholeness (which, after the archetypal pattern of dualistic monism, is a *complexio oppositorum*) is likewise unpredictable from the opposites in their contrariety. It appears as a *tertium non datur*.

The construction of the model presented here relies upon relating Balthasar's 'vertical' with Jung's 'horizontal' approach. It relies also upon accepting that Jung's insistence on the experience of good and evil as contrary opposites is not taken to imply that his ontology of the psyche is dualistic, since the archetypal structure of the psyche is that of a wholeness best understood as a dualistic monism. Nevertheless, Jung's contribution is thoroughly anthropological and relies on a theory of direct correspondence for connection to theology. Since Jung's psychology is based on a dualistic monism, his probable preferred option would be to develop a doctrine of God as a unity which is also a *complexio oppositorum*. However, I take a Balthasarian similarity-within-ever-greater-dissimilarity approach to be more satisfactory than direct correspondence, even though both are susceptible to exaggeration. Jung's linking of the human process of psychological development directly to the divine life is open to the criticism of being over-anthropomorphic or psychologically reductive, even though Jung protested that this was never his intention. This underlies Balthasar's resistance to any form of process theology: 'We cannot speak of a "process" in God, as if he could attain fullness only through the world's sinful alienation from him and through his Son's Cross' (*TD*5: 264). But there can be a danger in the other direction, from overemphasizing dissimilarity, in claiming, as Balthasar does – in line with the mainstream of Christian tradition – that although Christ was tempted in the same way that humanity is yet he did not commit sin. If this is handled without sufficient sophistication it can tend in the direction of docetic perfectionism.

My suggestion is that we allow (as Jung suggests) that on the Cross (as elsewhere during the incarnation) Christ experienced a real battle within himself between the opposites of good and evil (thereby suffering the trial common to humanity), and at the same time retain the restraint of a (Balthasarian) asymmetrical theory of analogy to prevent the imputation of that same struggle to God in Godself. Even if God's inner-trinitarian unity in some sense can be said to combine opposites it will not be (by direct correspondence) in the same way that those opposites (such as good and evil) are experienced in their worldly sense. Balthasar's discussion of the inner-trinitarian life is helpful since he envisages a divine love that allows for infinite distance/distinction (without alienation) existing together with complete unity. This intra-divine unity-in-difference (a form of *complexio oppositorum*) is revealed in the Cross-*descensus*-resurrection as love (held in unbroken bond) which is simultaneously kenotic and reconciling.

Because the divine bond of love holds through and beyond all the possible contradictions of sin, death and Hell (including the crucifying experience of contrary opposites), which in the Cross and *descensus* separate God from God, the resurrection takes place as a humanly unpredicted saving event offering the hope of inclusion in the divine life of the End for all finite creation. In this way God has become involved with evil and has overcome it by being defeated-and-yet-not-defeated, in that, in the resurrection, kenotic and reuniting love has made reconciling atonement an accessible reality: 'The Resurrection not only guarantees redemption: it enables the natural man to be whole' (*TD*2: 409). It is within this overall theological pattern of the redemption from contradiction that a psychotherapeutic process of individuating wholeness (healing the wound of the unresolved tension of contrary opposites) can offer its assistance to Christian practical theology, as Jung intended in the first phase of his project in relation to Christianity.

This cruciform model for God's involvement with evil drawing on both Jung and Balthasar raises a number of issues: the relationship of Balthasar as a type 2 contextualizing theologian and Jung as a type 4 reinterpretive psychologist; human experience and the divine action in relation to evil; how 'vertical' and 'horizontal' interrelate; the exception of the polarity of good and evil; and *descensus* in Balthasar and Jung.

The relationship between Balthasar as a contextualizing theologian and Jung as a reinterpretive psychologist

In the adapted Frei/Ford typology that I have used to frame the construction of a critical comparison between Balthasar and Jung, a notable feature of both a type 2 contextualizing theology and a type 4 reinterpretive psychology is that they give priority to the self-description of their own community of practice, whether the Roman Catholic Church and its theology or Jungian psychotherapy and its theory. If dialogue is to be maintained within this frame of reference it will have to endure a certain tension, avoiding either collapse into (a type 3) *ad hoc* complementarity or separation into (a type 5) mutual exclusion. The latter tendency is evident in both Balthasar and Jung. Jung begins with the human experience of duality between good and evil and proposes a process that allows for wholeness, and he uses this to propose an improved interpretation of the Cross-*descensus*, insofar as it exemplifies his theory of symbol formation, as a universal psychological process. Balthasar begins with the vision of trinitarian divine glory as infinitely free life and love, a unity which paradoxically includes distance/distinction. This is the truth that the trinitarian Christ-event reveals. It is the divine initiative in the theodramatic action that provides the enfolding within which the human experience of alienation discovers its meaning and resolution. There is, it seems, an either/or choice of starting point between a non-contingent divine initiative and a universal human process. Balthasar thinks that if we start with the human experience, we shall lose sight of the divine action: 'The anthropocentric tendency will never be able to keep within view the Trinitarian background of the Cross' (*MP*: 140).

My model acknowledges that Jung's human process involves a 'vertical' as well as a 'horizontal' psychological dimension, and also avoids making this the direct basis of an account of inner-trinitarian life. Such a trade-off might well not have been acceptable to either Jung or Balthasar themselves. The model implies that on the Cross God in Christ took part in the human predicament, with a greater degree of psychological participation (through 'the pain of God') in the economic realm than Balthasar seems willing to accept. It also requires Jung to accept a Balthasarian view of analogy, such that even though the Cross involves God suffering the temptation of the tension of opposites as human beings do, this does not mean there are contrary opposites of good and evil within Godself.

This compromise provides a means by which to envisage the shape of Jung's process of symbol formation as enriching and complementing a Balthasarian theology of the Cross as the divine saving initiative. Jung claimed never to want to replace theology with psychology, but to offer insights that theology would find affirming of revealed truth. This might be acceptable to Balthasar if he were reassured that Jung was not trying to reductively entangle the Christ-event in the laws of human processes and that Jung was prepared to let the theologian speak in terms of divine transformation (without repeating too loudly his scientist's necessary agnosticism about such 'metaphysical' claims). The complexity of the challenge for a dialogue of this sort is clear, when Balthasar says:

> God, desiring to reconcile the world to himself (and hence himself to the world), acts dramatically in the Son's Cross and Resurrection. This dramatic aspect does not entangle the immanent Trinity in the world's fate, as occurs in mythology, but it *does* lift the latter's fate to the level of the economic Trinity, which always presupposes the immanent. This is because the Son's eternal, holy distance from the Father, in the Spirit, forms the basis on which the unholy distance of the world's sin can be transposed into it, can be transcended and overcome by it ... in the temporal acts of the concrete Christ-event and its consequences ... [not] ... reduced to philosophical or timelessly abstract principles.
>
> (*TD*4: 362)

This would call for a willingness on Jung's part to see that what Balthasar sees as the divine action encompasses without making redundant his analysis of the human predicament. Further, if the dialogue were to continue, Balthasar would need to exercise a certain reticence about the dangers he sees in the sort of spiritual exploration that Jung thinks is important, namely accepting that there has to be an engagement in the spiritual struggle between good and evil. For Balthasar this is a danger for those outside the (Catholic) Church, who risk not being brought into the arena of salvation.

> Whether he is aware of it or not, the sinner who deliberately leaves the area between himself and God in which God's Holy Spirit operates – communicating divine grace and a divine mission to him – enters a contrary realm inhabited by a spirit that is hostile to God. He finds himself under the spell of a contrary spirit and, like a sorcerer's apprentice, cannot extricate himself from it.
>
> (*TD*3: 486)

In such a mood, for Balthasar, it is a matter of choice between the non-believing world, which Jung's insights might well describe accurately (where people are in the grip of 'overwhelming power'), and the world that faith in Christ offers, since 'Christ died on the Cross … [there]by loosing us from the sphere of the anti-divine spirit' (ibid.).

Human experience and the divine action in relation to evil

In relation to the reality of evil, Balthasar thinks that some questions can be given 'no clear answer', for instance, 'whether, behind the destructive cosmic powers, there is a free intelligence unmistakably bent on evil' (*TD*4: 137). Nevertheless, he would agree with Jung about the importance of recognizing the anthropological reality of evil, even though he might be more optimistic than Jung about the universal, conscious level of awareness: [e]veryone knows that the powers of evil are not simply alien and external to him; everyone knows that there is a shaft in him that reaches down to the deepest abysses' (ibid.).

But Balthasar's own main focus in relation to the human experience of evil is on the misuse of the gift of finite freedom. Humanity 'knows from [its] own experience of [it]self that evil in the world comes from freedom' that gives in to the 'temptation to evil', which is to use power as 'a means of domination' (ibid.). As a consequence humanity is '[subject] to death, free to commit evil and implicated in the world's suffering' (ibid.: 201). This is a perversion of the finite freedom which was intended, rather, to be used to find meaning and fulfilment in relation to the God who is love. Evil is '[humanity]'s revolt against [its] essential structure', in which 'the self tries to prescind from its rootedness in God and establish its own autonomy' (ibid.: 147; cf. *TD*4: 137–201), snatching after power. This includes humanity arrogating to itself the authority to define goodness, setting '[it]self up as the standard of the good, thus subordinating goodness to [its] own exercise of power' (ibid.: 151) rather than, as in God's creating intention, 'know[ing] that [its] personal autonomy is a gift and allow[ing] the image of God to radiate through [it]' (ibid.: 155).

Balthasar does not underestimate the challenge that evil represents. Existence presents the deepest of riddles of 'labyrinthine complexity' (ibid.: 489). We have to ask, 'Is our guilt not inextricably matted with the whole sickness of being, and hence irredeemable?' (ibid.: 490). This has significant resonance with the insistence in Jung's question, in *After the Catastrophe*, about how humanity can live in the face of horrendous evil.

Balthasar's response differs from that of Jung in two major ways: first, although Christ, in becoming sin, took on the problem of evil, he did not participate in it intrapsychically as the rest of humanity has to (as the tension of contrary opposites); second, although Balthasar acknowledges the force of the question – '[H]ow dare we give the name of "Love" to [such a world's] Originator?' (ibid.) – he resists any suggestion of a duality which accepting a Jungian dark side to God could imply. This raises questions about that aspect of the patristic tradition which presses for a fully human aspect to the incarnation on the grounds that only that which has been taken on can be healed.

How 'vertical' and 'horizontal' interrelate

In the *Epilogue* to his trilogy Balthasar relates the distinction between a 'vertical' dialectic of contradiction and a 'horizontal' experience of contrary opposites to different meanings of the 'polarity in being' (*EP*: 55–7 *passim*). The primary ('vertical') polarity of Being 'determines everything in the ['horizontal'] world', and the 'vertical' polarity is not an axis connecting equal and opposite poles but rather a link of similarity-within-ever-greater-dissimilarity between Being and beings: 'Being [*Sein*] gives to beings [*Wesen*] its own indivisibility, while the [uniquely indivisible] beings give to Being … its *real*-ization' (ibid.: 55). There are also polarities experienced in the 'horizontal' world. The polarity, for instance, between body and spirit is a matter of contrary opposites and the challenge is to seek 'a relatively secure tension-in-unity of these antitheses' (Przywara, 1935: 128). In this sense 'the creature [is] … *a being of tensions*' (ibid.). This is held within the greater 'vertical' polarity, which Balthasar (like Pzrywara) refers to as one of 'contradiction', between God and his creation, in which God, who is beyond creation, ('synoptically') holds the whole of creation and its contrary oppositions. Przywara identifies this as a Thomist Catholic philosophical approach rather than an Augustinian one, which sees the horizontal polarities as an aspect of the fallenness of creation. Balthasar follows Przywara in asserting that horizontal polarities 'must not be understood as a declension [*Abfall*] from the divine identity' (*EP*: 56). In the Thomist view, there is a more optimistic understanding that the horizontal polarities of contrary opposites (such as body–spirit) are a function of wholeness. The body–spirit polarity 'ultimately signifies the unity of the *unum ens* [one being] of the human being' (Przywara, 1935: 134). In the terms with which I have been describing Jung's ideas, this is a form of dualistic monism, a *complexio oppositorum*.

Balthasar hints at the primary basis on which the two sorts of polarity are linked, that is, by the nature of the divine love, which persists both in the experience of difference in worldly polarities and in their fulfilled 'perfection' (that is, in Jungian terms, when they relate as opposites and find wholeness):

> If this difference [between the two sorts of polarity] really is the presupposition for the interconnectedness, communication, and mutual exchange among the [finite] entities … then this difference forms the ontic first step of what love is among free entities. … [And] we can ask … whether and how this intraworldly perfection can be grounded in love.
>
> (*EP*: 56)

Balthasar develops this not philosophically (or psychologically) but in terms of the Christ-event and what it reveals about the inner-trinitarian love. Christ recapitulates, gathers up and transfigures the human experience of polarity into that paradox of love which is 'the infinite distance between the Divine Persons in the identity of the divine nature' (*TL2*: 315).

The occasional metaphors that Balthasar uses to describe the connection between the two polarities are cruciform, representable graphically as a cross set within a globe or sphere (which is also an archetypical image Jung invokes to express wholeness). Balthasar speaks of the action of God 'englobing' the human predicament, with a 'stepwise' or a 'perpendicular' interrelation between the vertical and horizontal dimensions.

The 'vertical' direction of travel (the analogical basis on which God and humanity are connected) requires that the life of God, which is unity-in-difference, be lived out on the world stage where the effects of humanity's No to God have to be taken into account. It is what the Son endures in the life of the world that links these two dimensions (*TD5*: 257). Within the Trinity, distance/distinction is an aspect of divine (kenotic) love. In the fallen world it is experienced as alienation, which changes the direction of orientation. This calls for a 'stepwise' involvement, accepting the worldly reality of alienation:

> The Son is eternally begotten by the Father: within the infinite divine nature, in other words, one Person is 'let be' in absolute Otherness; what deep abysses are here! God has *always* plumbed them, but once a finite world of creatures has been opened up, these depths must be traversed stepwise as forms of alienation [*schrittweise als Formen der Entfremdung durchwandert* (Balthasar, 1983: 459)]. Nonetheless these steps can only be taken as part of a journey already (and always) accomplished in the infinite Trinity. And when the particular mystery of the Son's Incarnation takes place, he traverses [*durchschreitet* (ibid.)] – as man and together with all sufferers and on their behalf – the realms of forsakenness that, as God, he has already (and has always) traversed.
>
> (*TD5*: 502)

It may be at this point that Balthasar is indicating that a journey through alienation has to be undertaken step by step, rather than, as it were, at right angles. However, on another occasion, he uses just such a geometrical metaphor when he speaks of the divine action related as 'perpendicular' (at right angles) to the human predicament:

> We must not be afraid to utter the harsh truth. In making his provocative claim to have reconciled the world in God, Jesus never suggested that he was creating an earthly paradise. The kingdom of God will never be externally demonstrable (Lk. 17:21); it grows, invisibly, perpendicular to world history [*es wächst, unsichtbar, quer durch die Weltgeschichte hindurch* (Balthasar, 1980: 413)] ... Man responds to this provocation by attempting to manufacture the kingdom of God on earth, with increasing means and methods of power; ... this power that resists the powerlessness of the Cross is bound to destroy itself, for it bears the principle of self-annihilation within it by saying No to the claim of Christ. ... [Mankind] has already decided its own fate.
>
> (*TD*4: 442)

In a passage in Przywara's *Deus Semper Maior*, there is a similar allusion to the way in which the 'vertical' (divine) and 'horizontal' (human) dimensions intersect in the Cross and so metaphorically in a cross-wise fashion. There is a 'double rhythm' [*Doppelrhythmus*] held together in the Cross as 'intersection [*Kreuzung*]', in which God's participation in the 'rift [*Riß*]' between the Creator and the fallen world both bears and redeems the polarities of contrary opposites (such as body and spirit, man and woman, individual and community) which are constitutive of humanity. Thus these 'contraries are atoned for in the beams of the Cross [*dann ... beide Gegen erlöst werden zu den Balken des Kreuzes*]' (Przywara, 1938: 71–74 *passim*[1]). Jung, in his Eranos lecture on the Trinity, refers to this passage ('Przywara's meditation on the Cross and its relationship to God' (*PCT*: 28 n. 24; cf. *PADT*: 170 n. 10)) as supporting his view that the Cross 'represents ... God's suffering in direct collision with the world' (ibid.: 21). In this, Jung and Balthasar both see the 'vertical' divine action and the 'horizontal' human experience relating to one another at right angles.

But what is the meaning to be ascribed to this cruciform interaction? Balthasar's theory of analogy could allow that even though divine kenosis (on a 'vertical' axis) is different from, set at right angles to, human alienation (on a 'horizontal' axis), yet they are connected by some similarity. Can human experience provide metaphors that give reliable insight into the divine nature? In principle, Balthasar would say yes, though with provisos. For instance, 'the creaturely process of becoming' can provide 'an "image" of [the] primal life' of the Trinity (even though 'the Trinity must not under any circumstances be described as a "becoming"')' (*TD*2: 261).

He notes, further, that Aquinas envisages the possibility of polar opposites in God. A consequence of asserting the primacy of divine Being was the impulse to include in God all forms of being, even those that contain internal contrariety, resulting in the suggestion that in God there is an interpenetration of opposites: 'things which are "manifold and opposed" in themselves (*diversa et opposita in seipsus*) are one and joined (indeed, they interpenetrate) in God' (*TD*1: 549). However, Balthasar is always clear that this is not to open a door to theological dualism. He and Jung both alike hold a dualistic monism. For Jung this is the wholeness of a *complexio oppositorum*; for Balthasar it is the principle of unity-in-difference, both within creation and in the divine life. Balthasar says: 'genuine unity always creates and sustains difference; this is true of what arises from below, from organic nature and human society, but also of what comes from above, from the kingdom of eternal, triune love' (*TD*4: 409). For Balthasar the inner-trinitarian life is both sufficiently distinct/distant to be referred to in terms of opposition and simultaneously a completely interpenetrating unity. In the Trinity, '[t]he hypostatic modes of being constitute the greatest imaginable opposition to one another, ... in order that they can mutually interpenetrate in the most intimate manner conceivable' (*TD*2: 258).

It is important, however, not to stress the similarity of this aspect of the divine inner life in a way that links it, by direct correspondence, to the human experience of the tension of opposites. Balthasar's understanding of what constitutes the inner-trinitarian life and love provides a different way of envisaging the understanding of a dualistic monism within which Jung frames the human tension of opposites. He would not want to speak in Jungian terms about dualistic monism in relation to God as a unity which holds together both good and evil within the divine life. It is, nevertheless, possible to speak in Balthasarian terms about the nature of the love of God in a way that is likewise consistent with dualistic monism. The divine love for Balthasar is kenotic. In the intra-divine processions this love allows for both the infinite difference/distance of Father and Son and also for the most intimate and unbroken (comm)union maintained in love through the Spirit. It is this intra-divine dualistic monism of kenotic–uniting love which also characterizes the missions of Son and Spirit. Human contrariety and its consequences, the irresolvable tension of contrary opposites, are enfolded/englobed by divine action within the 'vertical' dimension of the contradiction of the No to God. It is important for Balthasar that this is effected by the dissimilarity of divine love, as it were at right angles in relation to the tragedy of the human condition, as well as that this 'vertical' love in action should reach right under the entire depths of human sin and suffering to death – and beyond.

The exception of the polarity of good and evil

This aspect of dissimilarity is a key feature of Balthasar's approach. He resists any suggestion that in this action Christ is participating in the human predicament of (what Jung seems to imply by) a crucifying involvement in both evil and good. Balthasar's view is that the 'suffering of the Lord' was unique and 'not just an intensification of common human suffering', and it must be explained 'on trinitarian lines' (Balthasar, 1965: 73). It is not easy to discover what Jung intends by his interpretation of the Cross as Christ bearing the suspension between the opposites of good and evil (exemplified by one thief who is promised Paradise and the other, by implication, Hell (Luke 23:32–43)). Although Jung does not articulate a developed christology, he occasionally refers to the crucifixion as 'God's suffering' (*PADT*: 157). It seems to me that he is less interested in speculating, at the level of psychological consciousness, whether Jesus of Nazareth committed sin than in the symbolic value for humanity and for Christian believers of God in Christ bearing the pain of the humanly irresolvable tension of the opposites of good and evil. This puts Christ in the right starting position, according to Jung's theory of symbol formation, to move from dividedness to wholeness.

Though Jung does not expand on this in terms of the life and ministry of Jesus, it would not be inconsistent with a Balthasarian approach to the need for pedagogical 'accustoming' to suggest that it took time for Christ to discover what obedience to his mission would entail. In Jungian terms, when good opposes evil, part of what is taking place is projective splitting and in such situations it seems as though good could and should seek to defeat evil, rather than withdraw the (unconscious) projections and live with the irresolvable tension of opposites. Those aspects of the ministry of Jesus in which he banishes evil spirits that oppose him (such as in Mark 1:21–28, and 5:1–20) or utters woes against those who are currently enjoying prosperity (as in Luke 6:24–26) and against unrepentant cities (as in Luke 10:13–15) point to the reality of the experience of the unresolved tension of the opposites of good and evil. There is also, however, a recognition that evil cannot be got rid of but returns with greater force (as in Luke 11:24–26 // Matt. 12:43–45) and that from a human point of view the tension between good and evil, as when wheat and tares grow together in the same field, cannot be fully resolved until the End (see Matt. 13:24–30). This would exemplify Balthasar's view that in Christ God seeks to depotentiate rather than defeat evil. On a Jungian interpretation, the obedience that Christ came to realize and accept was that divine love responds to the challenge of evil by bearing the tension of the opposites, which might have had (Johannine) elements of serenity about it but could also be described in graphic terms as the agony of sweating blood (as in Luke 22:44).

It is not that Balthasar underplays the human conflict of good and evil. This is a matter of real experience, not just an intellectual exploration. What Balthasar emphasizes, however, is the 'vertical' dimension. Humanity is involved in the 'theodramatic war that has broken out between God, in his Logos, and hell's anti-logos' (*TD*4: 463). The provocation of 'Christ's utter Yes to God and to the world' produces an equal and contradicting opposite response, in that it 'drives the utter No – the demonic, anti-Christian No – out of its hiding place' (ibid.: 427). That battle of the Logos has to continue to the End. Balthasar's proposal is that the battle is already engaged and (in terms of realized eschatology) proleptically won. This takes place not by Christ engaging as the rest of humanity does, intrapsychically, in the conflict of contrariety between good and evil, but rather through the paradox of the powerlessness of kenotic and reconciling love, through Christ's utter Yes to God, bearing the full force of created humanity's No to God (with its associated tension of contrary opposites).

If that is Balthasar's positive reason for stressing the dissimilarity between the divine action and the human predicament, he has a further, more defensive, reason. In a situation in which theology lacks the bulwark of the analogy of dissimilarity, the admission of intrapsychic involvement in the tension of good and evil could easily result in the imputation of such contrariety within God, and hence lead to a form of theological dualism. For Balthasar, the distance/distinction between the Persons in the Godhead reveals God's nature as love and it does not signify contrary opposition. And such opposition is not to be read back from the incarnational kenosis: '[T]he renunciation of the "form of God" and the taking on of the "form of a slave" with all their consequences do not entail any alienation within the Trinitarian life of God' (*MP*: 208). For this reason, Balthasar is content to affirm Jung, when, in *Aion*, he argues for keeping the contrariety of good and evil within the psychological realm (*TD*1: 518). From Balthasar's perspective, 'Easter is the victory of the triune God over every contradiction', including sin and death. Nevertheless, even though 'the Lord brings the marks of his wounds into his victory and eternally remains the "Lamb as slain", [yet] it is surely not in order to integrate the contradiction of sin and hell into his heaven' (*TL*2: 359).

This is not to misrepresent Balthasar by claiming that he was not interested in the human predicament, or in creaturely growth and transformation. One of the reasons he writes about the saints is to show how human beings can be caught up into the movement of God's life as a consequence of being united with Christ in the theodrama. But priority is always given to the divine initiative which transforms (rather than defeats) all that is implied in humanity's contradictory No to God:

> Finitude, time and death are not negated: they are given a new value in a way that is beyond our comprehension. Indeed, even what is hostile to God, in all its profound abysses, is not abandoned; God does not turn his back on it: it is taken over and reworked.
>
> (*TD*4: 201)

Balthasar stresses that evil (all that is anti-God, the entire No to God) is met by the nature of the divine love itself. The kenotic nature of the eternal processions allows for God in the drama of the economy to suffer the complete alienation of becoming not-God, both in the dying abandonment of the Cross and in the descent to the realm of the dead. And yet, as in the eternal processions, the bond of love is not broken.

Balthasar does not romanticize the experience of Christ's passion. We should not 'reduce Christianity to "an unclouded harmony of God, the world, and man"' (*TD*1: 428). Christ's cry of dereliction is tragic. It is a '"being handed over to evil"' (ibid.: 429). It has 'certain parallels [with] the destinies of Christians and human beings generally' (ibid.) but it encompasses the human predicament of enduring the good/evil conflict. Yet 'God in the Cross abandoned by God' is 'more profound than anything we can imagine ... and underpins everything in the world that can be termed "tragic" … [and goes beyond] the mere opposition of human and divine freedom' (ibid.). God is addressing the consequences of the fallen nature of the world. His focus is not on Christ's psychological involvement in the human polarity of evil and good, but rather on the necessity of the initiative of grace:

> Christian theology alone can prevent the tragic dimension from this self-destruction [of collapse into a closed tragic world view] …; it can do this because it combines God's ultimate initiative on behalf of the world and his free creature with the *gratis* and unmerited quality of this loving self-gift.
>
> (ibid.: 433)

And what that act of grace reveals is the reality and the saving efficacy of the kenotic–reconciling love in the trinitarian passion-resurrection event: the 'counter-position of the wills' of the Father and the Son in the Garden of Gethsemane, 'the divine abandonment on the Cross', and the separation of God from God in the *descensus* are preparatory aspects of the revelation which 'only with the Resurrection … come[s] forth openly into the light' (*MP*: 212f.) to show the nature of the divine love.

Thus Balthasar's is on balance a 'vertical' rather than a 'horizontal' reading of the Cross. His focus is on God in Christ who suffers the trials and tribulations of the rift between God and humanity, the No to God, rather than on one who endures the human psychological crucifixion of wrestling with evil as the contrary opposite of good. Occasionally, Balthasar writes in terms that speak of Christ's full experience of the human condition:

> [God's] astounding masterpiece is to elicit the Yes of his free partner from the latter's innermost freedom. … [I]t takes all the mysteries of Christianity to achieve this: God must allow his Son to become man so that there may be a genuine dialogue between God in heaven and God as a human being on earth.
>
> (*TD*1: 34)

But the greater truth, for Balthasar, is that

> the entire abyss of man's refusal of God's love has been crossed over: in other words, that God is solidary with us not only in what is symptomatic of sin, the punishment for sin, but also in co-experiencing sin, in the *peirasmos* [trial] of the very essence of that negation – though without 'committing' (Hebrews 4.15) sin himself.
>
> (*MP*: 137)

Jung would be suspicious of this distinction, this avoidance of engagement with the psychological reality of evil.

The christological issue, which is beyond the scope of this book to engage with, is the central one of the two natures of Christ and their interrelation. Balthasar and Jung are not best suited as dialogue partners for such an exploration, since both give greater focus, in their own terms, on the divine nature of Christ. As regards his theodrama, what interests Balthasar is what the form of Christ reveals about the trinitarian life and love; for Jung it is how Christ functions as an archetypal symbol of the Self and (by direct correspondence) of God. They are, however, both interested in the practical theological question of whether and how the form of Christ or the Christ symbol enables people in general and Christian believers in particular to take up their own role in the drama of salvation or individuation. This is an area in which Balthasar allows that the 'vertical' divine and the 'horizontal' human predicament about good and evil co-exist in a complementary tension, in a manner compatible with the model constructed here, in living the Christian life.

There is a particular way in which the (Catholic (*TL2*: 357)) Christian can experience the sort of interaction between the horizontal and vertical dimensions, which Balthasar refers to on one occasion as 'the problem of contradiction in theology' (ibid.). Paradoxically, the believer is simultaneously both one with structurally sinful humanity and by grace also included in the saving action of the Son. The Christian 'has an affinity with his sinful brethren that is different from the ['perfectly sinless'] Lord's' (ibid.). It is not that Balthasar sees Christ's pattern as the mechanical unfolding of a predestined plan. Salvation for Balthasar is not predetermined. The human agenda remains a properly dramatic engagement between finite and infinite freedoms. If we see 'Adam's sin and all its consequences – including the Son's hell' somehow within the foreknowledge of God that makes it part of the Creator's 'plan', then we shall have put in place a 'closed system' (ibid.: 359f.) which would rob finite freedom of its genuine, if limited, autonomy, and would constrain the infinite freedom of the love of God in creation and redemption. Nor does Balthasar fall into the trap of giving human beings too exalted a role in salvation (as distinct from Jung in his pneumatology). God in Christ takes the initiative in the theodrama. The believer's is an important but supplementary role. Even though the Christian is enfolded in the grace of Christ, that person is not, however, a co-expiator; rather must he or she bear the 'insoluble conflict and contradiction' of contributing both to salvation history through 'what he suffers in Christ' and also to the problem that requires the independent divine initiative as a result of 'what he inflicts on Christ as a sinner' (ibid.: 358).

Jung sees the crucifying problem for conscious rationality of the tension of opposites arising from the lack of access to the life energy of the unconscious. Balthasar frames the problem in terms of reason and love. Whereas for Jung it is consciousness cut off from the unconscious that is in thrall to the tension of opposites, for Balthasar it is reason without love. In Balthasar's view, reasoning '(because love is lacking) is precisely "absurd"' (ibid.: 357 quoting Speyr), since in the world of contraries each pole contains a falsity (in that it is and is not) because of the existence of its opposite (ibid.: 357f.). To live in this situation may be humanly hopeless but it gains a new perspective through the grace of being in Christ. The Christian can 'experience existentially' things that 'resemble' Christ's experience of the Cross and *descensus*, when 'every love is withheld from him' (ibid.: 357). Humanity without the grace of Christ, though made in the *imago trinitatis* – in the image of the kenotic–reconciling infinite freedom of love – is now in the condition in which that 'image of God in man has become invisible', living in a state where 'everything is accordingly "twisted"' (ibid.: 358 quoting Speyr).

Descensus in Balthasar and Jung

Jung's 'horizontal' approach is itself dependent upon a 'vertical', psychological *descensus*. His theory of symbol formation involves, after the failure of conscious, 'horizontal', attempts to resolve the human predicament (that is, the crucifying tension between good and evil), a 'vertical' descent into the unconscious in order that a reconciled symbol of greater wholeness can emerge. Accepting the Balthasarian understanding of analogy, this is, of course, not to suggest that the unconscious and Hell are equivalent to one another on the basis of direct correspondence.

Nevertheless, for Jung and Balthasar, in contrast to the light of consciousness, the unconscious and Hell are both places of unknowing and darkness. As Balthasar puts it in relation to Hell, the realm of the dead, by Christ's *descensus* it is possible for God 'in his grace to envelop our sinful darkness in his greater darkness' (*TD*5: 265 quoting Speyr). Sinful humanity (in Balthasar's terms) or conscious humanity (in Jung's terms) cannot bear the idea that 'eternal love' (or psychic energy) 'needs its infinite places and its "darkness"' (or the unconscious) 'in order to "flow on eternally"' (ibid.).

Consciousness resists engagement with the unconscious and baulks at not being able to know all about it. When humanity chooses its No to God this is a violation of what God reserves to himself. In both situations there is a reaction, which needs to be understood and assimilated. In the Old Testament this was experienced in theological terms as the wrath of God. In Jung's psychology, when humanity chooses (through an exclusive overvaluing of consciousness) a No to the unconscious, or tries to engage it on its own consciously rational terms, there is likewise a compensatory reaction. This is what Jung means by the reality of the opposing spirit, the αντιμιμον πνευμα.

Both the wrath and the opposing spirit have to be appropriately integrated, for both represent a stage on the way to greater wholeness of understanding. In Balthasar's soteriology, the process of suffering the resulting contradiction on the Cross is penultimate, as, in a Jungian reading of the Cross, is suffering the tension of contrary opposites in the process of symbol formation. In Balthasar's terms the sin–wrath conflict is first accepted by Christ (in obedience to his mission) by 'experiencing on the Cross the Father's love in the form of his anger' against sin (ibid.: 267). But this is not a conflict of Father over against Son; rather, God in

Christ takes the punishing reaction upon himself. In Jung's terms this is like the person who has experienced the compensatory responses of the unconscious. The awareness of a struggle between good and evil has come into consciousness, but rather than continuing to engage in conflict between the 'I' and an opposing 'other', the person takes the opposition between good and evil into his or her own responsibility. As with Christ so with the person, this is crucifying and of itself does not fully resolve matters. Further help is needed. Consciousness needs the transcendent function to produce from within the unconscious a symbol of reconciled wholeness it cannot achieve by its own efforts. Contradicting humanity needs God who can endure all that is both anti-God and not-God in Hell to bring into resurrection the kenotic–reconciling life of love.

That is not to say, however, on the basis of direct correspondence, that God is to be equated with the unconscious, but rather that he is the One who makes the place within which the psyche, conscious and unconscious, together with all other aspects of creation, exists. In Balthasar's terms 'the Cross ... opens a path whereby men can get beyond their refusal and allow themselves' – as a psychic totality of individual consciousness and collective unconsciousness – 'to be drawn into God' (ibid.: 509).

Jung accepts that religion gives human beings access to the greatest totality imaginable. But even in his most expansive reflections on the unconscious, he is exploring something intra-cosmic. Even when Jung postulates, in his work on synchronicity, a psychoid realm (in which psyche and matter integrate), his aim is the assertion of the *unus mundus.* And although Jung argues that the unconscious operates acausally in relation to time and space, he is still putting forward an intra-cosmic concept, linked (in collaboration with Wolfgang Pauli) to the ideas of sub-atomic physics. Christ's descent to the realm of the dead, however, goes beyond all bounds of finitude (of matter and psyche), and thus God sets up a 'boundary stone marking the place where the lowest pitch is reached and the reverse movement set into operation' (*MP*: 167). Theology and psychology are not synonymous: humanity does not save itself; God is not another name for worldly processes. Jungian psychology might helpfully affirm aspects of the saving theodramatic action, but for it to be divine action God has to retain freedom of initiative. For Balthasar, the paradox of analogy persists. To be universal the Christ-event must be unique: 'the death of Christ, to be inclusive ... must be simultaneously exclusive and unique in its expiatory value' (ibid.: 168).

Despite the fact that Jung has very little to say about the resurrection of Christ that can be brought into the construction of this model of God's involvement with evil, Balthasar speaks of the resurrection in terms that could connect with seeing the Risen One as a Jungian symbol of greater wholeness. Balthasar's theme, again, is the divine love. As revealed in the Risen One, this is a love that holds together both entire separation and complete union, which is kenotic–reconciling. This is what Balthasar means theologically by the 'absolute uniqueness' of the Risen One as (what Jung would call) a symbol of wholeness (a *complexio oppositorum*),

> since in the greatest possible difference of conditions – deepest abasement and the highest exaltation, God-abandonment and union with God – is expressed … the supreme identity of the person … – an identity which John expresses in his unitary vision of the contraries as 'exaltation' and 'glorification', or in the image of the slain Lamb upon the throne. In both phases, what is involved is … the divinity of the Son's obedience as representation of the Trinitarian Love both in itself and for the world.
>
> (ibid.: 251f.)

For Balthasar, the inner-trinitarian distinction between Father and Son is an eternal '*locus*' which provides the space for a created world to exist and is also where 'its sinful alienation from God' is 'solved' since '[t]he creature's No resounds at the "place" of distinction within the Godhead' (*TD*4: 333f.). Again, this is not to assert, as Balthasar stresses, that there is a battle between opposites in Godself, for we must exclude from Godself 'all intramundane experience and suffering' and yet that same inner-trinitarian life 'presuppos[es] … the possibility of such experience and suffering' (ibid.: 234). As Friesenhahn notes, the processions within the immanent Trinity 'provide the condition for the possibility' (Friesenhahn, 2011: 151) for such an experience in the economic trinitarian Christ-event. And although this is experienced as an externalized (projected) Christ/Antichrist struggle, in Jung's reading of the Cross, Christ draws this into himself, bearing the suffering of the contrary opposites. This could be an aspect of trinitarian economic experience which also resounds in the place of distinction within the processions of the Godhead, though it does not get its origin there.

Balthasar's account of the *descensus* has resonances with Jung's comments on the Cross in the light of his theory of symbol formation. In Jung's terms the victory of the Prince of this world consists in the inability of Christ at the conscious level of the economy to resolve the tension of opposites between good and evil. From a human point of view, this is defeat. The more evil is opposed, the stronger it becomes. The rift between God and humanity remains unhealed. In the draining away of life in forsakenness and death, as the libido drops into the unconscious, the 'reversal' takes place because what could not be reconciled in consciousness cannot be separated in the unconscious. The true nature of the unconscious archetype holds. All dualities continue to be held in unity and from this unquenchable life energy there arises new life, manifesting in symbols of greater wholeness. The resonance can be maintained, however, only if the focus is on the Risen Lord bearing the marks of slaughter rather than, as Jung tended to prefer, on the Holy Spirit as a replacement for the Crucified One.

My suggestion is that there is in the nature of the divine love and in the eternal processions a capacity to enfold and transform what in the created and fallen world is experienced as the tension of contrary opposites. The divine love is both kenotic and uniting; the bond of love holds together what, in worldly terms, is a paradox of infinite distance/distinction and entire communion/unity. In the created world, structurally deformed by the No to the God of kenotic–reuniting love, paradox is experienced as the tension of contrary opposites, set as it were at right angles to the divine–human axis. We can use Jung's reading of the Cross in terms of symbol formation as a reassurance that the outcome of this tension is a wholeness, which is a dualistic monism and not dualism, together with Balthasar's insistence that we see the human experience in the light of the divine reality and do not project the human experience into the divine life.

However much of an accommodation such a model can achieve between Balthasar's 'vertical' and Jung's 'horizontal' accounts of the Cross-*descensus* as the focal point of God's involvement with evil, it is important to keep alive to the sense of the ongoing drama of salvation and individuation. For Jung the process of individuation does not come to completion, though it is sustained in hope by symbols of wholeness in the service of integrated living. For Balthasar the theodrama and human participation in it continues until the end of the final act, sustained in hope by the resurrection vision of God who is kenotic–reconciling love. The tension needs to be maintained between Balthasar's analogy of being (rather than Jung's analogy of direct correspondence) and Jung's dualistic monism, so that the conscious experience of good and evil, through the transformative process of symbol formation, offers a vision of unity-in-difference that avoids imputing duality to God. And, given these cautions, we may read the Cross as simultaneously the trinitarian action, effectively addressing humanity's contradictory No to God, and also as God in Christ participating in the human predicament of the crucifying tension of the contrary opposites of good and evil.

Concluding illustration: 'The Crucifix that Spoke to St Francis'

As a concluding illustration of this final point, I use the image called 'The Crucifix that Spoke to St Francis'.[2] A kneeling theology, such as that of Balthasar, will find resource in an image explored through prayer in interaction with doctrinal statement. This offers the opportunity to hold together the divine action and the human predicament. It is also part of the Jungian method of active imagination to allow an image to connect with a person's psyche in terms of bringing into consciousness unconscious contents for integrative reflection.

For Balthasar, when a person comes in prayer before an image of the Cross, what is revealed is that, in Christ, God takes 'an inner, divine, absolute part … in the drama of mortal existence without threatening his absolute nature' (*TD*2: 45) and the person brings to that prayer his or her experience of the human predicament, borne by God in Christ. For the 'tragic dimension of personal existence is not softened; in fact, it is wrenched to its very limit: in the Cross' (ibid.: 49). The use of an image by someone in prayer (not created by that person's consciousness, but given from the collectivity of the tradition) can be received as if, as with a dream image, from the unconscious, and can be reflected on (through Jungian active imagination) with an openness to its richness of archetypal meaning. For Jung, numinous, archetypal images 'have the significance of ikons' (*L2*: 606).

The image of the crucifixion, to which Jung pointed in conversation with Uhsadel in 1938, is a copy of a stained-glass window in the medieval Imperial monastery at Königsfelden in Switzerland (Uhsadel, 1966: 121; cf. Schwarz, 2008; Anon., 2009). A striking feature is the exaggeration of the blood gushing from the wounds of the still-dying Christ. This resonates with Jung's emphasis on Christ undergoing an ordinary experience of dying, and by implication the psychological suffering that it entails. Königsfelden is a Franciscan foundation and the emphasis in the stained glass on Christ's bleeding wounds evokes in an exaggerated way the still-bleeding figure of Christ which is a feature of the 'Crucifix which Spoke to St Francis' around the turn of the thirteenth century in the semi-derelict San Damiano chapel just below the walls of Assisi. This icon is not just an 'unequivocal expression of the Easter mystery' (Duffy, 2005: 131), but rather a paradoxical symbol of Christ simultaneously dying and rising.

The San Damiano icon can be read in terms of a number of themes in the model constructed in the present chapter. The 'englobing' of the divine 'vertical' initiative begins in heaven and reaches to the depths of Hell. In the semi-circle at the top of the icon is the golden hand of the Father, extended from heaven in blessing. Below the foot of the Cross (now mostly lost) is a shattered rock sepulchre, from the depths of whose darkness are emerging the first to be raised from among the dead with Christ. The Cross and the descent to the dead are held together with the resurrection in a single image. The Christ depicted here is one whose crucifixion wounds are still bleeding. This resonates with the reality of the passion of the God-in-Christ who (for Balthasar) became sin for us and who (for Jung) underwent the suffering of the tension of the opposites of good and evil. The resurrection, from within the realm of the dead, is part of the same Christ-event, symbolized by the divine nimbus around his head – the circle quartered by the cross. In Jungian terms the entire Christ-figure is a transcendent symbol of greater wholeness, a *complexio oppositorum* of body and spirit, good and evil, life and death, consciousness and the unconscious, human and divine. In Balthasarian terms we are offered an icon of kenotic–reconciling love that redeems the divine–human contradiction and draws us into the life of God. In Christ we see that we are made in the '*imago trinitatis*' and that the completion of human destiny is to share in 'the fount of [the triune] God's life' (*TD*5: 56, 57).

Jung's response to his own question at the end of the Second World War – how we can live in the face of evil – was to point to the Cross in hope, based on the greater wholeness for which we are intended, through the individuation process. Balthasar's vision is perhaps more grounded in the reality of human death. Balthasar recalls Paul's assertion that even 'all the suffering of the world, of "creation groaning under bondage to decay"' is not only 'slight' in relation to the glory to be revealed but is also a preparation for entering into that glory (ibid.: 498f. citing 2 Cor. 4:17 and Rom. 8:18). If Jung offers a way to live hopefully, Balthasar sees that that includes learning how to die well:

> Might it not be, in the end, that this baffling weight of suffering in the world is a feature of transcendence (of which we are largely unconscious), a way of training us for the great act of self-surrender that concludes our temporal life? … [E]ven … against a process that seems … pitiless and pointless? … Can the many tears that human beings shed, unfruitfully, … be transformed into something that is fruitful for eternity?
>
> (ibid.: 499)

He asserts this not perversely to glorify human suffering in the struggle between good and evil but to point to the paradox that it is only Christ's godforsakenness that reveals the fullness of the glory of God. Balthasar is not advocating 'glorifying earthly suffering' nor avoiding protest and fighting against 'worldly injustice' (ibid.: 500); rather, he is arguing for obedient openness, whether through 'militancy … [or] … endurance', to the fundamental values of the kingdom in which our cry of incomprehension is transformed by God in Christ enduring the godforsakenness of the Cross:

> if it is true that the suffering of the Crucified One can transform even worldly pain, unintelligible to itself, into a co-redemptive suffering, then the most unbelievable, most cruel tortures, prisons, concentration camps and whatever other horrors there may be can be seen in close proximity to the Cross, to that utter night, interrupted only by the unfathomable cry of 'Why?'
>
> (ibid.: 501)

In Balthasar's view, 'what the Son experiences on the Cross as total night is in God's sight the Son's ultimate obedience and hence his highest glory' (ibid.).

Balthasar's vision offers to enfold the processes that Jung counsels are necessary – withdrawing projections of evil, admitting that, of our own resources, we can neither resolve the conflict of good and evil nor stop ourselves from engaging in it, and need to trust in the unconscious psychological process of symbol formation – and asserts that they derive their fundamental efficacy from the theodramatic action of God's kenotic–reuniting love, reconciling the world to himself and himself to the world.

Notes

1 I acknowledge help from Jack Herbert with an English translation of this passage.
2 There are many images available on the web, to be found by entering 'San Damiano Cross image' into a search engine.

Chapter 10

Summary

The impetus for this study arose when I discovered that Jung undertook a project in relation to Christianity, which I have argued was not only psychotherapeutic in intention but also influenced by Jung's own theological orientation. Jung had a particular hope that his contribution would find resonance with Roman Catholic theologians. He published a set of essays, *Symbolik des Geistes*, which he had revised for the first phase of his project. A key feature of these essays was the question of God's involvement with evil. Balthasar gave significant attention in his theological project to Jung's psychology, and, more importantly, he saw Jung as a representative of an approach to the question of God and evil which he saw to be distinctively different from his own.

Both Jung and Balthasar wrote primarily for their own communities of practice, namely analytical psychology and the Roman Catholic Church. However, both sought to take the contribution of other disciplines sufficiently seriously to enable us to call Balthasar a contextualizing theologian and Jung a reinterpretive psychologist. Balthasar asserts strongly the priority of theological ideas. In Jung's case, his phenomenologically oriented psychology is set within a vitalist understanding of science, with prominence given to final causes. Furthermore, he not only has a metaphysical orientation, but also theological commitments. He can be located within the radical Protestant theological tradition as a 'prophetic or revolutionary spiritualist', and the shape of his theological orientation can be labelled 'Joachimite'.

Balthasar's reading of Jung's psychology represents something of a missed opportunity to see the similarities between their understandings of symbol and form, of the function of the ego/I in relation to social role/persona, with both only finding their fulfilment in relation to Christ as a factor other than consciousness, in terms of mission (for Balthasar) and the archetypal Self of the collective unconscious (for Jung). In the end I argue for holding these two understandings together in a cruciform tension in constructing a model for God's involvement with evil.

There are three major areas of divergence: analogy, polarity and theological orientation. Jung saw that theological discourse needs a working theory of analogy and paradox. He was not able himself to bring the two together. His working theory is one of similarity, the analogy of direct correspondence. Balthasar's approach is that of similarity-within-ever-greater-dissimilarity. In my view this would be beneficial for Jungian thinking about religion, in that it would provide a basis for escaping the inability to distinguish between Self- and God-images.

Balthasar and Jung both accepted the importance of contrary polar opposites in human experience. However, Balthasar was deeply suspicious of the use of this to imply that there are polar opposites within the Godhead. On the one hand, his theory of analogy cautions against any attempt by Jung to make such a move. On the other hand, Jung is not to be understood as a theological dualist, since for him symbols of wholeness represent a new unity made up of resolved contrary opposites, a *complexio oppositorum*. Jung's essay on Mercurius in *Symbolik des Geistes* forms part of his argument for this position. This dualistic monism has a marked similarity with Balthasar's understanding of the inner-trinitarian divine life, which holds together infinite distance/distinction between the Persons within an unbroken bond of love. If Jung is interested in the 'horizontal' polarity of contrary opposites, Balthasar is primarily concerned with the more fundamental and all-encompassing polarity between God and humanity, which he handles by developing a dialectic of contradiction.

Balthasar's and Jung's approaches to analogy and polarity, though divergent, could be brought together creatively. The same could not be said of their differing theological orientations. Jung's 'Joachimite' view envisages three successive ages of the Father, the Son and the Holy Spirit, with the second and third each needing to address significant shortcomings in its predecessor. Balthasar's *corpus triforme* view envisages three aspects of the same trinitarian life, expressing the interpenetration of Father, Son and Holy Spirit, all understood christologically. This results in three manifestations of the same Body: Old Testament Scripture, looking towards the Body of the incarnate Son (in the New Testament), and continuing in the life of his Body, the Church. It seems to me that, even if Jung and Balthasar were able to find ways of relating psychology and theology by creative use of their different approaches to analogy and polarity, there is very little chance of fruitful dialogue based on their differing theological orientations. I use the essay on Satan in the Old Testament, from the *Symbolik des Geistes* collection, as a case study of these areas of divergence.

When it comes to the question of God and evil, neither Jung nor Balthasar is engaged in an attempt to develop a theodicy, in the terms set by Enlightenment philosophy. They agree on the importance of human responsibility for the origin of evil, but Jung seeks to moderate this by asserting God's, usually surreptitious, involvement. Likewise, both are committed to an understanding of the reality of evil, though both struggle to elucidate their view. Jung's collaboration with the Roman Catholic theologian Victor

White foundered because of their failure, in a discussion of the doctrine of evil as *privatio boni*, to find a mutually satisfactory way of talking about the reality of evil. Balthasar seeks to establish the reality of evil, in part over against Barth's idea of *Das Nichtige*, but in his own terms Balthasar has to give up the attempt to allow demons a role as *dramatis personae* in the action of the theodrama.

Balthasar thought that Jung's essay on the Trinity (in *Symbolik des Geistes*) could be read solely as an attempt to produce a Quaternity which included the Devil within the Godhead. The Quaternity suggestion needs to be understood as part of a larger and more complex agenda. Jung accepted the archetypal provenance of the Trinity symbol and the positive contribution of Church Fathers in developing the doctrine. This set him the challenge of understanding why the collective unconscious should produce both threefold and fourfold archetypal images. He hoped to engage Christianity in this exploration by using his psychotherapeutic method to interpret the Trinity symbol. Jung's suggested interpretations were, however, also examples of his own theological approach. It seems clear that none of them would have appealed to Balthasar. He links the trinitarian drama to a version of human psychological development, which uses the analogy of direct correspondence and has a 'Joachimite' rationale of the need for the successive unfolding phases. In particular, the Quaternity suggestion focuses on the phase in the process in which Christ cannot by his own efforts resolve the conflict with his hostile brother, the Antichrist. Again, in 'Joachimite' fashion, it is human beings in collaboration with the Holy Spirit who must attempt to take the process of salvation forward.

Although, up to this point, critical comparison of Jung and Balthasar on the question of God's involvement with evil seems to be failing to promise any fruitful, mutual collaboration, how Jung and Balthasar understand the Cross opens up new possibilities. In Jung's case it is a minor feature of his essays in *Symbolik des Geistes*. For Balthasar, Christ's death on the Cross, his descent to the dead and his resurrection are central to his understanding of God's involvement with evil, because he sees them as trinitarian events. A key feature is that Jung interprets the Cross as an experience of the 'horizontal' tension of contrary opposites. Balthasar reads it as the experience of the 'vertical' contradiction that separates God and humanity. For both, a descent is required before resolution appears. In Jung's case this is linked to his theory of symbol formation. Consciousness cannot resolve the conflict of contrary opposites. Psychic energy descends into the unconscious, whence unexpectedly there can arise a new symbol of wholeness, a *complexio oppositorum*. For Balthasar, the Cross and the descent to the dead is the trinitarian experience by God of godforsakenness. This is the experience for the economic Trinity of the alienation which is not a feature of the life of the immanent Trinity, even though that life is characterized by distance/distinction. In inner-trinitarian life the bond of love is not broken. It is likewise not broken on the Cross or in the descent to the dead, though this is only, and unexpectedly, revealed in the resurrection.

I conclude this critical comparison by suggesting a cruciform model of God's involvement with evil, holding together in tension a Balthasarian understanding of the Cross as addressing the contradiction of the divine–human relationship and a Jungian view of the Cross as the start of the process of movement towards wholeness, which the conflict of contrary opposites calls for.

There are a number of areas for further study which have been opened by this critical comparison of the works of Jung and Balthasar. I have argued for the importance of recognizing Jung's own theological commitments. I brought forward evidence for these from his early student lectures through to just a few years before his death. A thorough theological reading of Jung's *Red Book*, which has recently been published, would enable a more subtle tracing of the development of these commitments. I focused my discussion on the essays in *Symbolik des Geistes* and *Aion*. It would be important to see whether this understanding of Jung's theology could further inform the interpretation of his late works, *Answer to Job* and *Mysterium Conjunctionis*.

Within the framework of a typology for relating psychology to theology, I have explored some possibilities for the mutual reception of Balthasar and Jung. This approach could be extended to other modern theologians, both those who have themselves given explicit attention to Jung and those whose interests overlap with those of Jung, no doubt revealing a variety of areas of convergence and divergence. These further researches would contribute to Jungian studies and to the dialogue between analytical psychology and Christian theology, to which this book has sought to make a contribution.

Bibliography

Anon. (2009) (Book review) 'Glass for Emperors: The Glazing of Königsfelden Abbey', *Vidimus: the only on-line magazine devoted to medieval stained glass*, 25 (January), www.vidimus.org/issues/issue-25/feature/

Bair, D. (2004) *Jung: A Biography*, London: Little, Brown.

Balthasar, H. U. von (1965) 'Theology and Sanctity', in *Word and Redemption: Essays in Theology 2*, trans. A.V. Littledale and A. Dru, New York: Herder and Herder.

—— (1980) *Theodramatik: Dritter Band: Die Handlung*, Einsiedeln: Johannes Verlag.

—— (1981) *Pâques, Le Mystère*, trans. R. Givord, 2nd edn, Paris: Les Éditions du Cerf.

—— (1982) *The Glory of the Lord: A Theological Aesthetics*, Volume I: *Seeing the Form*, trans. E. Leiva-Merikakis, J. Fessio and J. Riches (eds), 2nd edn, Edinburgh: T. & T. Clark and San Francisco: Ignatius Press.

—— (1983) *Theodramatik: Vierter Band: Das Endspiel*, Einsiedeln: Johannes Verlag.

—— (1984) *The Glory of the Lord: A Theological Aesthetics*, Volume II: *Studies in Theological Style: Clerical Styles*, trans. A. Louth, F. McDonagh and B. McNeil, J. Riches (ed.), 2nd edn, Edinburgh: T. & T. Clark and San Francisco: Ignatius Press.

—— (1986a) 'In Retrospect', trans. K. Batinovich, in J. Riches (ed.) *The Analogy of Beauty: The Theology of Hans Urs von Balthasar*, Edinburgh: T. & T. Clark Ltd.

—— (1986b) 'Another Ten Years – 1975', trans. J. Saward, in J. Riches (ed.) *The Analogy of Beauty: The Theology of Hans Urs von Balthasar*, Edinburgh: T. & T. Clark Ltd.

—— (1986c) *The Glory of the Lord: A Theological Aesthetics*, Volume III: *Studies in Theological Style: Lay Styles*, trans. A. Louth, J. Saward, M. Simon and R. Williams, 2nd edn, Edinburgh: T. & T. Clark and San Francisco: Ignatius Press.

—— (1988) *Theo-Drama: Theological Dramatic Theory*, Volume I: *Prolegomena*, trans. G. Harrison, San Francisco: Ignatius Press.

—— (1989a) *The Glory of the Lord: A Theological Aesthetics*, Volume IV: *The Realm of Metaphysics in Antiquity*, trans. B. McNeil, A. Louth, J. Saward, R. Williams, and O. Davies, J. Riches (ed.), Edinburgh: T. & T. Clark and San Francisco: Ignatius Press.

—— (1989b) *The Glory of the Lord: A Theological Aesthetics*, Volume VII: *Theology: The New Covenant*, trans. B. McNeil, J. Riches (ed.), Edinburgh: T. & T. Clark.

—— (1990a) *The Scandal of the Incarnation: Irenaeus against the Heresies*, trans. J. Saward, San Francisco: Ignatius Press.

—— (1990b) *Theo-Drama: Theological Dramatic Theory*, Volume II: *The Dramatis Personae: Man in God*, trans. G. Harrison, San Francisco: Ignatius Press.

—— (1990c) *Theologie der Drei Tage*, new edn, Freiburg: Johannes Verlag Einsiedeln.

—— (1991a) 'A Résumé of My Thought', trans. K. Hamilton, in D. L. Schindler (ed.) *Hans Urs von Balthasar: His Life and Work*, San Francisco: Ignatius Press.

—— (1991b) *The Glory of the Lord: A Theological Aesthetics*, Volume V: *The Realm of Metaphysics in the Modern Age*, trans. O. Davies, A. Louth, B. McNeil, J. Saward, and R. Williams, B. McNeil and J. Riches (eds), Edinburgh: T. & T. Clark and San Francisco: Ignatius Press.

—— (1991c) *The Glory of the Lord: A Theological Aesthetics*, Volume VI: *Theology: The Old Covenant*, trans. B. McNeil and E. Leiva-Merikakis, J. Riches (ed.), Edinburgh: T. & T. Clark.

—— (1992a) *Theo-Drama: Theological Dramatic Theory*, Volume III: *The Dramatis Personae: The Person in Christ*, trans. G. Harrison, San Francisco: Ignatius Press.

—— (1992b) *The Theology of Karl Barth: Exposition and Interpretation*, trans. E. T. Oakes, San Francisco: Ignatius Press.

—— (1993) *Razing the Bastions: On the Church in this Age*, trans. B. McNeil, San Francisco: Ignatius Press.

—— (1994a) *Our Task: A Report and a Plan*, trans. J. Saward, San Francisco: Ignatius Press.

—— (1994b) *Theo-Drama: Theological Dramatic Theory*, Volume IV: *The Action*, trans. G. Harrison, San Francisco: Ignatius Press.

—— (1998) *Theo-Drama: Theological Dramatic Theory*, Volume V: *The Last Act*, trans. G. Harrison, San Francisco: Ignatius Press.

—— (2000) *Theo-Logic: Theological Logical Theory*, Volume I: *Truth of the World*, trans. A. J. Walker, San Francisco: Ignatius Press.

—— (2004a) *Theo-Logic: Theological Logical Theory*, Volume II: *Truth of God*, trans. A. J. Walker, San Francisco: Ignatius Press.

—— (2004b) *Epilogue*, trans. E. T. Oakes, San Francisco: Ignatius Press.

—— (2005a) *Theo-Logic: Theological Logical Theory*, Volume III: *The Spirit of Truth*, trans. G. Harrison, San Francisco: Ignatius Press.

—— (2005b) *Mysterium Paschale: The Mystery of Easter*, trans. and intro. A. Nichols, San Francisco: Ignatius Press.

Barth, K. (2009) *Church Dogmatics*, Volume III, *The Doctrine of Creation*, Sections 50–51, *The Creator and His Creature II*, trans. G.W. Bromily J.W. Edwards, O. Bussey, Harold Knight, J. K. S. Reid, R. H. Fuller, R. J. Ehrlich, A. T. Mackey, T. H. L. Parker, H. A. Kennedy and J. Martos, G.W. Bromily and T. F. Torrance (eds), study edn, London and New York: T. & T. Clark.

Becker, K. L. (2001) *Unlikely Companions: C. G. Jung on the* Spiritual Exercises *of Ignatius of Loyola: An Exposition and Critique Based on Jung's Lectures and Writings*, Leominster: Gracewing and New Malden: Inigo Enterprises.

Bishop, P. (ed.) (1999) *Jung in Contexts: A Reader*, London and New York: Routledge.

—— (2012) 'Jung's *Red Book* and its relation to aspects of German Idealism', *Journal of Analytical Psychology*, 57(3): 335–63.

Block, E. (ed.) (2005) *Glory, Grace and Culture: The Work of Hans Urs von Balthasar*, Mahwah: Paulist Press.

Brooke, R. (1991) *Jung and Phenomenology*, London: Routledge.

—— (ed.) (2000) *Pathways into the Jungian World: Phenomenology and Analytical Psychology*, London and New York: Routledge.

Buber, M. (1952) *Eclipse of God: Studies in the Relation between Religion and Philosophy*, New York: Harper.

Bulkeley, K. and Weldon, C. (eds) (2011) *Teaching Jung*, Oxford and New York: Oxford University Press.

Burns, C. P. E. (2011) 'Jung's Engagement with Christian Theology', in K. Bulkeley and C. Weldon (eds) *Teaching Jung*, Oxford and New York: Oxford University Press.

Casement, A. (2001) *Carl Gustav Jung*, London: Sage Publications.

Chapman, J. H. (1988) *Jung's Three Theories of Religious Experience* (Studies in the Psychology of Religion, Volume 3), Lewiston/Queenston: Edwin Mellen Press.

Charet, F. X. (1993) *Spiritualism and the Foundations of C. G. Jung's Psychology*, Albany: State University of New York Press.

Clark, M. (1998) 'God Could be Something Terrible', in I. Alister and C. Hauke (eds) *Contemporary Jungian Analysis: Post-Jungian Perspectives from the Society of Analytical Psychology*, London and New York: Routledge.

Copal, C. (ed.) (1990) *Hans Urs von Balthasar: Bibliographie 1925–1990*, Freiburg: Johannes Verlag Einsiedeln.

Crammer, C. (2004) 'One Sex or Two? Balthasar's Theology of the Sexes', in E. T. Oakes and D. Moss (eds) *Cambridge Companion to Hans Urs von Balthasar*, Cambridge: Cambridge University Press.

Dalzell, T. G. (1997) *The Dramatic Encounter of Divine and Human Freedom in the Theology of Hans Urs von Balthasar*, Berne: Peter Lang.

Davies, O. (2004) 'The Theological Aesthetics', in E. T. Oakes and D Moss (eds) *The Cambridge Companion to Hans Urs von Balthasar*, Cambridge: Cambridge University Press.

D'Costa, G. (2009) *Christianity and World Religions: Disputed Questions in the Theology of Religions*, Malden, Oxford and Chichester: Wiley-Blackwell.

Dourley, J. P. (1981) *C. G. Jung and Paul Tillich: The Psyche as Sacrament*, Toronto: Inner City Books.

—— (2008) *Paul Tillich, Carl Jung and the Recovery of Religion*, Hove and New York: Routledge.

Duffy, E. (2005) 'Worship', in D. F. Ford, B. Quash and J. M. Soskice (eds) *Fields of Faith: Theology and Religious Studies for the Twenty-First Century*, Cambridge: Cambridge University Press.

Dunne, C. (1987) 'Between Two Thieves: A Response to Jung's Critique of the Christian Notions of Good and Evil', in M. Stein and R. L. Moore (eds) *Jung's Challenge to Contemporary Religion*, Wilmette: Chiron Publications.

Edinger, E. (1996) *The New God-Image: A Study of Jung's Key Letters concerning the Evolution of the Western God-image*, Wilmette: Chiron Publications.

Ellenberger, H. F. (1970) *The Discovery of the Unconscious: The History and Evolution of Dynamic Psychiatry*, New York: Basic Books.

Ford, D. F. (1995) 'On Being Theologically Hospitable to Jesus Christ: Hans Frei's Achievement', *Journal of Theological Studies*, NS, 46(2): 532–46.

—— and Muers, R. (eds) (2005) *The Modern Theologians: An Introduction to Christian Theology since 1918*, 3rd edn, Malden and Oxford: Blackwell Publishing.

Forryan, B. and Glover, J. M. (comp.) (1979) *General Index to the Collected Works of C. G. Jung* (*Collected Works*, Volume 20), Princeton: Princeton University Press.

Foster, P. (ed.) (2008) *The Non-Canonical Gospels*, London and New York: T. & T. Clark.

—— (2009) *The Apocryphal Gospels: A Very Short Introduction*, Oxford: Oxford University Press.

Franz, M-L. von (1980) *Projection and Re-Collection in Jungian Psychology: Reflections of the Soul*, trans. W. H. Kennedy, Chicago and La Salle: Open Court.

Frei, H. W. (1992) *Types of Christian Theology*, G. Hunsinger and W. C. Placher (eds), New Haven and London: Yale University Press.

—— (1993) *Theology and Narrative: Selected Essays*, G. Hunsinger and W. C. Placher (eds), New York and Oxford: Oxford University Press.

Friesenhahn, J. H. (2011) *Trinity and Theodicy: The Trinitarian Theology of von Balthasar and the Problem of Evil*, Farnham and Burlington: Ashgate Publishing.

Giegerich, W. (2010) 'God Must Not Die! Jung's Thesis on the One-Sidedness of Christianity', *Spring: A Journal of Archetype and Culture*, 84: 11–71.

Gieser, S. (2005) *The Innermost Kernel: Depth Psychology and Quantum Physics, Wolfgang Pauli's Dialogue with C. G. Jung*, Berlin: Springer Verlag.

Gruchy, J. W. de (1984) 'Jung and Religion: A Theological Assessment', in R. K. Papadopoulos and G. S. Saayman (eds) *Jung in Modern Perspective: The Master and his Legacy*, Aldershot: Wildwood House.

Hardy, D. W. (2005) 'Karl Barth', in D. F. Ford and R. Muers (eds) *The Modern Theologians: An Introduction to Christian Theology since 1918*, 3rd edn, Malden and Oxford: Blackwell Publishing.

Hayman, R. (2002) *A Life of Jung*, London: Bloomsbury Publishing.

Henderson, D. (2010) 'The Coincidence of Opposites: C. G. Jung's Reception of Nicholas of Cusa', *Studies in Spirituality*, 20: 101–13.

Henrici, P. (1991) 'Hans Urs von Balthasar: A Sketch of His Life', trans. J. Saward, in D. L. Schindler (ed.) *Hans Urs von Balthasar: His Life and Work*, San Francisco: Ignatius Press.

Hick, J. (1968) *Evil and the God of Love*, London: Collins.

Higton, M. (2007) *Deliver Us: Exploring the Problem of Evil* (Church Times Study Guide), Norwich: Canterbury Press.

Hillman, J. (1975) *Re-visioning Psychology*, New York: Harper and Row.

Hitchcock, J. (1974) 'Why Communio?' *Communio: International Catholic Review*, 1(1): 112–3.

Homans, P. (1995) *Jung in Context: Modernity and the Making of a Psychology*, 2nd edn, Chicago and London: University of Chicago Press.

Hostie, R. (1957) *Religion and the Psychology of Jung*, trans. G. R. Lamb, London and New York: Sheed and Ward.

Howsare, R. A. (2009) *Balthasar: A Guide for the Perplexed*, London and New York: T. & T. Clark.

Hume, D. (1947) *Dialogues Concerning Natural Religion*, N. Kemp Smith (ed.) 2nd edn, Edinburgh: Thomas Nelson and Sons.

Hunsinger, G. (1993) 'Afterword: Hans Frei as Theologian', in H. W. Frei, *Theology and Narrative: Selected Essays*, G. Hunsinger and W. C. Placher (eds), New York and Oxford: Oxford University Press.

Huskinson, L. (2004) *Nietzsche and Jung: The Whole Self in the Union of Opposites*, Hove and New York: Brunner-Routledge.

—— (2006) 'Holy, Holy, Holy: The Misappropriation of the Numinous in Jung', in A. Casement and D. Tacey (eds) *The Idea of Numinosity: Contemporary Jungian and Psychoanalytic Perspectives*, Hove and New York: Routledge.

Jaffé, A. (1971) *From the Life and Work of C. G. Jung*, trans. R. F. C. Hull, New York: Harper and Row, London: Hodder and Stoughton.

—— (1972) 'The Creative Phases in Jung's Life', trans. M. Stein, *Spring: An Annual of Archetypal Psychology and Jungian Thought*, 34: 162–90.

—— (1986) *The Myth of Meaning in the Work of C. G. Jung*, trans. R. F. C. Hull, 2nd edn, Zürich: Daimon Verlag.

Jung, C. G. (1909/1949) 'The Significance of the Father in the Destiny of the Individual', in *CW*4: 301–23.

—— (1913) 'The Theory of Psychoanalysis', in *CW*4: 83–228.
—— (1914a) 'On Psychological Understanding', in *CW*3: 179–93.
—— (1914b) 'Foreword to "Psychologische Abhandlungen,"Volume I', in *CW*18: 825.
—— (1916a) *Collected Papers on Analytical Psychology*, C. E. Long (ed.), New York: Moffat, Yard, London: Ballière, Tindall and Cox.
—— (1916b) *The Structure of the Unconscious* in *CW*7: 269–304.
—— (1916/1948) 'General Aspects of Dream Psychology', in *CW*8: 237–80.
—— ([1916]/1957) 'The Transcendent Function', in *CW*8: 67–91.
—— (1916/1966) 'The Structure of the Unconscious', in *CW*7: 269–304.
—— (1917/1926/1943) 'On the Psychology of the Unconscious', in *CW*7: 1–119.
—— (1920/1948) 'The Psychological Foundations of Belief in Spirits', in *CW*8: 301–18.
—— (1927/1931) 'The Structure of the Psyche', in *CW*8: 139–58.
—— (1928a) 'On Psychic Energy', in *CW*8: 3–66.
—— (1928b) 'Psychoanalysis and the Cure of Souls', in *CW*11: 348–54.
—— (1928c) 'The Relations between the Ego and the Unconscious', in *CW*7: 121–241.
—— (1928/1931) 'Analytical Psychology and "Weltanschauung"', in *CW*8: 358–81.
—— (1929a) 'Commentary on "The Secret of the Golden Flower"', in *CW*13: 1–56.
—— (1929b) 'Freud and Jung: Contrasts', in *CW*4: 333–40.
—— (1932) 'Psychotherapists or the Clergy', in *CW*11: 327–47.
—— (1934a) 'The Soul and Death', in *CW*8: 404–15.
—— (1934b) 'The Practical Use of Dream-Analysis', in *CW*16: 139–61.
—— (1934c) 'A Review of the Complex Theory', in *CW*8: 92–104.
—— (1934/1950) 'A Study in the Process of Individuation', in *CW*9(i): 290–354.
—— (1934/1954) 'Archetypes of the Collective Unconscious', in *CW*9(i): 1–72.
—— (1936a) 'Wotan', in *CW*10: 179–93.
—— (1936b) 'The Concept of the Collective Unconscious', in *CW*9(i): 42–53.
—— (1938/1940) *Psychology and Religion* in *CW*11: 3–105.
—— (1938/1954) 'Psychological Aspects of the Mother Archetype', in *CW*9(i): 73–110.
—— (1939) 'What Can India Teach Us?' in *CW*10: 525–30.
—— (1939/1954) 'Psychological Commentary on "The Tibetan Book of the Great Liberation"', in *CW*11: 475–508.
—— (1940) *The Integration of Personality*, trans. S. Dell, London: Routledge and Kegan Paul.
—— (1942) 'Paracelsus as a Spiritual Phenomenon', in *CW*13: 109–89.
—— (1942/1948) 'A Psychological Approach to the Dogma of the Trinity', in *CW*11: 107–200.
—— (1942/1954) 'Transformation Symbolism in the Mass', in *CW*11: 201–96.
—— (1943) 'The Psychology of Eastern Meditation', in *CW*11: 558–75.
—— (1943/1948) 'The Spirit Mercurius', in *CW*13: 191–250.
—— (1944) 'The Holy Men of India', in *CW*11: 576–86.
—— (1945a) 'After the Catastrophe', in *CW*10: 194–217.
—— (1945b) 'Marginalia on Contemporary Events', in *CW*18: 591–603.
—— (1945/1948) 'The Phenomenology of the Spirit in Fairytales', in *CW*9(i): 207–54.
—— (1945/1954) 'The Philosophical Tree', in *CW*13: 251–349.
—— (1946) 'The Psychology of the Transference: Interpreted in Conjunction with a Set of Alchemical Pictures', in *CW*16: 163–323.
—— (1947/1954) 'On the Nature of the Psyche', in *CW*8: 159–234.
—— (1948a) *Symbolik des Geistes: Studien über psychische Phänomenologie mit einem Beitrag von Dr. phil. Riwkah Schärf* (Psychologische Abhandlungen, Band VI) [Symbolism of the

Spirit: Studies on the Phenomenology of the Psyche, with a Contribution from Dr. Riwkah Schärf (Psychological Papers, Volume 6)]. Zürich: Rascher Verlag.
—— (1948b) 'Foreword to Jung: "Symbolik des Geistes" (1948)', in *CW*18: 649f.
—— (1951) 'On Synchronicity', in *CW*8: 520–31.
—— (1952a) *Answer to Job* in *CW*11: 355–470.
—— (1952b) 'Synchronicity: An Acausal Connecting Principle', in *CW*8: 417–519.
—— (1952c) 'Religion and Psychology: A Reply to Martin Buber', in *CW*18: 663–70.
—— (1952d) 'Foreword to White's "God and the Unconscious"', in *CW*11: 299–310.
—— (1952e) 'Foreword to Werblowsky's "Lucifer and Prometheus"', in *CW*11: 311–15.
—— (1954a) 'Letter to Père Lachat, 27 March', trans. A.S.B.G., in *CW*18: 679–91.
—— (1954b) 'On Resurrection', in *CW*18: 692–96.
—— (1958a) 'Jung and Religious Belief', in *CW*18: 702–44.
—— (1958b) 'Flying Saucers: A Modern Myth of Things Seen in the Skies', in *CW*10: 307–433.
—— (1959) 'Good and Evil in Analytical Psychology', in *CW*10: 456–68.
—— (1960) *The Psychogenesis of Mental Disease* (*Collected Works*, Volume 3), London: Routledge.
—— (1961) *Freud and Psychoanalysis* (*Collected Works*, Volume 4), London: Routledge and Kegan Paul.
—— (1966a) *Two Essays on Analytical Psychology* (*Collected Works*, Volume 7), 2nd edn, London: Routledge.
—— (1966b) *The Practice of Psychotherapy: Essays on the Psychology of the Transference and Other Subjects* (*Collected Works*, Volume 16), 2nd edn, London: Routledge.
—— (1967a) *Alchemical Studies* (*Collected Works*, Volume 13), Princeton: Princeton University Press.
—— (1967b) *Symbols of Transformation: An Analysis of the Prelude to a Case of Schizophrenia* (*Collected Works*, Volume 5), 2nd edn, Princeton: Princeton University Press.
—— (1968a) *The Archetypes and the Collective Unconscious* (*Collected Works*, Volume 9(i)), 2nd edn, London: Routledge.
—— (1968b) *Aion: Researches into the Phenomenology of the Self* (*Collected Works*, Volume 9(ii)), 2nd edn, Princeton: Princeton University Press.
—— (1968c) *Psychology and Alchemy* (*Collected Works*, Volume 12), 2nd edn, London: Routledge.
—— (1969a) *The Structure and Dynamics of the Psyche* (*Collected Works*, Volume 8), 2nd edn, London: Routledge.
—— (1969b) *Psychology and Religion: East and West* (*Collected Works*, Volume 11), 2nd edn, Hove: Routledge.
—— (1970a) *Civilization in Transition* (*Collected Works*, Volume 10), 2nd edn, Princeton: Princeton University Press.
—— (1970b) *Mysterium Coniunctionis: An Inquiry into the Separation and Synthesis of Psychic Opposites in Alchemy* (*Collected Works*, Volume 14), 2nd edn, Princeton: Princeton University Press.
—— (1971) *Psychological Types* (*Collected Works*, Volume 6), Princeton: Princeton University Press.
—— (1973-75) *C. G. Jung Letters*, 2 vols, trans. R. F. C. Hull and J. Hulen, G. Adler (ed.), Princeton: Princeton University Press.
—— (1977) *The Symbolic Life: Miscellaneous Writings* (*Collected Works*, Volume 18), London: Routledge.

—— (1978) 'Approaching the Unconscious', in C. G. Jung, M-L. von Franz and J. Freeman (eds) *Man and His Symbols*, London: Pan Books.

—— (1983) *The Zofingia Lectures* (*Collected Works*, Supplementary Volume A), trans. J. van Heurck, intro. M-L. von Franz, London: Routledge and Kegan Paul.

—— (1990) *Analytical Psychology: Notes of the Seminar given in 1925 by C. G. Jung*, transcript C. F. de Angulo, W. McGuire (ed.), London: Routledge.

—— (1991) *Psychology of the Unconscious: A Study of the Transformations and Symbolisms of the Libido: A Contribution to the History of the Evolution of Thought* (*Collected Works*, Supplementary Volume B), trans. B. M. Hinkle, intro. W. McGuire, Princeton: Princeton University Press.

—— (1995) *Memories, Dreams, Reflections*, trans. R. Winston and C. Winston, A. Jaffé (ed.), London: Fontana Press.

—— (1998) 'On the Psychology of the Concept of the Trinity', trans. G. V. Hartman, *Quadrant: Journal of the C. G. Jung Foundation for Analytical Psychology*, XXVIII(1): 7–29.

—— (2001) *Modern Man in Search of a Soul*, trans. W. S. Dell and C. F. Baynes, London and New York: Routledge.

—— (2009) *The Red Book: Liber Novus*, trans. M. Kyburz, J. Peck, and S. Shamdasani, S. Shamdasani (ed. and intro.), New York and London: W. W. Norton and Company.

—— and Jaffé, A. (unpublished) 'Protocols of *Memories, Dreams, Reflections*', Manuscript Division, Library of Congress.

Kelsey, M. T. (1984) 'Jung as Philosopher and Theologian', in R. K. Papadopoulos and G. S. Saayman (eds) *Jung in Modern Perspective: The Master and his Legacy*, Aldershot: Wildwood House.

Kerr, F. (1997) *Immortal Longings: Versions of Transcending Humanity*, London: S.P.C.K.

Kilby, K. (2000) 'Perichoresis and Projection: Problems with the Social Doctrines of the Trinity', *New Blackfriars*, 81(956): 432–45.

—— (2003) 'Evil and the Limits of Theology', *New Blackfriars*, 84(983): 13–29.

—— (2004) 'Balthasar and Karl Rahner', in E. T. Oakes and D. Moss (eds) *The Cambridge Companion to Hans Urs von Balthasar*, Cambridge: Cambridge University Press.

—— (2012) *Balthasar: A (Very) Critical Introduction*, Grand Rapids and Cambridge: Wm. B. Eerdmans Publishing Co.

Kirsch, T. B. (2000) *The Jungians: A Comparative and Historical Perspective*, London and Philadelphia: Routledge.

Kluger, R. S. (1967) *Satan in the Old Testament*, trans. H. Nagel, Evanston: Northwestern University Press.

Lammers, A. C. (1994) *In God's Shadow: The Collaboration of Victor White and C. G. Jung*, New York and Mahwah: Paulist Press.

—— (2005) *'The Missing Fourth' in the Jung–White Letters* (Lecture no. 287), London: Guild of Pastoral Psychology.

—— and Cunningham, A. (eds) (2007) *The Jung–White Letters*, Hove and New York: Routledge.

Larrimore, M. (ed.) (2001) *The Problem of Evil: A Reader*, Oxford and Malden: Blackwell Publishing.

Lubac, H. de (1938) *Catholicisme: Les Aspect Sociaux du Dogme* [Catholicism: The Social Aspects of Dogma], Paris: Éditions du Cerf.

—— (1979–1981) *La Postérité spirituelle de Joachim de Flore* [The Spiritual Posterity of Joachim of Fiore], 2 vols, Paris: Lethielleux, Namur.

—— (1991) 'A Witness of Christ in the Church: Hans Urs von Balthasar', trans. J. R. Dunne and A. Emery, in D. L. Schindler (ed.) *Hans Urs von Balthasar: His Life and Work*, San Francisco: Ignatius Press.

MacKenna, C. (2012) 'What Implications Does *The Red Book* Have for My Clinical Practice?' *Journal of Analytical Psychology*, 57(4): 477–82.

MacKenna, C. (2013) 'Jung's Divine Madness' in J. Gale, M. Robson and G. Rapsomatioti (eds) *Insanity and Divinity: Studies in Psychosis and Spirituality*, London: Routledge.

Main, R. (2004) *The Rupture of Time: Synchronicity and Jung's Critique of Modern Western Culture*, Hove and New York: Brunner-Routledge.

—— (2006a) 'Religion', in R. K. Papadopoulos (ed.) *The Handbook of Jungian Psychology: Theory, Practice and Applications*, Hove and New York: Routledge.

—— (2006b) 'Numinosity and Terror: Jung's Psychological Revision of Otto as an Aid to Engaging Religious Fundamentalism', in A. Casement and D. Tacey (eds) *The Idea of the Numinous: Contemporary Jungian and Psychoanalytical Perspectives*, Hove: Routledge.

McGuire, W. (ed.) (1974) *The Freud/Jung Letters: The Correspondence between Sigmund Freud and C. G. Jung*, trans. R. Manheim and R. F. C. Hull, London: Hogarth Press and Routledge and Kegan Paul.

McLynn, F. (1996) *Carl Gustav Jung: A Biography*, London: Bantam Press.

Melville, H. (1986) 'Billy Budd, Sailor (An Inside Narrative)', H. Hayford and M. M. Sealts (eds) in F. Busch (ed.) *Billy Budd and Other Stories*, London: Penguin Books.

Metzger, B. M. and Murphy, R. E. (eds) (1991) *The New Oxford Annotated Bible, with the Apocryphal / Deuteroncanonical Books: New Revised Standard Version*, New York: Oxford University Press.

Mongrain, K. (2002) *The Systematic Thought of Hans Urs von Balthasar: An Irenaean Retrieval*, New York: The Crossroad Publishing Company.

Nagy, M. (1991) *Philosophical Issues in the Psychology of C. G. Jung*, Albany: State University of New York Press.

Nichols, A. (1998) *The Word Had Been Abroad: A Guide Through Balthasar's Aesthetics*, Edinburgh: T. & T. Clark.

—— (2000) *No Bloodless Myth: A Guide Through Balthasar's Dramatics*, Edinburgh: T. & T. Clark.

—— (2001) *Say It Is Pentecost: A Guide Through Balthasar's Logic*, Edinburgh: T. & T. Clark.

Oakes, E. T. (1994) *Pattern of Redemption: The Theology of Hans Urs von Balthasar*, New York: Continuum.

—— (2006) '"He Descended into Hell": The Depths of God's Self-Emptying Love on Holy Saturday in the Thought of Hans Urs von Balthasar', in C. S. Evans (ed.) *Exploring Kenotic Christology: The Self-Emptying God*, Oxford: Oxford University Press.

—— (2007a) 'The Internal Logic of Holy Saturday in the Theology of Hans Urs von Balthasar', *International Journal of Systematic Theology*, 9(2): 184–99.

—— (2007b) 'More on Balthasar, Hell and Heresy', in *First-Things: A Monthly Journal of Religion and Public Life* (January), http://www.firstthings.com/article/2009/02/003-more-on-balthasar-hell-and-heresy-39

—— and Moss, D. (2004) *The Cambridge Companion to Hans Urs von Balthasar*, Cambridge: Cambridge University Press.

Olney, J. (1980) *The Rhizome and the Flower: The Perennial Philosophy – Yeats and Jung*, Berkeley and London: University of California Press.

Otto, R. (1958) *The Idea of the Holy: An Inquiry into the Non-rational Factor in the Idea of the Divine and its Relation to the Rational*, trans. J. W. Harvey, 2nd edn, London: Oxford University Press.

Phillips, D. Z. (2005) *The Problem of Evil and the Problem of God*, Minneapolis: Fortress Press.

Pitstick, A. L. (2007) *Light in Darkness: Hans Urs von Balthasar and the Catholic Doctrine of Christ's Descent into Hell*, Grand Rapids: Eerdmans.

Plantinga, A. (1975) *God, Freedom and Evil*, London: Allen and Unwin.

Przywara, E. (1923) *Gottgeheimnis der Welt: Drei Vorträge über die geistige Krisis der Gegenwart* [The Mystery of God in the World: Three Lectures on the Current Spiritual Crisis], München: Theatiner Verlag.

—— (1935) *Polarity: A German Catholic's Interpretation of Religion*, trans. A. C. Bouquet, London: Oxford University Press.

—— (1938) *Deus Semper Maior: Theologie der Exerzitien*, Drei Bände, Freiburg im Breisgau: Herder & Co.

Quash, B. (2004) 'The Theo-drama', in E. T. Oakes and D. Moss (eds) *The Cambridge Companion to Hans Urs von Balthasar*, Cambridge: Cambridge University Press.

—— (2005) 'Hans Urs von Balthasar', in D. F. Ford and R. Muers (eds) *The Modern Theologians: An Introduction to Christian Theology since 1918*, 3rd edn, Malden and Oxford: Blackwell Publishing.

Ress, L. (comp.) (1979) *General Bibliography of C. G. Jung's Writings* (*Collected Works*, Volume 19), London: Routledge.

Rodin, R. S. (1977) *Evil and Theodicy in the Theology of Karl Barth*, New York: Peter Lang Publishing.

Roten, J. (1991) 'The Two Halves of the Moon: Marian Anthropological Dimensions in the Common Mission of Adrienne von Speyr and Hans Urs von Balthasar', in D. L. Schindler (ed.) *Hans Urs von Balthasar: His Life and Work*, San Francisco: Ignatius Press.

Rowland, S. (2005) *Jung as a Writer*, London and New York: Routledge.

Samuels, A., Shorter, B. and Plaut, F. (eds) (1986) *A Critical Dictionary of Jungian Analysis*, London and New York: Routledge and Kegan Paul.

Sanford, J. A. (1981) *Evil: The Shadow Side of Reality*, New York: Crossroad.

Schärf, R. (1948) 'Die Gestalt des Satans im Alten Testament', in Jung 1948a: 151–319.

Schlamm, L. (1994) 'The Holy: A Meeting-Point between Analytical Psychology and Religion', in J. Ryce-Menuhin (ed.) *Jung and the Monotheisms: Judaism, Christianity and Islam*, London and New York: Routledge.

Schwarz, B. K. (2008) *Die Mittelaterlichen Glasmalereien der Ehemaligen Klosterkirche Königsfelden* (Corpus Vitrearum Medii Aevi: Schweiz, II) Berne: Stämpfli Verlag.

Segal, R. A. (1992) *The Gnostic Jung*, London: Routledge.

Shamdasani, S. (1995) 'Memories, Dreams, Omissions', *Spring: A Journal of Archetype and Culture*, 57: 115–37.

—— (1998) 'From Geneva to Zürich: Jung and French Switzerland', *Journal of Analytical Psychology*, 43: 115–26.

—— (2003) *Jung and the Making of Modern Psychology: The Dream of a Science*, Cambridge: Cambridge University Press.

—— (2005) *Jung Stripped Bare: By His Biographers, Even*, London: H. Karnac (Books) Ltd.

—— (2009) 'Liber Novus: The "Red Book" of C. G. Jung', in *RBLN*: 193–226.

—— (2012a) 'After *Liber Novus*', *Journal of Analytical Psychology*, 57(3): 364–77.

—— (2012b) *C. G. Jung: A Biography in Books*, New York and London: W. W. Norton and Company.

Smith, R. C. (1996) *The Wounded Jung: Effects of Jung's Relationships on His Life and Work*, Evanston: Northwestern University Press.

Speiser, A. (1942) 'Die Platonische Lehre vom Unbekannten Gott und die Christliche Trinität [The Platonic Doctrine of the Unknown God and the Christian Trinity]', *Eranos-Jahrbuch 1940/1941*, Rhein-Verlag: Zürich.

Speyr, A. von (1966) *Kreuz und Hölle* [Cross and Hell] *I* (vol. 3 of *Die Nachlasswerke* [The Posthumous Works]), Einsiedeln: Johannes Verlag.

Stein, M. (1985) *Jung's Treatment of Christianity: The Psychotherapy of a Religious Tradition*, Wilmette: Chiron Publications.

—— (1987) 'Jung's Green Christ: A Healing Symbol for Christianity', in M. Stein and R. L. Moore (eds) *Jung's Challenge to Contemporary Religion*, Wilmette: Chiron Publications.

—— (1990) 'Jung, Psychologist and Theologian', in R. L. Moore and D. J. Meckel (eds) *Jung and Christianity in Dialogue : Faith, Feminism and Hermeneutics*, New York and Mahwah: Paulist Press.

—— (1995) 'Introduction', in M. Stein (ed.) *Jung on Evil*, London: Routledge.

—— (1998) *Jung's Map of the Soul: An Introduction*, Chicago and La Salle: Open Court.

—— (2001) *A Changing God Image: What Does It Mean?* (Lecture no. 278), London: Guild of Pastoral Psychology.

—— (2012) 'How to Read *The Red Book* and Why', *Journal of Analytical Psychology*, 57(3): 280–98.

Stepansky, P. E. (1992) 'The Empiricist as Rebel: Jung, Freud and the Burdens of Discipleship', in R. Papadopoulos (ed.) *Carl Gustav Jung: Critical Assessments*, vol. 1: *Jung and His Method in Context*, London and New York: Routledge.

Stevens, A. (1990) *On Jung*, London and New York: Routledge.

Storr, A. (1996) *Feet of Clay: A Study of Gurus*, London: Harper Collins.

Tacey, D. (1997) 'Jung in the Academy: Devotions and Resistances', *Journal of Analytical Psychology*, 42(2): 269–83.

—— (2004) *The Spirituality Revolution: The Emergence of Contemporary Spirituality*, Hove and New York: Brunner-Routledge.

Taylor, E. (1998) 'Jung before Freud, not Freud before Jung: The Reception of Jung's Work in American Psychoanalytical Circles between 1904 and 1909', *Journal of Analytical Psychology*. 43: 97–114.

—— (1999) *Shadow Culture: Psychology and Spirituality in America*, Washington: Counterpoint.

Uhsadel, W. (1966) *Evangelische Seelsorge* [Protestant Pastoral Care] (*Praktische Theologie*, Band 3), Heidelberg: Quelle and Meyer.

Ulanov, A. B. (1997) 'Teaching Jung in a Theological Seminary and a Graduate School of Religion: A Response to David Tacey', *Journal of Analytical Psychology*, 42(2): 303–11.

—— (2006) 'Theology after Jung', *Journal of Jungian Theory and Practice*, 8(1): 61–8.

Voogd, S. de (1984) 'Fantasy versus Fiction: Jung's Kantianism Appraised', in R. K. Papadopoulos and G. S. Saayman (eds) *Jung in Modern Perspective*, Hounslow: Wildwood House.

Weldon, C. (2007) *Fr. Victor White, O. P.: The Story of Jung's "White Raven"*, Scranton and London: University of Scranton Press.

White, V. (1952) *God and the Unconscious*, London: Harvill.

—— (1960) *Soul and Psyche: An Enquiry into the Relationship of Psychotherapy and Religion*, London: Collins and Harvill Press.

Wigley, S. (2007) *Karl Barth and Hans Urs von Balthasar: A Critical Engagement*, London and New York: T. & T. Clark International.

—— (2010) *Balthasar's Trilogy: A Reader's Guide*, London and New York: T. & T. Clark International.

Wilhelm, R. and Jung. C. G. (1962) *The Secret of the Golden Flower: A Chinese Book of Life*, trans. R. Wilhelm, foreword and commentary C. G. Jung, trans. C. F. Baynes, new, revised and augmented edn, London: Routledge and Kegan Paul.

Williams, G. H. (1992) *The Radical Reformation* (Sixteenth Century Essays and Studies, Volume XV), 3rd edn, Kirksville: Sixteenth Century Journal Publishers.

Williams, R. (2004) 'Balthasar and the Trinity', in E. T. Oakes and D. Moss (eds) *The Cambridge Companion to Hans Urs von Balthasar*, Cambridge: Cambridge University Press.

Zacharias, G. (1954) *Psyche und Mysterium: Die Bedeutung der Psychologie C. G. Jungs für die christliche Theologie und Liturgie* [Psyche and Mystery: The Meaning of C. G. Jung's Psychology for Christian Theology and Liturgy] (Studien aus dem C. G. Jung-Institute, V), Zürich: Rascher Verlag.

Zaunert, P. (ed.) (1912) 'Die Prinzessin auf dem Baum [The Princess in the Tree]', in *Deutsche Märchen seit Grimm* [German Fairy Tales since Grimm], Jena: E. Diederichs.

Index

For Product Safety Concerns and Information please contact our EU representative GPSR@taylorandfrancis.com
Taylor & Francis Verlag GmbH, Kaufingerstraße 24, 80331 München, Germany

www.ingramcontent.com/pod-product-compliance
Ingram Content Group UK Ltd.
Pitfield, Milton Keynes, MK11 3LW, UK
UKHW011006180926
475701UK00004B/591
* 9 7 8 0 4 1 5 7 9 1 7 8 6 *